BEHIND THE CASTLE GATE

In this engaging book Matthew Johnson takes a look *Behind the Castle Gate* to discover the truth about castles in England at the end of the Middle Ages. How were they used? What influenced the way they were built? Why were they modified and who did it? In answering these questions a new and exciting way of thinking about castles emerges.

Traditional studies of castles have seen them as compromises between the needs of comfort and of defence. They were either statements of wealth or of power or both. Johnson rejects familiar narratives of 'military decline' on the one hand or 'social display' on the other. Rather he encourages the reader to dig deeper into the history, architecture and physical setting of castles. By so doing we discover that when a castle is viewed in relation to the identities of the people who used them and lived in them a whole new vantage point is uncovered.

Castles acted in part as stage-settings – as backdrops against which people played out roles of lord and servant, husband and wife, father and son, soldier and gardener, in both everyday and ceremonial contexts. The daily raising and lowering of the gate, the passage from one courtyard to another, the views of the surrounding landscape – all this was manipulated by the architecture of the castle and the choice and modification of its landscape setting. We see how the changing identities of the occupants were reflected in radical change in the physical attributes of these castles with the transition from the medieval to the Renaissance eras. Building, rebuilding and living in a castle was every bit as complex a set of experiences as a piece of medieval art or a Renaissance play.

Behind the Castle Gate brings castles alive as well as the people who lived in, worked on and modified them. Combining ground-breaking scholarship with fascinating narratives this book will be read avidly by all with an interest in castles.

Matthew Johnson is Professor in Archaeology at the University of Durham, where he has taught since 1991. He has published three books: *Housing Culture: Traditional Architecture in an English Landscape* (Routledge 1993), *An Archaeology of Capitalism* and *Archaeological Theory: an Introduction*.

BEHIND THE CASTLE GATE

From Medieval to Renaissance

Matthew Johnson

London and New York

First published 2002
by Routledge
2 Park Square, Milton Park, Abingdon, Oxon, OX14 4RN

Simultaneously published in the USA and Canada
by Routledge
270 Madison Ave, New York NY 10016

Routledge is an imprint of the Taylor & Francis Group

Transferred to Digital Printing 2006

© 2002 Matthew Johnson

Typeset in Garamond by
Florence Production Ltd, Stoodleigh, Devon EX16 9PN

British Library Cataloguing in Publication Data
A catalogue record for this book is available from the British Library

Library of Congress Cataloging in Publication Data
A catalog record for this book has been requested

ISBN 0–415–26100–7 (pbk)
ISBN 0–415–25887–1 (hbk)

Printed and bound by CPI Antony Rowe, Eastbourne

TO SARAH

CONTENTS

ACKNOWLEDGEMENTS

Scholarship is a team effort, even when the team has never met, and even when its constituent members have very different ideas about the material they are working on. One of the constant and most pleasant surprises for me as a researcher is the way senior colleagues in castle studies and landscape archaeology have given freely of their time, thinking and 'raw data'. Far more of the ideas presented here originated in discussions with other 'castle buffs' than from solitary theoretical excursus. Those to be thanked for such discussions include Dave Austin, Charles Coulson, Chris Taylor, Brian Dix, and Paul Everson. Michael Prestwich pointed out to me that we must explain why castles are different, one from another. I cannot remember whether it was Philip Dixon or I who first suggested that castles were deliberately left unfinished, and he noted the parallel of Cartington with Warkworth before I did, much to my chagrin. Richard Britnell generously made available references he had unearthed to activities of homage that probably took place in halls, which I discuss in Chapter 3. Tadhg O'Keeffe pointed out to me the implications of the use of the term 'feudal' in Chapter 4 and arranged a tour of Irish castles and towerhouses that restored my faith in castle studies at a critical moment. I have never met Anthony Emery, but the accounts of Tattershall and Raglan in this book could not have been written without his scholarship.

Chris Constable's ideas on eleventh- and twelfth-century castles in the north of England, and Adrian Green's on ideas of downward social diffusion and the process of architectural change more generally, have developed in parallel with my own; the point that the image of the castle arose at the very moment of its dissolution is derived from Adrian's work. The work of Pam Graves and Mark Douglas on religious buildings also influenced my thinking.

Staff of the then Royal Commission on Historical Monuments at Swindon (now English Heritage) provided much help in going through the archives. In particular, I was fortunate to encounter Donnie McKay while I was working on the Swindon archives, and to be alerted to his account of work at Whorlton. Giovanna Michelson discussed her work at Leeds with me, and pointed out the existence of the 'viewing point' to the south of Kenilworth mentioned in Chapter 6. Several anonymous reviewers made valuable comments.

Many of the ideas here have been presented at various seminars, and feedback from those discussions was invaluable. These include students and staff at the Department of Anthropology, University of California at Berkeley; the Departments of Archaeology at the Universities of Reading, Glasgow and Cambridge; Wesleyan and Brown Universities; the Durham Centre for Medieval and Renaissance Studies; University College Dublin; and the University of Siena School in Archaeological Theory. The Department of Archaeology, University of Durham made a Young Scholar's Grant to support this work.

This book is dedicated to my sister Sarah Johnson, who as a child cheerfully if noisily tolerated being dragged round cold, wet ruins by her anorak-clad elder brother. I doubt she would have showed as much equanimity if she had realised he was to be as tedious on the subject in adulthood.

How does one acknowledge one's partner without committing a solecism? I can only record that my wife Becky made comments and suggestions on various drafts, copy-edited and proof-read the manuscript, and compiled the index. These were all important activities, but more important were her enthusiasm for Sunday castle-visiting and her fresh approach and ideas 'on site'. More important still has been her constant and unfailing support over the last ten years. I could not have done it without her.

Matthew Johnson
Durham
September 2001

FIGURES

PREFACE

Behind the gate at Cooling

I first visited Cooling in February 1998. I drove there from Rochester, that castle which forms the linchpin of so many traditional narratives of castle development, with its square *donjon*, rebuilt circular corner turret and curtain wall studded with flanking towers. Cooling was meant to be a cursory visit; the brief manner in which published sources dealt with the structure suggested that little interesting remained; it was another building to be checked off the list, to be entered into the archives and used rhetorically to establish one's academic credentials – 'Oh yes, not much to see, but I have made the effort to visit it. Shame about all the nettles. Somebody should do a proper plan . . .'

In the event, Cooling turned out to be much more interesting than Rochester. I stayed there for the rest of the day, making notes and sketches in the sunshine in a pale winter light. What lay behind the gate at Cooling was quite surprising, quite fascinating, and turned out to be absolutely central to this book. The centrepiece of Cooling, and the subject of the view most frequently reproduced in published accounts, is that of the south façade of its gate flanked by towers (Figure 0.1). The 'gatehouse' faces south, with expansive and sweeping views across the north Kentish countryside. Its two towers are crowned with elaborate machicolations, an ornament that has been castigated on aesthetic grounds by other scholars as being slightly too exuberant, a little too large in scale, out of proportion with the towers (Coulson 1992). The battlements are executed in a different technique from the walls and appear to be partly restored.

We 'know' who built Cooling, because building accounts and other historical records survive, carefully archived in the dusty backrooms of the Public Record Office. The 'licence to crenellate', a document giving permission to fortify the manor house, is made out to John de Cobham and dated to 1381. Various named architects and stonemasons were involved in its construction, the most famous being Henry Yevele, builder of Westminster Palace hall roof and Canterbury Cathedral nave; building accounts run to 1385 (Newman 1969: 229–32). We 'know' even more, because on close inspection of the eastern tower of the gatehouse the visitor discovers a copper

Figure 0.1 The front of Cooling outer gate, from the south.

Figure 0.2 The copper plate on the eastern tower of Cooling outer gate.

plate, apparently original (Figure 0.2), whose words proclaim to us the purpose of the castle in the contemporary legal jargon ('charter and witnessing'):

Knowyth that beth and schul be
That I am mad in help of the cuntre
In knowyng of whyche thyng
Thys is chartre and wytnessyng.

So the meaning of Cooling castle is quite transparent – it is sited close to
the Thames estuary; and we 'know' (that word again) about French raids
along the Thames during the 1380s. Cooling was 'obviously' (another word
we shall revisit several times in this book) intended to defend the estuary
just as its contemporary Bodiam Castle defended the south coast. In 1380
and 1381 John de Cobham headed commissions to survey possible landing-
places and to fortify them (Coulson 1992: 92).

But any visitor who takes the trouble to examine the rear of the 'towers'
will have this picture shown to be rather more complex (Figure 0.3; a view

Figure 0.3 Rear view of Cooling gate.

which I have never seen reproduced in any text). The towers are not circular. In fact, they have no rear walls at all; they appear to be hollow. There is no trace on their inner faces of any wall now removed, or even mortises for timber-framed walls. From the front, Cooling presents a bold, martial face; it appears to be a huge gatehouse of similar form to the great gates of the Edwardian castles of Wales; from the rear, it is revealed as a stage setting, a joke even. Whatever else it might be, the gate at Cooling is certainly a fraud.

As the visitor explores Cooling further, he or she makes a passage through a series of illusions and revelations of this kind. Impressive as it is, the gatehouse is but the entrance to the outer courtyard. Walking through the gatehouse arch and turning right, one finds that the corner towers of this outer courtyard sport keyhole-shaped gunports of the latest 1380s' style – but the towers are again hollow on the inside, and horseshoe-shaped rather than truly circular. Going forward from the gate, and trying to 'think away' the modern house in front, one finds oneself passing alongside a wide moat to the left, now partly drained, with a second impressive gatehouse leading to the inner court rising from that moat (Figures 0.4 and 0.5). Yet once viewed from the rear, even this gatehouse is also a fraud; the gunports here are almost impossible to use and one flanking tower is merely the housing for a circular or 'newel' staircase. It has no portcullis groove and no indication of housing for a drawbridge chain.

The castle of Cooling, then, reveals itself gradually to the visitor, who moves across decayed and surviving moats, along carefully defined and delimited causeways, below apparently mighty arches, to finally arrive in the middle of the structure, within four walls forming a rectangle, each corner studded with a circular tower. On the way, the visitor sees grotesque faces and creatures carved into the fabric, and notes the prominent use of reused masonry. But even here, at the centre of the courtyard, Cooling's secrets are not exhausted.

The walls are too thin to support a fighting parapet; if such a parapet existed, it must have been a timber hoarding. The towers, frankly, are very small, and it is not entirely clear that there ever was a tower in the northeast corner. Instead, in this corner, there is a rectangular structure distinctively marked out by chequer-work in flint and ashlar.

To the north of the castle lie yet further surprises. Cooling is not sited on the estuary at all; it is at present five kilometres south of the coast. Much of this area is marsh. Immediately to the north of the castle, however, is high ground – so high that at one point it overlooks the earthen ramparts of the outer court, hardly a recipe for military impregnability. Yet the defences are not oriented towards this weak point or towards the hypothetical path of invading hordes of Frenchmen. Rather, the towers of the gate point south. I suggest that *Cooling is a castle that is meant to be seen from the south, rather than defended to the north*. There is a double ditch on the north side of the inner court, but only the one tower at the north-west corner. Would this

Figure 0.4 Front view of Cooling inner gate,
from the south.

tower have enjoyed an unimpeded view to the Thames estuary? It is possible,
but unlikely.

This complex and fascinating structure is little known or cited in the standard textbooks. When it is cited, the front view of the gatehouse is
reproduced. I have never seen the rear view of the gatehouse published
anywhere, or any interior view of the castle. Cooling is privately owned and
not open to the public. Though the owner was perfectly happy to let me
roam, she probably thought I was slightly mad.

What are the lessons of a visit to Cooling? Most fundamentally, we must
look *behind the gate*. Cooling stands as an exemplar and metaphor for the
way we look at individual castles, and the way we think about complex
pieces of architecture generally. A casual glance at the exterior of Cooling
is enough to fit it into a generally known and accepted story or narrative of
architectural development. The more closely we look, the more this narrative begins to look just a little more complex. The story fragments; from

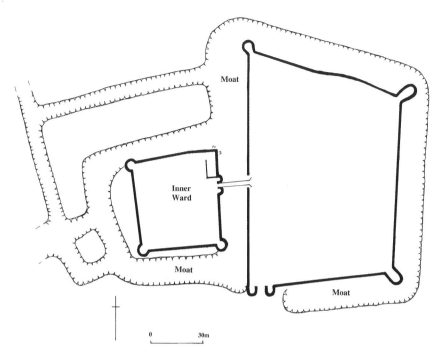

Figure 0.5 Plan of Cooling castle (After Page 1908).

being a coherent whole, it becomes a series of disjointed pieces.

Second, Cooling is half-forgotten, being in a hidden corner of England; it is hard to find today, tucked behind Rochester in a maze of country lanes. In its own way, it is just as fascinating as the more famous Bodiam. And yet it is little known. To what extent have archaeologists and architectural historians written the story of architectural development as a series of anecdotes or little stories, focusing on the biggest and best known sites, those most accessible and on public display? Nikolaus Pevsner (1976) argued for a view of architectural development derived from Darwin, that building types were like species, with one 'type' evolving into another; we will return to this view in Chapter 5, but we might also characterise existing approaches using literary analogies. Do we have a 'canon' of castles like a canon of literary texts? If so, can we criticise the way that canon is made up, just as literary scholars have criticised theirs? If we can, how does this change our perception of the past?

Third, how do we interpret the copper 'document' on the gate, particularly when we place it against the context of the structure of Cooling as a whole? Do we still read it literally, or do we dismiss its assertions as a piece of self-conscious bravado, just another fraudulent piece of 'display'? Or do we look for a third way to see its meanings, taking its assertion that Cooling was made 'in help of the cuntre' at a series of different levels of readings?

If we move towards a more complex and multi-layered reading of this document, what are its more general implications for the way we practise archaeology and documentary history? Cooling suggests that documents do not in fact record what is 'true' and that we cannot fit our archaeology around them – a familiar enough point. However, Cooling also suggests that archaeology – in this case, the physical fabric and form of the structure – also cannot be read literally. So we have no certainty, no unproblematic baseline from which to do medieval or historical archaeology. In the absence of such certainty, how do we practise our craft?

One way to rephrase this problem is to ask: how do we *explain* Cooling? We might write: 'Cooling was built near the coast; its licence to crenellate is dated two years after documented French raids.' The narrative mode of this sentence deftly conceals its status as an explanation or theory. Could or should we explain archaeological sites like castles with reference to historical events?

Fourth, which parts of Cooling do we concentrate on? The lines of the outer walls are clear enough, and in the view of one scholar the ramparts should always be the centre of scholarly study of castles (Thompson 1994). However, the ramparts are pierced with traces of other buildings – fireplaces, doors, gates, roof lines, windows are inscribed on their surface like a palimpsest. With a little work, the attached buildings within the courtyard can be reconstructed. We must also look *outside* – at the landscape context of castles. Cooling is surrounded by a complex system of moats and ponds, now partially overgrown. It stands at one end of the church and hamlet of Cooling, with wide views to the south.

Cooling, then, raises all sorts of questions about how we should look at castles. When I arrived at Cooling, all appeared 'obvious'; we 'knew' about the history and purpose of the structure; Cooling fitted clearly in to a narrative about late medieval architecture and warfare. As we leave the structure, we find that everything is thrown into doubt. *And doubts and uncertainties are raised not because of some new, fashionable theoretical perspective, but through a close examination of the fabric of Cooling itself.* Close examination has replaced certainty with doubt; in a sense, we know less as we leave than when we arrived. Perhaps, though, close examination has also made Cooling a little more interesting in the process.

So how should we understand castles at the end of the Middle Ages? What should we be looking for when we wander round buildings? What are castles' histories and forms 'charter and wytnessyng' to? What new things might we find when we start looking behind the gate?

1

INTRODUCTION

Casting our eyes upon sconces

ALONZO: De Flores.
DE FLORES: My kind, honourable lord?
ALONZO: I am glad I ha' met with thee.
DE FLORES: Sir.
ALONZO: Thou canst show me
　　The full strength of the castle?
DE FLORES: That I can, sir.
ALONZO: I much desire it.
DE FLORES: And if the ways and straits
　　Of some of the passages be not too tedious for you,
　　I will assure you, worth your time and sight, my lord.
ALONZO: Puh, that shall be no hindrance.
DE FLORES: I'm your servant, then.
　　'Tis now near dinner-time; 'gainst your lordship's rising
　　I'll have the keys about me.
ALONZO: Thanks, kind de Flores.
DE FLORES: (*aside*) He's safely thrust upon me beyond hopes.
　　　　　(Middleton and Rowley, *The Changeling*, Act II,
　　　　　　　　Scene ii, 1622; Daalder 1990: 44)

This book is about castles, and what happened to castles at the end of the Middle Ages. It will concentrate on England in the period running from roughly 1350 to 1660, covering both the later medieval period and the Renaissance.

I start by talking about late fourteenth- and fifteenth-century castles such as Cooling, Bodiam, Warkworth and Tattershall (Figure 1.1); I go on to look at what happened to castles in the sixteenth and early seventeenth centuries. I offer some thoughts on a wider theme: I reconsider through the medium of castle studies how we might rethink the 'medieval to Renaissance transition' as archaeologists. In this latter part of the book I will look at castles such as Kenilworth, old and ancient medieval piles that were reused in new, Renaissance contexts.

1

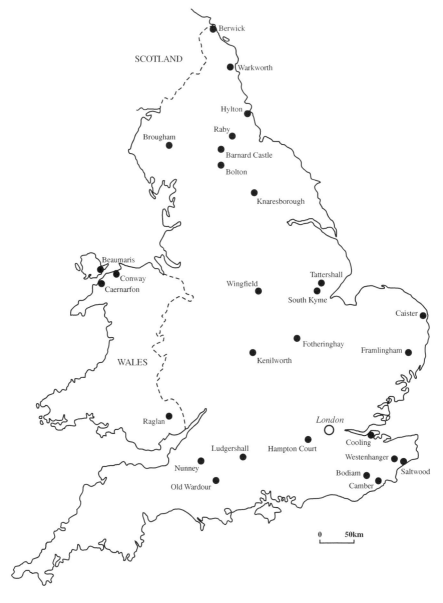

Figure 1.1 Location map of the principal castles mentioned in the text.

This book is not an attempt to reassess individual castles; nor does it attempt to claim particular new insights into particular structures. Its motivation and theme are more general. I try to look afresh at what these buildings meant to contemporaries, and how now, as we think and write in the present, archaeologists and architectural historians might best understand or approach them. Castles, I suggest, were not simply defensive structures. Equally, they were not built simply to passively fulfil certain functions like meeting a need for a certain standard of accommodation or to 'reflect' social status. Castles did do all these things, but they did much more besides. They were active and complex pieces of landscape and material culture.

A guiding metaphor for this complexity will be this: castles acted in part as stage settings. If we want to understand how they worked as elite structures, we have to understand them as backdrops in front of which and through which the identities of men and women were 'played out'. And those backdrops were manipulated with all the care and skill of a theatre production. As the identities of the protagonists changed, so did the meanings of the physical structures, even where their form remained the same.

I utilise several recent practical and theoretical developments in telling this story. First, recent archaeological fieldwork on the landscapes surrounding castles has shown that their surroundings often contained formal elements – causeways defining patterns of ceremonial movement, sheets of water, landscape elements 'framing' the castle. Second, recent theoretical stress within archaeology on 'agency' and 'lived experience' – the importance of studying how people moved through buildings, what they saw from different vantage points, and the stress on everyday practice – plays a role here. Third, interdisciplinary work on the Renaissance by New Historicists, Cultural Materialists and others suggests that forms of buildings – architecture – and elite identity and power – who people were, how they negotiated their social surroundings – were interwoven and unstable in the sixteenth century, and before that period.

Such a story is an incredibly wide-ranging and difficult one to tell, both practically and theoretically. It covers a wide base, encompassing the territories of both medievalists and Renaissance specialists, students of both the 'castle' and the 'country house' or 'domestic residence' (though I will be deconstructing these categories). It must equally be set within the intellectual context of contemporary theories of architecture and architectural change, changing interdisciplinary understandings of the Renaissance, changing historical and archaeological theory.

And most importantly, such a story cannot be reduced to one simple baseline or reality or final explanation. Castles are not 'basically about conspicuous consumption' or 'essentially about social status' or 'at heart about balancing defence and comfort' or 'fundamentally symbols of power'. I am going to argue that they were all these things, but basically or fundamentally none of them. At the risk of sounding pretentious, it seems apparent to me that the study of castles, and of the world in general, has moved well beyond the point where it can be reduced to a few core or basic essentials in this manner.

If the burden of this book is complex, it is tempting then to start with a long excursus on where this book stands theoretically. I do not want to do this, however; instead, I want to present changing views of medieval and Renaissance architecture as arising out of more complete, deeper, better understandings of the data, the buildings and landscapes themselves. I have already discussed Cooling, and in the next chapter move on to the reassessment of Bodiam now well known to castle specialists. However, before we can get on to the buildings, it is necessary to make a few comments on the present state of castle studies.

No real doubt

Some people know exactly how to look at castles, even before they start. For the Royal Archaeological Institute, at the outset of their research project into castle origins, a castle is a 'fortified residence which might combine administrative and judicial functions, but in which military considerations were paramount' (Saunders 1978: 2). For Michael Thompson, 'there is no real doubt about a castle, no doubt for the medieval scribe nor for ourselves, a house in which the defensive features completely overshadow the domestic one' (1998: 5). Allen Brown writes:

> The difference [between Norman and earlier defences] lies in the intention and hence the scale, strength and design of the enclosure. The dividing line between the castle . . . and the unfortified residence is always going to be hazy, but on either side of that dividing line there is really no confusion.
>
> (1973: 79)

How do they know this? How can such certainty be attained, even before research has begun in the case of the Royal Archaeological Institute?

In part, this certainty can be understood with reference to the historical context of castle studies. A generation of scholars working on castles were military men. They chose to pursue historical interests in retirement; and the obvious place to look for evidence of changing medieval techniques of warfare was the castle. Castles, then, were understood in military terms almost by definition; if it wasn't military, it wasn't 'really' a castle.

I want to stress right at the outset that *the military view is not so much wrong as only part of the story*. Many castles did play important 'military' roles; as we shall see, many of their features have a clear military intent; the definition of a castle is indeed bound up with what today we call the martial. For the time being, I will simply raise a series of problems with the military view, to be explored in later chapters.

Perhaps the most fundamental problem is one of circularity. Castles are primarily military. Ah, but what happens when we point out one that is not? Oh, the military men reply, but if it is not really military, then it is not really a castle. Bound up with this circularity is the difficulty of mentalist explanation: if we define a structure or artefact with reference to a 'need ' or 'intention' on the part of its builders, in this case an intent to defend, we are defining castles with reference to something that is inherently unknowable. In other words, we make assumptions about motivations and mentalities – what was inside the heads of medieval people before we have started the research.

Tom McNeill has pointed out the limitations of this view elegantly:

> [W]hen we are studying castles . . . what we are studying are the structures of power, literally and metaphorically, in the society of the middle ages . . . The nature of that power will be reflected in the structure of the castle, and so we should be able to deduce it from the study of the structure. Until then, *the castle is dumb*, so we must not carry to the castle preconceived notions of its role.
>
> (1997a: 235; emphasis mine)

But we cannot even go as far as McNeill suggests. Stand in front of a castle's ruined walls, or stand within its shattered vaults, and however carefully you listen, you will hear absolutely nothing, not even structures of power. (Not always; at Bolton, you will hear taped prayers in the chapel, and taped screams from the dungeons). So any meanings that we attach to the castle come from us, in the here and now.

Second, the military view can be argued to be a strong view of castle development up to *c.*1300, but weakens thereafter. Between the introduction of the castle to England at the Norman Conquest and the construction of Edward I's Welsh castles, according to the military narrative, we see the replacement of passive defence with active defence, the 'evolution' of the *donjon* and towers from vulnerable square forms to circular ones without weak angles, the proliferation of projecting towers providing flanking fire along the walls, the development of systems of concentric defence, and so on. At the same time there are well-documented and clearly desperately serious sieges in which many soldiers and others lost their lives, of Rochester, Kenilworth, Dover and many others. So a military view of twelfth- and thirteenth-century castle development is apparently very strong, at least at first sight; and for some, interest in the development of castle architecture ends there. Allen Brown writes of Rochester in terms that could easily be extended to castles in general that 'after the end of the 14th century, at least in military terms, the rest is anti-climax, and certainly the architectural development of the castle was at an end' (1986: 18).

The military view, however, visibly weakens when we turn to the fourteenth and fifteenth centuries. All sort of odd things start to happen. The *donjon* or an architectural form very like it comes back into fashion; walls get thinner; military commanders apparently prefer military engagement in the field to the security of the castle. We shall see in Chapter 5 how the period 1350–1500 has been characterised, I will suggest rather awkwardly, as a 'transitional period' between the military perfection of Edward I's Welsh castles and the advent of the Renaissance house.

Part of the problem here would be recognised by the structural anthropologist Edmund Leach from his work on how humans classify the world around them (1976). The military men have created two structurally opposed categories: castles and unfortified houses. The category of the castle works quite well for the twelfth and thirteenth centuries. Thereafter, its edges are increasingly fuzzy, and by 1550 or so we have clearly moved to the unfortified house, built according to 'Renaissance' principles. The 'in-between' period thus defined is difficult to classify. It becomes marginal, liminal, 'transitional'.

One way to explain this 'transitional period' is in terms of neither being militarily serious on the one hand, nor a complete sham on the other. The phrase often used here is 'defence against casual violence', in which reference is made to the peasant revolt and unrest of the later Middle Ages. For Thompson, 'the enemy was at the gate, but ill-armed and ill-equipped; he was not a military enemy to be fought, but to be overawed by fierce-looking buildings' (1998: 108). I will suggest later that castles are indeed intended to convey ideas and messages to the lower social orders, though whether these were blindly accepted by the lower social orders, or on the other hand resisted, is quite another matter. However, the idea that late medieval castles acted as a kind of social deterrent is again at best only part of the story.

I find this view of the mentalities and capabilities of lower social orders, apparently so easily overawed by the odd machicolation, unconvincing. Even within the military view's own terms, the 'enemy at the gate' of yeomen and others has been seen in other contexts as the finest archery in Europe, enjoined by Edward III and Henry V to practise military skills every Sunday and capable of beating massively superior forces of trained French knights mounted on specially bred steeds. If the lower social orders were so overawed by crenellations at Cooling, how on earth did they manage to stand up to French finery at Agincourt?

An exclusively military view of castles is therefore now in headlong retreat, though rumours of its death have I feel been exaggerated; there is a degree of interpretive 'doublethink' in which assertions of military primacy are overtly denied, but slipped in through the back door through implicit assumptions. I shall discuss such doublethink in Chapter 5. Of more interest to our present purpose are recent, more 'social' interpretations.

Social interpretations

Over the last decade or so, castle studies have explored other themes in addition to the military, looking at the 'social' functions of the castle. I would pick out several elements in these new views: interest in circulation patterns and the organisation of space; stress on castles as reflective of social status; and the castle as theatre.

The interest in circulation patterns is actually quite long-standing. Forty years ago Peter Faulkner published two influential articles centring on Goodrich on the Welsh border and Bolton Castle in Yorkshire. He looked at the circulation patterns within this late fourteenth-century structure and argued that its increased provision of 'private' lodgings and for domestic comfort was one point in a slow evolution of domestic provision stretching back to the thirteenth-century structures of Conway and Goodrich and forward to the Renaissance unfortified house (1958, 1963).

Faulkner's work was extremely influential and continues to be cited as a central text today. His suggestions were expanded by Graham Fairclough (1992), who extended the analysis of Bolton through the use of more sophisticated 'penetration diagrams' of the sort that have seen increasing popularity among theoretically minded archaeologists in recent years (Hillier and Hanson 1984; Gilchrist 1993; Mathieu 1999). Castles, being structures with complex circulation patterns whose subtleties are not immediately apparent to the casual modern visitor, are very suitable for these sorts of analyses; though I often think that the complex circulation patterns they describe still remain to be explained after the penetration diagram has been outlined (see Chapter 3).

Close structural analysis of buildings, often done on a stone-by-stone basis using new techniques of photogrammetry, has also led to new views of castles. This is most obvious in the work of Philip Dixon and Pamela Marshall (1993a, 1993b), who have made the point that very famous, high-status buildings still have secrets to yield to us; millions of people troop by the Tower of London every year, but until the last decade, archaeologists and historians included, few pause to examine the stonework in any detail; the new discoveries at the Tower testify to the power of such techniques (Impey and Parnell 2000). Dixon, Marshall and others have shown how apparently well-known buildings actually have very surprising structural sequences and initial forms. They make the point that we think that castles' fabrics have been 'studied to death' – that because they are so famous, we already know everything they have to offer – but in fact there is still much to observe and discover.

And when we observe and discover new features, we are led on to rethinking our wider ideas about castle development. The close empirical reanalysis proposed shows that castles do not fit into the easy typologies and interpretations of the past, and lead us to new insights in the present. For example, the work at Hedingham (Dixon and Marshall 1993a) and Norham

(Dixon and Marshall 1993b), combined with similar work at the Tower of London, has shown that the image of the Norman 'tower-keep' or *donjon* conceals a far more complex reality. Norman builders did not have a set idea of a *donjon* in the form of a tower which they simply reproduced on the other side of the Channel; instead, a variety of architectural forms were seen before the appearance of the classic form of the *donjon* in the early twelfth century. Builders changed their minds during the construction process, and evolved new forms very rapidly, as happened at the late thirteenth and fourteenth centuries at Aydon Castle (Dixon 1988).

Changing techniques of survey and interpretation go hand in hand with changing theoretical perspectives. In this case, the practical demonstration that the classic *donjon* was a 'late' development out of more diverse forms means that we can begin to understand tower keeps in part as an ideology – just as the early twelfth century saw the creation of a 'Norman myth' in historical texts, so Norman barons created an image of themselves through their architecture. Again, Dixon's (1990) re-analysis of the tower at Knaresborough in Yorkshire proceeds from a close analysis of its layout and an appreciation of its social context to an interpretation of how the building acted as a stage setting for the staging of the identity of Piers Gaveston as a great lord in the North.

If Dixon and others have shown us that architectural forms do not fall into such easy categories, Charles Coulson has achieved a similar task with documents – in particular 'licences to crenellate'. I will discuss Coulson's work in more detail in the next chapter, but his central point is worth inscribing on the study door of every writer on castles: that we cannot read off in a simple way the self-evident, literal meanings of documents, for example, those indicating an apparent military intent (Coulson 1994).

If we must look more carefully at the castle's fabric and its documentation, we must also look more carefully at its context within the landscape. David Austin has pointed out that in our urge to classify one castle form against another, we often forget about the castle's immediate context within an urban or rural landscape. Austin (1984) explores these points in a discussion of his excavations at Barnard Castle, where a large and impressive oriel window gives a view over the medieval deerpark beyond the castle. To understand the architecture at Barnard Castle, then, we have to think not in terms of wall and turret but in terms of human figures moving across a landscape: the lord's host 'riding out' to hunt in the deerpark, observed perhaps by figures at the windows.

The analysis of castles must also be gendered. They are also not simply sites for predominantly or exclusively male activities; Roberta Gilchrist has pointed out that where women were involved in building or living in a castle, distinctive patterns of spatial organisation can be seen. She identifies particular architectural features, such as gardens and covered walkways, that can be identified with women living and working in castles (1999: Chapter 6).

Even where castles were mostly occupied by men, this should be the starting point of a gendered analysis, not its end. Castles are structures that played a part in defining and renegotiating unstable social identities, one dimension of which was masculinity (Hadley 1999).

Many of these points were crystallised in a pivotal review article by David Stocker entitled 'The shadow of the general's armchair' (1992). In this review Stocker traced some of the intellectual roots of the military view (in particular pointing to nineteenth-century ideas of evolution, to which we shall return: see Chapter 5) and looked at some recent books on the subject. He gloomily noted that while the elements of a more fully social view of castles had been individually published, none of the syntheses he was reviewing had done anything to pull them together. Intellectually the flaws of the military view were there for all to see, claimed Stocker, but recent monographs had simply ignored these flaws and the contrary literature: their eyes firmly fixed on the distant prospect of sconces and munition, they had not yet appreciated the difficulties lurking behind them.

To return to *The Changeling*:

DE FLORES: All this is nothing; you shall see anon
    A place you little dream on.
ALONZO: I am glad
    I have this leisure; all your master's house
    Imagine I ha' taken a gondola.
DE FLORES: All but myself, sir – (*aside*) which makes up my own safety.
    (*to Alonzo*) My lord, I'll place you at a casement here
    Will show you the full strength of the castle.
    Lord, spend your eye a while upon that object.
ALONZO: Here's rich variety, De Flores.
DE FLORES: Yes, sir.
ALONZO: Goodly munition.
DE FLORES: Ay, there's ordnance, sir –
    No bastard metal – will ring you a peal like bells
    At great men's funerals. Keep your eye straight, my lord,
    Take special notice of that sconce before you.
    There may you dwell awhile. (*takes up the rapier*)
ALONZO: I am upon't.
DE FLORES: And so am I. (*stabs him*)
ALONZO: De Flores! O, De Flores!
    What malice hast thou put on?
                    (Middleton and Rowling, *The Changeling*, Act III,
                              Scene ii; Daalder 1990: 46)

Alonzo, perhaps, should have been less fixated on the sconces and munition of Vermandero's castle, and more conscious of the hidden complexities, sentiments and motivations of the human beings living there.

Back to basics

So what is a castle, really? *The Shorter Oxford English Dictionary* states:

> From Old Northern French var. of chastel; latin castellum; middle
> English biblical use rendering Latin castellum in the sense 'village'
> (1564) and as trans. of castre = camp (1483).

> 1. A large building or set of buildings fortified for defence; a fortress.
> Retained as name for feudal mansions which were formerly feudal
> castles. OE.

> 'a castel al of lime and ston' Chaucer
> The Castle: govt of Ireland

> Verb: to enclose in, or as in, a castle 1587
> to ornament with battlements (Chaucer)

> in chess 1656

There are several dangers in both 'military' and 'social' views of castles. First, of essentialism: both these views of castles see castles as 'essentially' this or 'essentially' that. I suggest that the search for a set of fundamental or essential features to a castle may miss the most basic point about late medieval architecture. One of the striking features of castles, so obvious that it is often ignored, is that each one is *different*, one from another. This one is 'regular'; that one 'irregular'; this one has square towers, that one round. There are differences in function also: this one was a hunting lodge, that one part of an urban centre; this one a royal stronghold, that one a 'private' residence. If we really want to understand castles, we have to think about and explain that difference. The problem of essentialism is, of course, a quite complex topic in postcolonial theory which I will discuss in Chapter 4.

Second, our accepted definitions of 'castles' are historical, not archaeological. The definition of a castle is derived from documentary sources rather than the physical fabric. We might see castles very differently if we were working within a prehistoric period. Would the prehistorian group the grassy, uninspiring lumps and bumps of Hen Domen in the same class as Windsor or Raglan? Would she or he really start their analysis by placing South Wingfield 'Manor' and Wingfield 'Castle', two grand late medieval buildings of courtyard plan, in different classificatory categories, as Thompson does (1987: 1)? Castle interpretation is similar in this way to a wide range of other issues in the relationship of archaeology and documentary material. For example, the study of Roman villas is tied in to problems of definition from documentary sources, and via such problems of method into a complex historiography of the debate over Romanisation (Millett 1990).

Late medieval and early Renaissance masons worked on a variety of projects, and do not seem to have specialised particularly in genres of architecture. The career of the famous Henry Yevele spanned over forty building and monumental projects; Yevele built bridges, palaces, churches, castles, funerary monuments, and engaged in modification and repair work on buildings of all genres, moving from project to project with no discernible pattern (Harvey 1944: 80). His castles ranged from the circular Queenborough to the quadrangular Bodiam and Cooling; it also included city walls. Italian Renaissance architects similarly worked on different classes of architecture; specialisation into recognisably modern categories did not start till the mid-sixteenth century at the earliest (Duffy 1979: 40; see also Chapter 5).

Castle terminology used by medieval and Renaissance writers is notoriously 'imprecise', in England as it was in other countries (cf. Dean 1984: 147–74; Poklewski-Zoziell 1996 on Poland). Even apparently factual contemporary accounts seem to obscure more than they reveal. A Tudor survey may have described the Knaresborough *donjon* as 'a marvelous hous of strength . . . strongly fortified with worke and man's ingyne to abide all assaults' but even the military man Allen Brown points out it has a 'very unmilitary quality' (cited in Allen Brown 1970: 140).

I suggest that the apparent imprecision of such contemporary documents, the frustrations they present to modern castle scholars, is revealing. It suggests that the search for a tight definition or classification of species or sub-species of form is unhelpful. There is no one essential category of 'castle'. It was a fluid idea in the medieval mind; it changed in the course of the fifteenth and sixteenth centuries; and of course, different social groups had different categories and classifications. In this book, I shall use the term 'castle' very loosely, and use examples from structures considered by many not to be 'palaces' or 'houses' rather than 'castles' where appropriate.

Trying to separate out 'core' or 'essential' features of a castle is like trying to define intrinsic characteristics of a social group such as 'knights' or 'gentry' or 'yeomen'. Social historians have moved away from the attempt to define social groups in absolute terms to a more nuanced understanding of how membership of a social group was in part a staged performance, and involved subtlety and ambiguity (Isaac 1982). To be a 'yeoman' in the late sixteenth century was not simply to be possessed of certain economic means; the term implied a certain mentality or world-view as well. 'Yeomen' or 'gentry' were defined in part performatively; that is, they acted the part on an everyday basis, through where they sat in church, who they doffed their hat to, how they behaved at festivities. A failure to act the part could lead to a loss of social status (Barry and Brooks 1994). And so it is with castles.

'Tys made Roger'

The view that comes closest to the one I want to pursue here is that described by Philip Dixon (1990) as the 'castle as theatre'. Castles were theatrical in that they served as stage settings. The social identities thus staged were unstable, and the staging itself was constitutive of that status. The ambiguity of the early fourteenth-century inscription over the gate at Brougham – 'Tys made Roger' – encapsulates the recursive nature of material things and social identities. If Roger made the castle at Brougham, the castle made Roger. The example is not an isolated one. There is an unreliable story that William of Wykeham inscribed *hoc fecit Wykeham* on Windsor castle walls. Upon being accused of arrogance, Wykeham asserted that the words meant 'this castle made Wykeham', not 'Wykeham made this castle' (Hayter 1970: 15).

I want to take this analogy further and deeper than Dixon does. We noted in the last section that social identities were in part the result of performances at an everyday and ceremonial level. Who people were, then, depended on these performances. An eighteenth-century gent who started behaving like a yeoman, adopting a certain lifestyle, behaviour, set of attitudes, eating and acting towards social superiors, equals, or inferiors in a certain way, might cease to be a gent. Contemporaries were certainly capable of making quite nuanced judgements about 'civility' in this way (Elias 1978). Similarly, being a medieval knight or a noble was also in part a performative category. Obviously, performances are structured by the world in which they are set, and architecture is a way of manipulating that world.

The documentary evidence as well as the architectural can be seen in terms of such staging, such manipulation. Brougham was given a licence to crenellate in 1309; the licence was granted to Roger Clifford, who was subsequently killed at Bannockburn. We can better understand such licences if we think of them in part as stage props, for example being ceremonially stamped with the Great Seal, or laboriously unfurled and read out loud in County Court, or displayed in the castle (Coulson 1993). Documents have a physical presence which needs to be explored further.

Such points are very familiar to a generation of archaeologists raised on the work of the 'postprocessual school' of prehistoric archaeology (Johnson 1999: 101–8), or theoretically informed work in historical archaeology outside Europe (cf. the studies in Leone and Potter 1999; Yentsch and Beaudry 1992); they are still novel and radical in certain quarters of English medieval and postmedieval archaeology. I shall explore them further in the course of this book, but for the time being I want to make the point that *castles are made by people, but make people in their turn*. This making and remaking unites everyday and ceremonial. It is the everyday rhythms of castles that are important here but which can be seen as little ceremonies; the values that they embody are all the more powerful for being implicit, accepted, part of routine practice. The daily raising and lowering of the gate, the movements of different members of the household, the regular gathering for dinner in the hall; the seasonal or annual arrival and departure of the lord, the regular holding of court – all these physical activities created the castle and the landscape beyond, created the identities of the participants. In this sense, social identities were performative, to borrow a term from sociology (cf. Goffman 1959; 1971). To be a lord was not simply an intrinsic quality of birth and blood, however much the lord might want observers to believe this. It was a series of social roles that were played out each day in ceremonial ranging from the everyday and apparently trivial to highly charged annual or life-changing ceremonies such as the 'dubbing' of knighthood or the meting out of justice in the Great Hall.

These everyday routines and specific acts of pomp and ceremony involved a bundle of actions and meanings. We must avoid therefore either/or questions like 'is this castle military or residential in function?' because both the castle and its owner's social standing were by definition rooted in both; and must avoid questions like 'how did the castle reflect social status?' because the castle *was* in part that person's social standing, was in part constitutive, not reflective of social status.

What I am getting at here is that current debates about castles are currently portrayed as a simple 'military versus social' dichotomy. A common remark made to me while I was preparing this book was 'Oh, we all know now that castles were not just military; recent work has looked at their social functions and symbolic aspects as well.' But castles are much too complex – and too interesting – to be portrayed in such simple terms. They deserve a more subtle approach. To ask 'was this or that castle primarily military in intent, or was it social/symbolic?' is to bring a set of twentieth-century preconceptions to a late medieval context.

Let me take a different analogy to explore this point. In the early days of castle excavation, much harm was done by the desire of particular scholars to follow where a wall went, or the desire of the then Ministry of Works to display wall foundations at castle sites in their care. To do this, narrow trenches were dug on either side of extant foundations in order to follow the line of the wall when it disappeared above ground. Now every field archaeologist knows that this is bad practice, since such a trench systematically cuts through and destroys the relationship of the wall to the adjacent below-ground archaeological deposits. The correct way to 'understand' a wall through excavation is to dig a section *across* it, so as to expose the relationship of the wall to the below-ground archaeology, or even better to open up a whole area. This produces a more complex but more accurate and truthful picture – for example, showing that stone curtain walls are not the only archaeological feature on castle sites, that castles were often densely packed with less substantial timber buildings (Higham and Barker 1992).

Thus it is with interpretation of castles. Those stressing the 'military' function of castles, or equally those stressing 'social' functions, have been guilty of interpretive wall-chasing. In their urge to find out where the wall goes, they have overlooked the relationship of 'the military' to all sorts of other phenomena, arguably hidden from view below turf, but nevertheless there. It is not enough now to say 'OK, let's chase walls in other directions – the social, the symbolic.' We need to interpret *across the wall*, looking *contextually* at all aspects of castles and their relationship. The picture thus produced will be more complex, and possibly less unified and coherent, but ultimately richer, more faithful to the evidence, and more interesting.

It is worth noting in passing how different strands of thinking have come together in this debate. Empirically-minded 'castle buffs' (and there is a part of us all that fits into this category) have seen that the evidence simply does not add up to the military story. Royal Commission scholars have used their long-tested techniques of landscape survey and analysis to note some very odd things going on around castles. At the same time, a changing theoretical environment has made archaeologists more sympathetic towards questions of symbolic meaning, structure and practice, and more sceptical towards the idea of finding one final answer or solution. It is fruitless to ask which of these three elements came first, whether the 'evidence' is driving changes in 'theory' or vice versa; all these practices are structured within a changing twenty-first-century intellectual and cultural environment which forsakes easy narratives and accepted identities.

Castles as anecdotes

In this book, I want to build on and extend many of the insights discussed above. First, our assumption that castles have been 'studied to death' applies not only as Dixon has shown to the fabrics of well-known structures, but also to the way certain famous examples of castles are cited again and again in support of a larger narrative. As a result, buildings that are less well known get a mention in passing, but are rarely studied in the depth that they deserve. Bodiam is very well known, but Cooling is less so.

Yet I think there is more to this selective use of castles than simply over-emphasis on certain classic case studies. The use of castles can be seen as anecdotal. That is, castles are deployed as illustrative examples of certain trends or processes. Syntheses make a few general remarks about late medieval towers or *donjons*, and then include a page or two on Tattershall supplemented by a photo and plan. They go on to make a few general remarks about courtyard houses, supplemented by a page or two on Bodiam supplemented by a photo and plan. They mention 'the Northern preference' for square towers, illustrated by a page or two of discussion of Bolton.

As a result, stories we tell about castles can be quite unverifiable. For every Tattershall or Bodiam or Bolton one might cite a counter-example (in the respective cases cited above, South Wingfield, Raglan, Alnwick ...). One simply has to rely on the authority of the narrator; one has to trust their implicit word that they have selected 'typical' examples. *Therefore, the stories told appear to be empirical but are actually deeply theoretical* because implicitly theoretical criteria always underlie the selection made. To clarify, the bulk of such a text is taken up with archaeological minutiae; the text is garnished with lovingly prepared pictures and plans with a direct appeal to 'the evidence'. Kick a castle and it hurts; but if the reader is given no yardstick to measure how far examples have been chosen to fit the underlying story, the reader has no clue as to what other elements of 'the evidence' have been left out. They simply have to trust the authority of the writer, an authority that is partly social (is the writer a 'respected' member of the academic or professional community?).

I would go further. The same examples recur again and again. In this sense, the history of castle design is built on a *canon* of particular examples, much as traditional literary history is based on a canon of 'great texts'. The well-known critique in English literature of the idea of the canon (Gates 1995) is, I suggest, directly applicable to castle studies. I suspect that if we were to explicitly draw up such a canon of castles, it would be skewed towards the south of England and towards English Heritage-owned sites. Such a bias is entirely understandable; many of the most noted authorities on castles work for English Heritage or used to work for its ancestor bodies, and are based in the south.

Castles in the landscape

I also want to build on the insight that castles must be placed in their landscape. In Chapter 2 I build on observations of landscape to ask what those landscapes meant to contemporary observers. Here, I take the insights of the Royal Commission and extend them to think about how people move through space and how they attach meanings to what they see. Chapter 3 takes the same ideas but applies them to the internal architecture of the castle; how one moves around the spaces and what those spaces 'meant' to observers and participants.

If early castle studies were dominated by wall-chasing, later studies have been dominated by the plan view and of the aerial photograph. We often forget that such views of a castle and its landscape context were never seen by contemporary observers before the invention of the balloon. The plan view was only seen by builders, and even then only arguably so. In this sense, all the wonderful reconstructions by Alan Sorrell and latterly by the artists of English Heritage are lovely to look at but deeply problematic. To plausibly represent 'Baconsthorpe Castle as it appeared in 1500' one has to give a ground view rather than an aerial view by definition.

A new view of castles

How might we then go about constructing a new view of castles? Here are some of the elements that might make up a bare minimum. First, a definition of a new sample based on strictly archaeological criteria, not dependent on documentary references; second, intensive structural analysis along the lines pursued by Dixon and others of a rigorously defined sample of structures; third, intensive excavation of some structures; fourth, detailed analysis of their landscape context beyond the collection of case studies we currently have; fifth, a full consideration of contemporary mentalities both elite and common, including late medieval vernacular texts; sixth, full consideration of castles across Europe, treating so-called 'Celtic fringes' equally with 'heartlands'; seventh, consideration of artistic portrayals of castles from items such as the *Duc de Berry* and Renaissance portrayals; eighth, consideration of social identity as expressed in other classes of material and textual culture, for example, funeral monuments (Llewellyn 1993).

This book is only a very tiny part of such a project. It concentrates on one country, England, with a brief excursion into Wales to discuss Raglan. It looks at one phase of castle studies, the late medieval and Renaissance periods. Within this period, it makes no attempt to be exhaustive in its coverage. It will have succeeded in its purpose if it encourages others to take up other elements of this project, even if every one of the ideas and interpretations suggested within its pages is rapidly superseded.

My main interest is in late medieval castles and what happened to the castle at the Renaissance. The book follows this path as follows. Chapter 2 will tell the story of changing scholarly views of Bodiam Castle, the classic case study of its kind. We will see the debate between 'military' and 'symbolic' views of Bodiam played out, and the way the evidence of the castle itself, its surrounding landscape, and the documentary record can be mobilised to support different understandings. The second part of this chapter will take the lessons of Bodiam and apply them to many different castle sites where 'watery landscapes' played a key role. Chapter 3 will consider what happens within the moat and walls – how we should understand the plan and layout of castles. In both these chapters I will stress how castles acted as stage settings.

Chapter 4 is a kind of interlude. It takes the lessons learnt from the previous two chapters and applies them to ways we might think about the medieval/Renaissance transition in architecture and material culture generally. Here I bring in bodies of theory developed in related disciplines, particularly postcolonial theory, New Historicism and literary Cultural Materialism, to begin to look at how we might understand architectural change between 'medieval' and 'Renaissance', and with it 'the decline of the castle', in a new way. This chapter is necessarily dense and theoretical, as it deals with very difficult underlying conceptual issues of how we explain architectural change, conceptual issues that have been raised by the problems of the evidence discussed in the preceding chapters.

Chapter 5 applies the lessons to a specific castle – Kenilworth – and looks at the famous visits of Queen Elizabeth I to that structure in the 1570s. I argue that we cannot understand the ceremonial of those visits without looking at the material backdrop of the castle and its surroundings. I suggest that we can only do so through a fully archaeological and contextual account of those surroundings. Kenilworth is thus an 'evidence house', an empirical illustration of the theoretical points made in the previous chapter.

If we want to consider fully what castles meant to people, we have to look at readings other than those of the dominant patriarchal classes – we must consider gender, other social classes, questions of how people of other social classes and statuses understood what they were looking at. Chapter 6 explores these issues. It concludes that questions of social identity of this sort cannot be seen clearly by archaeologists and historians using traditional ideas. For example, we can only ask meaningful questions about how architecture relates to social status if we rethink deeply held notions about 'vernacular' and 'polite' design.

In several of these chapters, I try to start with the castles themselves – what can be seen on the ground now – before moving on to wider interpretations. In part, this is an attempt to follow McNeill's injunction to study the castle without a set of preconceived theories about its function, but it is also an attempt to avoid abstract theorising. If others have started with 'no real doubt' before they even started their researches, here I want at least to look at the buildings before making assertions about what they might mean.

My aim in writing the book is not to persuade the reader towards a particular viewpoint about castle design. If what follows merely sows some seeds of doubt in their minds about accepted narratives, 'what we know' about 'clear military intent' or 'obvious social display', it will have served its purpose. One of the problems with recent work on the late medieval and Renaissance periods, I suggest, is that it has claimed to have moved forward, but in fact merely replaced one set of easy buzz phrases with another. We all know that we can no longer talk about 'comfort and convenience' or 'progress', so we talk instead of 'the rise of the individual', 'competitive emulation' and 'conspicuous consumption'. I am not sure that this represents progress in our understanding of the material. In what follows I shall try to stress the unfamiliar, to move away from easy readings, to interpret castles 'against the grain', just as the literary critic Jonathan Dollimore suggests we should read Renaissance literary texts against the grain (1992).

And, even if the reader is not convinced, we will have looked at some really wonderful buildings along the way. One of the chief strengths of castle studies is that it is *fun*. People love clambering around old ruins, pacing up and down shattered halls, looking out from crumbling battlements. The stress on the subjective experience of castle-visiting and appreciation is not new; rather, it was a central part of traditional writing on castles and was only recently excised from academic writing. As late as 1960, Douglas Simpson could feel free to allude in print to the devastation of his study by an escaped circus monkey, refer to the London and North-Eastern Railways poster of Tattershall, and make aesthetic value judgments in his introduction to the Tattershall building accounts (Simpson 1960: v, xvi). Why do properly detailed, empirical accounts have to be impersonally written and frankly boring in order to be taken seriously by the scholarly community?

I have written before that there is something wrong with our disciplinary practices if we want the study of the past to be easy (Johnson 1997); there must be something very wrong if our study is, by definition, uninteresting, devoid of pleasure; or if we cannot try to communicate that pleasure to our audience; or if writing in such a manner is somehow considered unscholarly. We love casting our eyes upon sconces; we do not have to follow De Flores' example and stab the interest to death before it has had time to blossom.

2

WATERY LANDSCAPES

The castle of Bodiam is in Sussex, close to the Kentish border and the south coast of England, directly south of London (Figure 1.1). It is owned by the National Trust; the area around the castle is open to the public without charge, kept neatly mowed and maintained in the manner of an English Heritage site, and frequented even in the dead of winter by retired couples walking their dogs.

The car park is at a little distance from the monument; one walks up to the castle, and having walked around the moat to the other side of the building, one can take a little footpath up the rise beyond. At the top of this rise, one can turn and look back to see Bodiam Castle framed against what many might consider to be a quintessentially English landscape: the meandering River Rother fringed by green fields and rolling hills (Figure 2.1). The only discordant note (for some) is the hexagonal concrete World War Two pillbox a little south of the castle.

Guidebooks and local tradition proudly proclaim that Bodiam is the finest surviving late medieval castle in England. It is certainly the most written about, and the most controversial. The evidence of Bodiam – its architectural details, its landscape context, and its associated documents – has been interpreted in different ways. These different interpretations embody not just different views of the monument itself, but different ways of thinking about the later Middle Ages, and different ways of thinking about the nature of archaeological and historical evidence in general.

Towers in a landscape

Bodiam gives the lie to the notion that symmetrical design arrived with the Renaissance (Figure 2.2). It is planned as a rectangle. At each corner is a circular tower. On two opposed sides are the gateways; one the main entrance, flanked by rectangular projections, the other the 'postern' or rear gate, placed within a square tower. The use of square forms is echoed on the other two sides where rectangular interval towers have been placed. The exterior is thus carefully composed of alternating circular and rectangular tower forms. The

Figure 2.1 Bodiam Castle, as viewed from the 'Gun Garden' to the north.

fenestration of the castle is, however, not symmetrical: from the outside, windows appear to be placed in a superficially random pattern.

Inside the walls of the castle, the disposition of rooms is also not symmetrical. The arrangement of rooms characteristic of a typical high status late medieval domestic building is laid out around a courtyard. As we look at buildings from the fourteenth to the sixteenth centuries in the course of this book, we shall find these rooms coming up again and again, as common elements of what might be termed a 'spatial grammar' or 'language', a system of organising space that the builders of such structures employed time and time again. The specific sizes and arrangements might vary; the different elements might be stacked in a tower, or placed end to end, or placed within an H-plan; but they are almost always there. It is an arrangement which is specific to England; the 'grand salle' of France and its attendant rooms had a rather different set of forms and functions (Girouard 2000: 42).

At Bodiam, these elements include the hall; the cross-passage at the lower end of the hall, here giving direct access to the postern gate, the kitchens placed on the other side of the cross-passage from the hall, 'private' chambers for the lord at the other, 'upper' end of the hall, and guest chambers. The overall scale of the domestic accommodation can be judged from the presence of thirty-three fireplaces and twenty-eight latrines. The latrines discharge directly into the moat, in contrast with the usual medieval practice of simply discharging down the slope of the wall and berm.

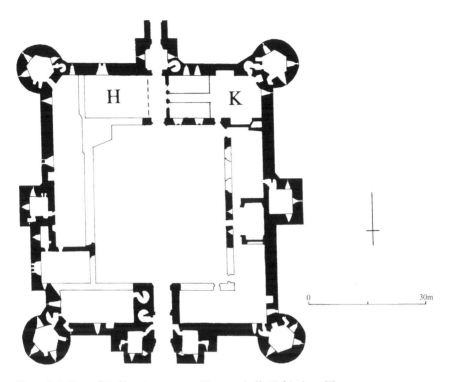

Figure 2.2 Plan of Bodiam inner court. H: great hall; K: kitchen. The postern gate opens on to the cross-passage between at the lower end of the hall; three doors open off the cross-passage leading to pantry, kitchen and buttery.

This late medieval house is surrounded by a wall, surmounted by battlements and studded with towers. The only element to disturb the external symmetry is the chapel, which projects outside the line of the curtain into the moat. It is easily recognisable as a chapel from the outside by its large and distinctive window with unusual tracery. The forms of the gates are again readily intelligible to anyone familiar with late medieval castles. The postern gate is housed within a tower, while the pair of 'towers' of the main gate are actually projections to the gatehouse itself. The housings of the gates have vertical grooves apparently to enable a portcullis or grille to be raised and lowered, and keyhole-shaped gunports around their base.

But the most striking feature of Bodiam is without doubt the moat or small lake which surrounds it. There is no berm, and so the castle appears to rise directly from the moat; it appears to be joined directly to its reflection in the water. This moat was created artificially; the site of the castle in a small natural basin was carefully selected. The site of Bodiam as a whole lies on a shallow slope; the moat is fed by a stream from the west. The builders of

21

Figure 2.3 The south and east fronts of Bodiam, as featured in a brochure for National Westminster Bank. The caption below reads: "Reflect on the strength of our investment portfolio service".
(Courtesy of NatWest Bank Plc. NTPL – Photography: O.Benn/A Olgilvie (1997)).

Bodiam constructed an earthwork-retaining bank to the south and east, and the whole site was excavated to enhance the natural basin. There is no berm; the plinth of the castle is partly submerged, as at the thirteenth-century castle of Leeds, Kent. This means that the latrines to the castle are 'flushed out' by the water, and therefore that this moat can be seen as an open sewer. Despite such unpleasant realities, today the image of Bodiam rising from its reflection is a famous motif, being used for example to sell investment policies on the back of its apparent military strength (Figure 2.3).

The documentary record states that Bodiam was built by Sir Edward Dallyngrigge or Dallingridge (like Shakespeare, his name could be spelt in several different ways). If the spatial grammar at Bodiam is one that will be familiar by the end of this book, elements of the biographies of men like Dallyngrigge will become almost tedious.

Dallyngrigge was a younger son, denied the prospect of his father's estate under the prevailing practice of primogeniture; he served in the French wars from 1359 to 1387. He returned from France a rich man; popular tradition states that he made his money from ransoming innocent French maidens. There is no evidence to support such a tradition, but there is no question that much building in this period was funded by loot from the French wars. McFarlane makes the pertinent point that though the English were eventually driven from France at the close of the Hundred Years War, they pursued the admirable policy of fighting the war largely on French soil and benefited financially in various ways, including those of ransoms of hapless French noble prisoners brought home (McFarlane 1973: 27–32). Dallyngrigge married an heiress of the de Wardeleu family, who brought him substantial estates as dowry and also provided a son and heir. He was active in local and national politics; he was Knight of the Shire for Sussex 1379–88, was involved in various local disputes including a quarrel with John of Gaunt's agents in Sussex, and played a national political role during the regency of Richard II's childhood.

Does the castle really work?

We can walk around and admire this fascinating castle endlessly; one of the few areas of agreement in Bodiam's interpretation is that, in aesthetic terms, it is an exceptionally fine piece of late fourteenth-century architecture. But how can we understand or explain it?

The orthodox view has been to see Bodiam in military terms. The castle is sited close to the south coast; at the time it was built, English fortunes in the French wars were at a low ebb, and the area was susceptible to French raids. The wide moat, the towers, the elaborate entry into the main gatehouse, all these features can be seen as intended to make penetration into the castle difficult. The quadrangular plan would make it easy, it has been suggested, for a small group of defenders to move from point to point on the parapet, defending where need be.

The final confirmation of the military thesis comes from an historical document, a 'licence to crenellate [fortify]'. Translated from the Latin, it states apparently quite unequivocally that Sir Edward Dallyngrigge sought and duly obtained licence in October 1385 'to fortify with a wall of stone and lime the dwelling-place of the manor of Bodiam next to the sea . . . and to construct and make thereof a castle for the defence of the adjacent countryside' and for the 'resisting of [the king's] enemies' (Coulson 1993). Here is a clear, irrefutable statement of the military purpose of the castle.

Opposition to this military view started early, in the late nineteenth century. In 1966 Hohler called Bodiam an 'old soldier's dream house' (Hohler 1966: 140). But a serious rethinking of Bodiam and what it meant has come over the past fifteen years from two sources working to some extent independently: the scholar Charles Coulson, working on the architecture and the documentary record, and from the Royal Commission on Historical Monuments, working on the landscape context of the castle.

First, the licence to crenellate. The problem with such an interpretation is that it fails to consider the nature of such licences in general. Licences to crenellate were given to monasteries, towns, builders of clearly non-military structures in general. Bodiam is not 'next to the sea'; it is ten miles away. The meandering River Rother is hardly a route of major strategic importance, going nowhere in particular. Documents of this kind cannot be taken at face value as prehistorians might suppose. Coulson (1994) suggests that the production of such documents was largely part of a system of chivalric honour, and the references to defensive intent were part of a knightly code that cannot be taken at face value or seen as a straightforward reflection of reality.

Coulson moves on from a reassessment of the licence to a reassessment of the architecture. The most obvious 'defensive' feature, the moat, is retained by an earthen bank that is utterly undefended; it has been estimated that it would take a dozen men to cut through the bank in a single night. Most window loops are inconveniently placed or downright unusable for archery, while large windows lighting the hall and the chapel pierce the curtain wall. He goes on to examine almost every element of the architecture in some detail, arguing that flanking towers do not really flank; evidence for drawbridges is equivocal; portcullis grooves and 'murder holes' are unusable; the parapet is not easily accessible for defence, and in any case is commanded by higher ground within crossbow range; and so on (1992).

The castle as a whole has a series of features that make the structure appear larger than it really is. The reflection of the castle in the surrounding water magnifies its image; to achieve this effect, Bodiam has been revetted in a very similar way to the 'gloriet' at the late thirteenth-century Leeds Castle. The circular corner towers resemble thirteenth-century examples, and yet are much smaller than their Edwardian counterparts; the battlements on their projecting stair turrets are purely decorative. One tower doubles as a dovecote. The battlements are slightly smaller than they really should be; they are not high enough to cover a man standing upright. Upon entry to the inner courtyard, the castle appears decidedly modest, no more than a large manor house. Other structures of this type generally have an outer court of some kind, as at the much larger early fourteenth-century castle at Bampton in Oxfordshire (Youngs *et al.* 1988: 268–9) and nearby Westenhanger.

Moving through landscapes

What lends Coulson's views additional strength is that a similar view of Bodiam has emerged from work at Bodiam that was initially carried out independently. In the 1980s the Royal Commission on Historical Monuments (England) carried out a survey of the immediate landscape context of the castle (Figure 2.4).

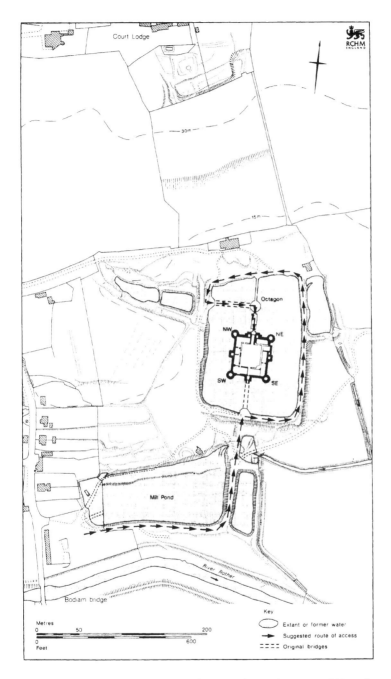

Figure 2.4 Royal Commission plan of earthworks, with suggested line of approach indicated. (After Everson 1996: Figure 1.)

This survey revealed a complex series of earthworks surrounding the castle and its moat that were interpreted as part of a formal landscape. To the south of the castle were a series of rectangular ponds; fishponds were placed on the east and west sides of the castle also; there appeared to be a cascade or series of ponds created to the north-west. To the north of the castle, an ornamental terrace, a little way off the modern path, gave a view from above of the whole composition in all its glory (Figure 2.1). This earthwork is known as the 'Gun Garden' after its mistaken identification by earlier scholars as a Civil War gun platform (O'Neill 1960: 107). Excavations on this platform, however, revealed traces of a medieval building, interpreted as a possible banqueting hall. Guests of Dallyngrigge, then, could ascend the hill and look down admiringly on his carefully composed creation as they dined.

The most interesting aspect of this earthwork survey for our present purpose, however, is the importance it places on movement across the landscape and the way that movement is controlled and delimited. As a result, views of the castle are carefully constructed as part of a progression, an stage-by-stage unveiling of the building. The late medieval visitor to Bodiam, let us say a knight and prospective guest of Dallyngrigge, might arrive from the south. From there his path was delimited by a causeway south of one sheet of water before a sharp left turn along a causeway between pools and up to the south front of the building.

On mounting the hill, our visitor is met with a surprise: it is only at this point that the moat is visible; at first sight, the castle is without a moat. The knight's movement is again controlled as he sets off again, this time around the moat to the right (no guest of honour would enter straight ahead via the postern). Another left turn and the projecting chapel is revealed to the left, another pool to the right; yet another left turn around the corner of the moats and the north front is revealed. On this front, the merlons and crenels of the battlements are set slightly closer together; Coulson suggests that Dallyngrigge retainers could have manned the battlements at this point, their own bodies becoming features of display in welcoming our guest.

But the processional route is not ended. Our knight admires the symmetry and composition of the front before being forced to turn again and move to a point beyond the north-western corner of the moat to access the causeway bridge. From this point he can see the succession of ponds leading up the slope to the west. Mounting the causeway, he makes yet another turn, on the octagonal platform, before finally entering the gatehouse and emerging into the courtyard beyond. Once in the courtyard the whole layout of the castle is finally revealed.

Bodiam, Froissart and Kafka

So Bodiam is revealed, stage by stage, to our knight; but can we say that the 'true meaning' of Bodiam is revealed to the modern scholar? Clearly not.

The crude, exclusively military view of Bodiam has been comprehensively discredited. The only architectural element of the Bodiam landscape that fits neatly into such a perspective is the rather forlorn twentieth-century pillbox. There is less certainty, however, about what to put in the place of the military view. Much of Coulson's work has been a detailed rebuttal of Bodiam's supposed military effectiveness. When it comes to how, then, we might better interpret Bodiam, his writing becomes more equivocal – and, it seems to me, more suggestive and less conclusive:

> The wisest course is to resist the temptation to write off any feature as 'sham', or to take any element as purely 'functional' (by which 'defensive' is intended normally). It is an artful combination which expresses . . . all the complex seigniorial associations of the medieval castle-image, which included the deterring (and, if necessary, the defeating) of attack at whatever level was appropriate . . . the bravado of double portal chambers, 'murder holes' and three portcullises is mere *rodomontade* when the lateral doors are so weak. There is no 'military' logic in trebling the main closures while leaving a short and direct approach to a weak back door (Postern) which entirely lacks elaboration. But there is powerful psychological sense nonetheless: is it closer to Jean Froissart (and perhaps also to Franz Kafka) than it is to Vegetius or to the Sieur de Vauban. The fairy-tale element is here, allusive and romantic . . . 'Fortification' was surely metaphysical as well as material; a matter of imagery and symbolism, not just of technology.
>
> (Coulson 1992: 66 and 83)

Elsewhere, Coulson insists:

> The difficulty lies in discerning how far the visual impact and the symbolic significance inherent in battlemented panoply have affected particular features and exaggerated them in the familiar contemporary fashion whereby art enhanced structural function. Working the same transformation upon the defensive elements of fortification . . . can so perfectly integrate the military and the psychological that separately analysing the contribution of each becomes very difficult . . . Given that the age of Richard II was one of the most sophisticated and cultured in the whole of medieval European civilisation, it would be as well to jettison the crude dichotomy [of military versus residential].
>
> (1992: 66)

Elsewhere, he notes 'conflicting and simultaneous signals' and even suggests Bodiam may have been built with a sense of humour (ibid.: 106 and 102). Frustratingly, however, Coulson ends his analysis at this point.

The contrast between the depth and confidence of Coulson's architectural analysis, and his brevity and equivocation when he comes to ask what it might mean, is very striking. Why is he so equivocal, having spent so much time in a comprehensive, to my mind irrefutable, point-by-point demolition of the military case? Because, I suggest, Coulson's detailed and deep knowledge of late medieval fortification and its social context suggests that *when we consider medieval architecture there are no easy, bold statements to be made.* Things are never that simple; analysis of late medieval mentalities can never be reduced to either/or comparisons or easy reference to a 'range of functions'.

Bodiam, like Cooling, started off in our account as obvious and familiar: first, obviously military, then obviously sham; it is neither. As with Cooling, when we look at Bodiam more closely, we move from the familiar to the unfamiliar, the obvious and 'easy' to the counter-intuitive and 'difficult'. There are a series of aspects to Bodiam Castle that need to be thought through before a better account of its many meanings can be offered.

What did Bodiam mean?

First, we can look at the immediate social and landscape context of Bodiam. Dallyngrigge sat in an ambiguous position in local and national politics. In broad terms, he was a 'new man', a younger son who had made his political and financial fortune through astute moves in war and marriage. Within the local context, his sway over the local community was far from complete; he was required to share the local parish church, and much local land was controlled by a nearby monastery. He was thus denied the opportunity to show patronage in the church and to make a private park out of extensive tracts of land, two of the most familiar ways in which late medieval nobles expressed their identity.

Dallyngrigge did transform the local landscape where he could. Three months after the licence to crenellate was issued for Bodiam, he obtained a licence to divert a watercourse from 'Dalyngreggesbay' to power the water-mill in the *vill* of Bodiam. Together with the recent grant of a market, 'we see in these three grants evidence for the plantation of a planned, almost model village on the bank of the Rother – moated castle, mill, cottages and market-place' (Whittick 1993: 122). He did this, we should note, at a time when according to landscape historians (Roberts 1987), wholesale layout of such planned landscapes had been almost non-existent in the English landscape for over a century, if indeed it was present before this.

Dallyngrigge also lacked another element available to many elite builders at this time – an old building. For every castle built afresh during this period, many more old castles were altered. And while it is debateable how far medieval people were conscious of anachronism in architectural style in the manner of modern observers, old fabric was used and deployed to emphasise the ancient nature of the lineage in many instances. For all the ostentation of the heraldry around its front gate, Bodiam was not an old and ancient pile when it was finished. Its power had to be expressed in other ways. In its symmetry, Bodiam forsakes the symbolism of other old and ancient piles; it is at one level loudly and assertively new, of one build.

Of course, what Bodiam was taken to 'really mean' would vary from observer to observer. In the first place, Dallyngrigge could have used his castle and landscape in different ways, choosing to ride out to greet his guests at different points – by the river before the full view of the castle was apparent, at the postern, or within the castle itself. The octagonal platform in front of the main gate appears a perfect placement for a ceremonial reception; the north front of the castle would act as a backdrop for the bodies of Dallyngrigge and his party. The non-elite visitor, on the other hand, may have had to make do with the postern gate from which he or she could be ushered swiftly into the service range, or be denied access entirely. There are possible other routes to the castle, for example from the north-west along-side the 'cascade' (McNeill, pers. comm.).

But to ask 'What did Dallyngrigge really have in mind when he built this structure?' is an unanswerable question. We will never know what Dallyngrigge really had in mind. It is as meaningless as 'What did Chaucer really have in mind when he wrote *The Canterbury Tales*?' As poststructural-ists insist, the author, or in this case the owner or builder, is dead.

To clarify this point, regardless of what Chaucer's conscious intentions may have been, when we read *The Canterbury Tales*, we bring our ideas, atti-tudes, assumptions to it. Knowledge of the cultural and social context in which *The Canterbury Tales* were written can help enrich our analysis and locate sources of tension and contradiction within the text, and produce better, more accurate and fuller readings, but this is not the same thing as getting closer to what Chaucer 'really meant'. Similarly, we can explore the meanings of Bodiam through reference to its contexts – the ideas, values, tensions and contradictions of late medieval society and ideology. Such an exercise will help us understand Bodiam better, but must not be confused with a search for what the person Dallyngrigge, superficially so familiar to us in his *nouveau-riche* ostentation but actually a rather distant and enigmatic figure, 'really meant'.

Bodiam would have been read in different ways regardless of what Dallyngrigge had, consciously or unconsciously, in mind. Our knight is only one of many possible visitors to Bodiam; each visitor would have a different experience, according to their gender and social position. Anyone trained as a knight – in other words, elite men of the secular world – might admire the gunports on the gate, the very latest fashion in defence, while observing to their companions that the position of those gunports makes them almost impossible to use effectively, thus showing off their military knowledge. Visitors of a lower social order might be expected to enter via the postern, or (if they had horses or other mounts) to dismount earlier in their approach to the castle, it being disrespectful to ride directly up to the gate. The ordinary inhabitants of the late medieval community of Bodiam would experience the castle as part of an everyday landscape. We do not know how they felt about the military symbolism of the castle, but we do know that some contemporary pictures assigned the generic image of the castle to Hell (Warnke 1994).

To summarise, I suggest that the reason Coulson finds it so difficult to disentangle what he calls the 'military' and the 'psychological' is because the two were not easily separable in the late medieval ways of thinking. We must therefore turn to some account of those ways of thinking if we are to move towards any understanding of Bodiam, a structure at first so obvious and now so opaque.

Medieval masculinities

How did different genders perceive the military symbolism of the castle? It seems axiomatic to me that if we are to move beyond an either/or analysis of Bodiam, we must start with an account of late medieval elite masculinity. The 'military' conceptions of late fourteenth-century warfare were, I suggest, intimately bound up with late medieval ideas of masculinity, knighthood, and martial valour, ideas that were historically transient and which need placing in the context of late medieval society. In other accounts, the castle is gendered as feminine; it becomes the fortress which needs to be taken and possessed (Gilchrist 1999).

To be an elite man in the later Middle Ages was to be at the centre of a series of discourses about topics such as lordship and chivalry, discourses which were neither 'real' nor 'just fantasy'. They were complex pieces of ideological belief that on the one hand were idealisations, yet on the other hand guided everyday and ceremonial activities in a very real way.

'Chivalry' was a system of values explicitly addressed to the male knight. According to Keen, its substance is difficult to pin down:

> One can define within reasonably close limits what is meant by the word knight, the French *chevalier*; it denotes a man of aristocratic standing and probably of noble ancestry, who is capable, if called upon, of equipping himself with a war horse and the arms of a heavy cavalryman, and who has been through certain rituals that make him what he is – who has been 'dubbed' to knighthood. But chivalry, the abstraction from *chevalier*, is not so easily pinned down. It was a word that was used in the middle ages with different meanings and shades of meaning by different writers and in different contexts.
>
> (1984: 1–2)

Keen goes on to identify elements of blood and lineage, *prouesse, loyauté, largesse* (generosity), *courtoisie*, and *franchise* (which Keen defines as the bearing that goes with good birth and virtue). As such, chivalry was written on the body through armour and arms of war, as well as being indicated by bodily posture and behaviour. It was staged and re-staged through tournaments and other ceremonies, for example, Edward III's founding of the Order of the Garter, and was expressed in medieval Arthurian literature. Though the knight was part of a complementary tripartite structure of society (those who fight, those who work and those who pray), his role was closely linked and suffused with Christian values, particularly if obviously in the didactic writings of churchmen.

Huizinga (1924: 65) saw chivalry as a code of honour that glossed over the bloody realities in late medieval life; in this he is followed by Thompson and Platt who draw the implication that where we see a 'martial face' in later medieval castles it is pure 'make-belief' and 'fantasies' (Thompson 1987: 71; Platt 1982). I suggest, however, that, as Coulson implied of Froissart, chivalric values were more subtle and complex than this. As recent studies of late medieval literature have shown, knighthood was a complex construction, involving, for example, transvestism (Putter 1997). The pure fantasy element is an imposition of eighteenth- and nineteenth-century Romantic notions of chivalry; when modern scholars talk of fantasy, they have Tennyson in mind rather than Malory (cf. Girouard 1981). In this respect as in others the shadow of Victorian medievalism looms even further over castle studies than the general's armchair.

For Keen, chivalry occupied an uneasy space between ideal and reality; it suggested an ideal code of personal conduct for the male knight. As Keen points out (1984: 3), if it were pure fantasy, it would not be worth studying. A Marxist would rephrase this by saying that while a belief in chivalry is clearly ideological, and clearly serves to both legitimate and mask certain systems of power and inequality, this does not mean it is either completely 'untrue' or without any power (Eagleton 1991 discusses how beliefs can be simultaneously 'true' and ideological).

Chivalry occupied the conceptual space between ideal and real, as it did between abstract notions of political order and personal codes of conduct on the other. That is why chivalry is so difficult to classify and analyse. In this respect, it is just like the castle of Bodiam. Both stress martial values and ideas of honour in a way that is neither 'fantasy' nor 'real'. Both are gendered; both are the creations of men, and reflect men's idealised notions of themselves and their conduct. Both occupy an uneasy space between ascribed status (that of blood) and achieved status (Dallyngrigge's position as a younger son who made a career and married well).

Power and the state

Bodiam's meanings thus point towards the individual, to the personal conduct of the male knight. But they also point outwards to a larger scale, to the cultural patterns that underlay royal and state politics.

The 1380s were a moment of crisis in English politics, both in terms of political infighting and more fundamentally in social tensions; French raids of the Kent and Sussex coast were only one symptom of this. Other symptoms included the political youth of the King, Richard II; Richard's political career was to end in his deposition and probable murder; and striking more fundamentally at the heart of the social system, a series of peasant uprisings both in England and the rest of Europe. These uprisings saw the articulation of alternative models of society, and are often taken as the point of origin for popular protest and radical politics of the labouring classes in England (Hilton 1973; Poulsen 1984).

The period was therefore marked by a series of anxieties, both about dynastic politics, and about the subversion of the political system itself. Art and architecture are always expressions of social concerns, and it is no surprise therefore to find that the period sees a sudden burst of artistic activity (Williams 1980). Art and architectural historians view the existence of a 'court style' in Richard II's reign as a topic of controversy (Colvin 1983), but its elements might be taken to reflect this anxiety about relationships between court and country as they were to do albeit in a very different manner two centuries later. Artistic style was certainly not regarded as trivial, in an age when the smallest gesture was a source of cultural tension: later in his reign Richard II was condemned for 'strange and flattering' forms of address along with new powers (Saul 1995).

This set of anxieties may be reflected architecturally at Bodiam. Henry Yevele, one of the builders who regularly enjoyed royal patronage, was probably involved in the work at Bodiam; Coulson sees the aesthetic balance of the north front as a sign of his architectural genius at work. Leaving such a biographical footnote aside, we might ask what architectural choices were made at Bodiam, why the specific form was taken there. Bodiam could have been designed in the French manner; other castles have more extensive machicolation, usually cited as a French import, the most relevant example being the gatehouse towers at Cooling. Other late medieval castles such as Nunney and Raglan have very striking use of architectural features that are similar to or derivative of French practices.

In other respects, Bodiam Castle is less demonstrative than its contemporaries. As already noted, the scale of the domestic furnishings is not large. The hall is much less impressive than others of its period. The exterior of the castle has none of the decorative features found elsewhere, such as grotesques or carved figures on the battlements like those at Alnwick or Chepstow. The late fourteenth century was not a great period for sculpture

(Lindley 1995) but nevertheless the opportunities here for it are not taken. The style of Bodiam can be seen as part of a wider late fourteenth-century adoption of a style of Perpendicular Gothic that was particularly and assertively 'English' in a way that architectural historians have argued was not present in Gothic style before (Pevsner 1956). In this sense, Bodiam is the expression of ideas that have a national as well as social and political dimension.

What I have tried to do in my analysis of Bodiam is to start where Coulson and others stopped, with the observation that Bodiam is a carefully constructed landscape and monument; that 'military versus symbolic' debates are shallow; and that the meanings of Bodiam are intimately tied up with late medieval values of elite identity. These values are gendered, and have social and national connotations also.

In themselves, confined to the one site, the observations in the last few pages are merely speculation, though in themselves they are no more of a speculative leap than more mundane and commonly found assertions of 'conspicuous consumption' or 'desire to impress'. Their tenor will certainly be very familiar to late medieval literary scholars (cf. Kaueper 1999). We will never know for sure what was consciously or unconsciously in the mind of Dallyngrigge as he showed his visitors round, or for that matter in the minds of his guests as they viewed the building and heard his proud words; still less what was in the minds of those who were not elite men – peasants, women of all social classes.

This is one sense in which Bodiam is like Franz Kafka's castle; so apparently huge and physically dominating, it nevertheless remains an enigma – we wander round its complex landscapes and labyrinthine corridors searching for some essential identity or final meaning, a meaning that forever eludes us, that is always just around the next twist in the causeway or behind the next door. For Kafka, this lack of a final reference or anchor is the whole point; arguably, for Bodiam also.

So what we can do is take the possibilities raised at Bodiam and trace them through other sites; in other words, we can place Bodiam in its context. Bodiam is not unique; far from it. Its landscape of sheets of water, causeways, twists and turns is remarkably well preserved but parallels can be found in a whole series of castle and other high-status sites across England and beyond. I shall first review the archaeological evidence for some of these sites, and then ask what these features might mean.

Water and the Royal Commission

It is a commonplace in traditional garden history that large-scale formal gardens arrived with the Renaissance; this is simply not true. We have known for a long time about medieval gardens in documents; references to gardens are discussed in a variety of historical sources. And they are familiar allegorical and emblematic devices in medieval literature; gardens and garden imagery abound in the tales of Chaucer, in the Arthurian fantasies of Thomas Malory and the accounts of Jean Froissart. Medieval manuscripts and books of hours abound with pictorial representations of pleasure gardens; a series of treatises were written on gardens; most of these were in Latin, though one was translated into French in the late fourteenth century. These gave recommendations on how to arrange one's garden, and descriptions of existing layouts including mention of smaller residences in castle gardens (Whiteley 1999: 91, 97). And of course, no medieval theologian could fail to note that the first human habitation was the Garden of Eden; gardens recur throughout the Bible, most notably in the Song of Solomon, and embody a whole range of complex theological allusions. Gardens are the settings for the practices of courtly love, practices that themselves could take on Christian connotations (Johnson 1996: 145–9; Gilchrist 1999).

We have also known for some time about a whole series of surviving features in the landscape that are evidence of late medieval elite management of that landscape. The importance of hunting to the medieval elite household is seen in the profusion of 'forests' and other estates (Austin 1984). A forest, of course, was not simply a forest; it was an area of special rights and tenures, often royal. Thus village communities could exist within 'forests'. The more immediate context of the castle almost always had access to a park or managed estate, as well as a demesne farm.

Archaeologically we can trace the park pales that surrounded parks and estates, particularly from the late medieval period. We are also well aware of a series of earthwork remains associated with high-status sites relating to the management of its immediate surroundings. Sites of mills are well known, as are the complex system of leats and dams used to create millponds. Retaining dams for fishponds occur in abundance on sites of different social status, but most especially on the elite sites such as manor houses or monasteries (Aston 1988). Rabbit warrens were constructed throughout the late medieval period, particularly on 'marginal' land. Rabbits were not simply kept for their economic value; they were in part valued for their range of symbolic, theological associations, most notably at the Renaissance lodge and warren at Rushton in Northamptonshire (Stocker and Stocker 1996). And lastly though by no means least, moats and dry ditches surround rural sites. These moats again are found in different social contexts, but often around high-status sites (le Patourel and Roberts 1978).

What is new in recent scholarship is a recognition that these landscapes are much more extensive than previously realised and, further, are not simply utilitarian arrangements designed to meet the complex logistical requirements of feeding a large peripatetic household. Archaeological evidence exists for formal or 'pleasure' gardens, however defined, around a series of castles and other high-status sites.

Much of this evidence has been recognised, surveyed and collated by the scholars of the RCHME (Royal Commission of Historical Monuments of

England, now part of English Heritage), in particular those members who were involved at the survey work and subsequent discussions with Coulson at Bodiam. Examples are Stowe Park and Nettleham near Lincoln (Everson *et al.* 1991: 129–31; Taylor 1989); Somersham (Taylor 1998: 30) Cawood (Blood and Taylor 1992), and Alvechurch (Aston 1970). Now that some definite examples have been established, there has been a steady stream of further identifications. At Clun Castle, the City of Hereford Unit have interpreted the surroundings of a lodging range as a manipulated setting (Nenk, Margeson and Hurley 1993: 279–80); Shotwick (Everson 1998) is another example. Ludgershall is a site without water features but where 'a clearly designed and garden-like aspect from the beginning of the 13th century' has nevertheless been discerned (Everson *et al.* 2000: 102).

Designed landscapes can also be observed indirectly in the documents. The standardised format of the licences to crenellate discussed above also included routine references to the landscape beyond by the late medieval period. Coulson (1993) recounts Wingfield in Suffolk, where the 1385 licence to crenellate for Michael de la Pole, a 'new man' from a Hull merchant family, specified imparking also; Old Wardour; and Tonford Manor, near Canterbury, one of six sites licensed to Thomas Browne in 1448 with a common format including imparking, a free warren, and other rights (ibid.: 12–14).

Why have these complex, manipulated landscapes not been recognised until recently? There are several possible reasons. First, many such landscapes must have been rapidly replaced by later generations of landscape. Where a castle continued to be occupied into the sixteenth and seventeenth centuries, later styles of landscape garden would sweep away traces of earlier designs. The 'English landscape garden' style of the mid-eighteenth century onwards destroyed not just many sixteenth- and seventeenth-century formal gardens, but many traces of earlier landscapes as well. By the late eighteenth century, of course, many castle ruins were deliberately landscaped as romantic 'objects' in their own right, and had traces of earlier landscapes that did not fit with Romantic preconceptions obliterated in the process.

At Old Wardour in Wiltshire, for example, a fifteenth-century castle slighted in the Civil War was carefully maintained as a romantic ruin; woodland was laid out around it with various follies, including a druids' grotto and a miniature stone circle. The view of the old castle from the new country house was opened out, and new Gothick buildings added; the river was dammed to create a lakeside setting (Figure 2.5). Any analysis of earlier landscape settings for Old Wardour is thus rendered difficult if not impossible, though the hexagonal design of the castle and the layout of its outer ward suggest that this is an obvious place to look for the presence of a designed landscape beyond.

Wardour is certainly cleverly contrived for external viewing. The main front of the inner courtyard is carefully composed, with symmetrical rectangular projections flanking a ground floor entrance. The front is divided by an

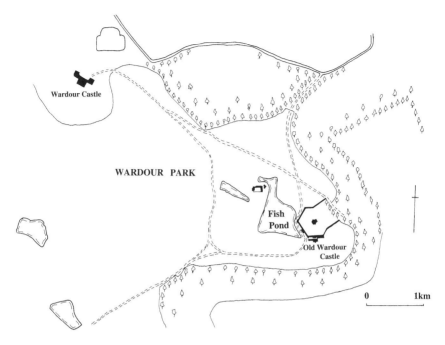

Figure 2.5 Old Wardour, Wiltshire. The hexagonal form of the fifteenth-century castle
suggests the possibility of a designed landscape beyond, but any such remains
are masked by the eighteenth-century layout of Wardour Castle and Park with
its driveways, areas of water and of woodland.

elegant string-course that was an integral part of the fourteenth-century
composition (Figure 2.6). Above this string-course is a row of tall windows
that the late medieval observer would correctly interpret as belonging to the
hall, with service chambers on one side and apartments on the other. Thus
does Wardour display itself. However, the interior of the hall reveals that the
windows are very steeply plunged; their lower base, and the floor of the
hall, are much lower than the external string-course implies. The hall is consequently much loftier, and would be a surprise to the visitor. It is worth
noting in passing that where a similar device is used at Trinity College Library
in Cambridge, it is cited as an example of the genius of its architect,
Christopher Wren (RCHME 1959: 237).

Again, at Raby Castle in County Durham, there are the clear signs of
a carefully composed landscape, in an artificially dammed body of water
below the ramparts, in the very low outer circuit of walls that form a platform
themselves and were lowered still further after the Middle Ages, a stage that
frames the inner buildings, and in the carefully composed plan which is a
combination of a regular interior studded with projecting towers (Figure 2.7).

Figure 2.6 Old Wardour, Wiltshire: façade.

Raby, however, is surrounded by a later, 'picturesque' landscape: ha-has ensure that Romantic views of the landscape are unimpeded, and green expanses run up to the walls. On the south-east side of Raby, the pasture runs over the earthworks of ridge-and-furrow agriculture; either Raby was surrounded by productive arable fields, or these fields were abandoned as part of a process of late medieval emparkment at the same time as the building of the castle. In other cases still more recent landscape modifications intrude: at the castle of Leeds in Kent they are partly hidden by remains of a modern golf course.

We do not have to wait until the eighteenth century for possible obliterations of earlier landscapes. At the fifteenth-century castle of Ashby de la Zouch, there is a garden with ornamental ponds to the south of the buildings, overlooked by Lord Hastings' great tower. The ponds are surrounded by a sixteenth-century wall and brick towers; it appears to be congruent with the towers, but no reason why the ponds cannot be earlier. There were certainly three deer parks in the late fifteenth century, named Great Park, Preston Park and Little Park, and a mill whose earthworks for leats survive (RCHME records, SE31 NE3).

Second, where visible earthwork traces do survive, they have often been assigned to later periods. Many may well be wrongly interpreted as Civil War emplacements. Bodiam 'Gun Garden' was seen as a Civil War emplacement

Figure 2.7 Raby Castle, County Durham, from the east. The outer walls were lowered in the postmedieval period. The apparent irregularity of the arrangements of the towers masks a regular internal courtyard plan.

by Douglas Simpson (Coulson 1992: 67). A raised terrace at Kenilworth has been routinely interpreted as such an emplacement, but there is evidence that it may be much earlier (see Chapter 5).

The third reason why such 'watery landscapes' have not been recognised is that they simply use sites that have bodies of natural water in front of or around them. The 'natural' setting of such castles does not invite comment by modern scholars until they are placed in the context of other landscapes. At Fotheringhay in Northamptonshire (Figure 2.8), the stone fabric of the castle is now almost completely destroyed. The first phase of occupation at Fotheringhay was an undistinguished motte-and-bailey castle; only these earthworks now survive from the inner bailey, together with a single lump of masonry, rather shapeless and forlorn, adorned with a plaque from the Richard III Society saying this was his birthplace. The River Nene flows past the site, spanned by a medieval bridge; earthworks to the immediate east of the site suggest a system of fishponds and leats. Within the castle walls, there is evidence for the layout of a fine range of domestic buildings (RCHME 1975).

In the later medieval period, Fotheringhay was transformed. A college and associated church were built at a little distance from the castle, together with ancillary ranges of guest lodgings. The whole site at this period was clearly

Figure 2.8 Fotheringhay: view from the south. The motte of the castle can be seen to the
right and the collegiate church to the left.

carefully composed, with the collegiate church at the same distance from the
river and with a series of outer courts and buildings interpreted as lodgings
on the other side of the complex. The bridge runs into the area between
college and castle, possibly within an outer court; the inner court consists of
a combination of buildings within a rampart, dominated by a D-shaped
polygonal *donjon* on the motte.

As a result, a visitor to Fotheringhay approaching across the flat lands to
the south would see the fine stone bridge ahead, the church to the left, and
castle to the right, both framed by the river in the front. The *donjon* on the
motte reflects the polygonal form of the tower of the church. Clusters of
buildings providing lodgings and stables are tucked away at the back from
this perspective. Further to the right, the system of ponds and leats creates
a setting for any visitor approaching from the east. So at Fotheringhay, the
meandering and placid River Nene does not excite our immediate scholarly
attention, but when considered as part of the whole is clearly again an integral part of a designed landscape.

Fourth, designed landscapes can be mistaken for earlier 'military' layouts.
Many complex systems of causeways and bridges over artificially created
bodies of water originated in the eleventh to thirteenth centuries; there, they
have often been interpreted in military terms, as barbicans or outer defences.

Figure 2.9 Barnard Castle, County Durham. The fifteenth-century window looking out
on to the deerpark.

This may be the case for these earlier periods; this question is outside the
scope of this book. What is clear, however, is that such complex systems
were used in ceremonial ways as settings for processions in later periods. The
most obvious example is again Kenilworth (see Chapter 6). It may be the
case in other examples that we have mistaken designed landscapes for military features. Whatever the case, many elements of late medieval designed
landscapes originated in this earlier period and have been interpreted in these
terms. Only in the few cases where castles were built on fresh sites, most
obviously Bodiam, do we not have this problem.

The use of impressive, precipitous locations may again have had an earlier
military intent but may have become part of a composed landscape by the fourteenth and fifteenth centuries. In the cases of both Warwick and Barnard
Castle (Figure 2.9), the original location may have been 'military' but carefully composed by the later medieval period. In both cases, windows do not
just look out over hunting grounds, but also act as features to be seen and
admired from below. The whole household was thus laid out for display; external observers could note the large windows at the upper end of the hall and
the chimneys indicating the internal disposition of rooms to the outside world.

Finally, the presence of designed landscapes has been overshadowed by
structures deemed to be of more importance on the site. At Saltwood, most

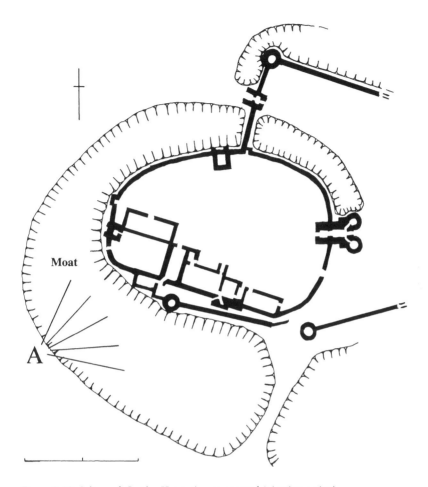

Figure 2.10 Saltwood Castle, Kent. A = suggested 'viewing point'.

scholarly attention has been focused on the gatehouse, with its tall twin towers; it has been argued on stylistic grounds that this impressive structure was built in the 1380s with the involvement of the ubiquitous Henry Yevele (Emery 1994). Saltwood also, however, has other features of interest, most notably a dam to one side to turn a small valley into a lake. A path runs around the perimeter of this lake from which composed views can be obtained of the main structure; at one point, one appears to be looking at a grand concentric castle studded with towers rather than what is actually quite a modest structure (Figure 2.10).

I suggest that there is a final and deeper reason, underlying all the others, why, in spite of all the evidence, we have failed to see these designed landscapes till recently. Archaeologists and historians have tended to assume that medieval landscapes are primarily functional and utilitarian. It is a matter of official policy for the Society for Medieval Archaeology (1987: 5) that 'the main medieval industry was agriculture', rather than being a medium for the expression of cultural values. As a result, the first port of call in explaining landscape features has consistently been a utilitarian one. For example, the rectangular mounds at Bolingbroke castle were seen by Thompson (1966: 152–8) as enclosing a watering-pond for impounded animals, an interpretation that was repeated by Beresford and Hurst (1979: 50–2) before the earthworks were reinterpreted as part of a formal landscape by Taylor (1998: 38). Again, early work on fishponds made the assumption that islands found in the middle of fishponds were ornamental and therefore could not be medieval (Aston 1970: 200). As a result, where 'cultural' or symbolic aspects of these landscapes have been acknowledged, particularly in recent years, they have been seen as an 'add-on' to their utilitarian value. Consequently, the division between 'functional' and 'symbolic' has been assumed rather than questioned.

Obviously medieval people had to eat to live, and obviously it would be a mistake to forget about the requirements of feeding the large households of the later Middle Ages. The accounts of the aristocracy suggest that more money was spent on food than any other item (Dyer 1989: 55). Mertes (1988) has estimated that the late medieval noble household could contain up to 2,000 people; that is, a lot of mouths to feed. The estates and economic networks of the later medieval elite were clearly in part organised as a vast provisioning machine, so that elite households could be fed, clothed and given accommodation, and guests could be given the appropriate hospitality. It would be a great mistake to see these landscapes in terms of a vulgar and exclusive set of 'cultural meanings' devoid of their context within everyday routine.

What I do think is going on here is that 'economic' uses of these landscapes and their cultural meanings were tied up one with another, so that the need to feed a great household and the ordered presentation of the estate in terms of symbolic meanings cannot be easily distinguished. I have made similar points about the practice of agriculture before enclosure elsewhere (Johnson 1996) and I shall expand on this point below.

Textual sources are ambivalent on what, precisely, were the intentions of late medieval elites in designing and managing these landscapes. Elite men, trained in the values of chivalry discussed in the context of Bodiam above, were often enjoined not to be concerned with the everyday management of their estates (Archer 1992). Elite concern with well-ordered and productive estates only comes in the later sixteenth century according to some commentators, with refreshed attention to Classical texts enjoining great men to retreat to the countryside; this new cultural concern can be argued to have played a central role in the succeeding period of agricultural innovation and transformation (Thirsk 1992; see also Johnson 1996: 70–96). What may be going on then in part, particularly at sites so obviously and extensively designed, is a landscape that deliberately sets itself up in a way that distances itself from the mundane everyday activities of household management.

But in other architectural and social contexts it is difficult to avoid the conclusion that the productivity of the estate is emphasised. Hospitality is offered in the hall in the form of vast quantities of food, and the huge numbers of liveried retainers bustling about, many of them bearing great platters of meat and drink from kitchen to hall. At the palace at Nettleham, where Bishop Burghersh was given a licence to crenellate in 1336, the main approach was flanked by two large buildings that were probably barns; these would have dominated the first impression of the palace (Everson *et al.* 1991: 129–31). It could be argued that consumption rather than production is emphasised in these demonstrations. As usual, an ideology is rarely simply or unequivocally expressed.

The exterior of the castle itself, viewed from a distance, can be taken as a representation of the consumption of the household writ large. The observation may be distasteful to modern sensibilities, but it is worth noting that most of these castles had latrines that discharged directly into the moat. At Bodiam, they did so below the waterline, but the moat was nevertheless turned into an open sewer. At castles on rising ground like Conway and Brougham the sewage must have cascaded down the hill. The appearance from the outside must have been striking, to say the least. This was not simply a disregard for hygiene or for smell; several late medieval structures have careful provision for running rainwater through to 'flush' the latrines.

At South Wingfield, for example, the lodging tower is provided with an elaborate set of latrines associated with its stacked lodgings. These are elaborately designed so that they are flushed out by rainwater, and discharge directly down the hillside outside. While the main entrance to the house was on the other side of the building, this side is clearly viewed from the passing road; there are ponds and landscape features below the castle on the side; and of course the tower itself has clearly been placed on this side of the building for display. One meaning this might present is that of the castle as a huge body – in an age when the body was a social metaphor for the 'private' household and the nation–state (Camille 1994).

Westenhanger, near Saltwood, is a castle that might be argued to present different faces to different visitors. A visitor approaching through the lower court would see stables, barns, and other features of a great agricultural centre; someone approaching from the other side would see eight circular and square towers set in a moat and deerpark, similar in form to Bodiam. Westenhanger was known as 'Kiriel castle', after its gentry builder John Kiriel, who also constructed a chantry in the local church. There are indistinct traces of earthworks suggesting another formal landscape on this side of the castle. Whatever else it was, Westenhanger was hardly defensible.

It was broken into by John de Cornall in 1382 with the intention of forcing a marriage on Kiriel's widow; the widow 'hid in some water' and escaped (Coulson 1993).

The danger here is that in our eagerness to assemble a raft of conclusive evidence to affirm the symbolic aspects of these landscapes, we try to prove our case by assigning these features to a 'non-functional' category. In so doing, we fail to question and indeed reinforce an assumed, underlying division into 'functional versus symbolic'. We might do better to step back from such easy pigeon-holes for a moment and consider wider questions of that these landscapes might represent.

Watery meanings

We can start by looking at the historical origins of some of these elements. The deployment of sheets of water and the use of complex hydraulic systems are a hallmark of high-status structures in England and Europe since the thirteenth century onwards. Water was part of a series of Muslim features of garden design; Islamic gardens had a tradition of garden design that was related to the strategic manipulation of views to reinforce social rank stretching back to the tenth century at least and including the use of viewing platforms and belvederes (Ruggles 1994). This tradition was possibly brought to England by Eleanor of Castile and her household. The most obvious example is the watery landscape of Leeds Castle, known to be a favourite of Eleanor; another example is that in the barbican adjacent to the royal lodgings at Conway (Taylor 1998: 24). The form of the 'gloriet' at Leeds built around 1278–90 and appearing to rise directly out of the water had Islamic antecedents; the northern French castle at Hesdin also had a gloriet, Arabic water engines and by the mid-fifteenth century various other 'wonders, sports, artifices, machinery, watercourse, entertainment, and extraordinary things' according to Guillaume de Machaut (Harvey 1984: xiii; Whiteley 1999: 98).

However, this is merely a list of possible 'influences'. Archaeology, however, has long moved beyond simply dating and ascribing material and social change to 'influences' and prefers now to explain change in terms of internal dynamics (Renfrew 1973). What might we say about the changing organisation of landscapes around castles in the later medieval period?

Further observation on the origins and dating of these landscapes is hindered by two methodological difficulties. First, field observation of earthworks produces clear evidence of formal designs, but these are difficult to date without excavation; so there exists enough evidence to confirm the existence of such landscapes before the Renaissance, but not yet enough to suggest how landscape design changed *within* the Middle Ages. Even at Ludgershall, the late twelfth-century date is rightly only presented as a possibility (Everson *et al.* 2000). Second, as we have noted, earlier features may be reused in different ways; a twelfth-century moat might be a late medieval 'watery landscape' without any actual physical change at all.

Thus the castle of Framlingham has been identified as the centre of a designed landscape (Taylor 1998). It certainly has the right elements – a large body of water retained by a dam, in which the late twelfth-century walls of the castle are reflected; a causeway leading off from the north-west of the castle and running across this body of water and a lower court that had a garden in the sixteenth century (Figure 2.11). However, I suggest that the landscape may date to the very end of the Middle Ages, when the castle was given a major refitting in any case. It is well known that the Howard family coat of arms were placed over the main gate, and the towers were provided with dummy chimneys. However, this refitting is more extensive than is generally recognised. The battlements also appear to have been rebuilt at this point; they are much smaller than is practical, and thus give the castle the impression of being larger than it really is when viewed from a distance. Is the mere sixteenth century or is it earlier? Without excavation we cannot know (the castle was excavated by Group Captain Knocker, without clarification on this point). If it is earlier, was it originally intended as a designed landscape or did it simply come to be seen as such by the end of the Middle Ages?

Part of the answer to the question of chronology may lie in further exploration of examples where landscape change can be demonstrated within the medieval period. Two examples are Raby and Warkworth, both castles built or substantially altered in the late fourteenth and early fifteenth centuries. These are both castles whose settings were carefully composed in the later medieval period; and they are both castles with areas of extant ridge and furrow within visibility of their walls. In the case of Raby, the ridge and furrow runs up to the outer perimeter. When was the arable farming, presumably undertaken by peasants, abandoned? It is likely that this may have happened at or around the time these were transformed into late medieval palaces. At 'John O'Gaunt's House', a lodge or possible 'pleasance' at Bassingbourn in Cambridgeshire, a formal landscape has been argued to be fifteenth century on the basis of its form and the biography of its builder, who had knowledge of Italian Renaissance gardens (Oosthuizen and Taylor 2000).

Whatever their historical origins, the use of sheets of water around castles and other high-status buildings had become much more than a defensive exercise by the early fourteenth century. What did such sheets of water mean? Before we can go much further in such speculation it is necessary to reiterate two central points.

First, the central point of recent studies of eighteenth-century garden history needs to be repeated for this period: that gardens are not just about plants, they are about ideology and social power (Bermingham 1987; Barrell 1990). To clarify, the aesthetics and organisation of the garden need to be placed in their social context. Second, the central point of recent literary

Figure 2.11 Framlingham, Suffolk: view of the castle across the mere. The platform for the sixteenth-century garden, the dummy chimneys and remodelled battlements are all clearly shown.

criticism: we cannot explain these landscapes with reference to the intentions in the minds of their creators. Just as the author is dead in literary criticism, a point made above with reference to Dallyngrigge at Bodiam: what the individual creators of these landscapes may have consciously intended is both beyond us and not of primary relevance to our understanding of the gardens (Barthes 1977). What we can do, as we have already done at Bodiam, is draw out some of the meanings which the creators and observers of different social classes and genders, both literate and illiterate, might have seen in these landscapes

One might start by turning to a classic theme of literate medieval culture, humoural theory: earth, air, water, and fire. It was believed that the world was made up of these four elements, and that each was associated with a particular 'humour'. Water was associated with the feminine in medieval thought; Gilchrist has suggested that this is one meaning behind the association of water features with nunneries (1993). In religious terms, water was a symbol of salvation, most obviously in Psalm 23: 1–2. Everson has pointed out symbolism of animals involved: the flights of swans at St Hugh of Lincoln's park at Stow could symbolise purity, as well the Virgin, as well as alluding to chivalry and courtly love (1998: 33).

Moats feature prominently in literature, for example in *Piers Plowman* and *Sir Gawaine and the Green Knight*. In Capellanus' *The Art of Courtly Love*, written in the late twelfth century, the spatial layout of water is complex and suggestive. The Queen of Love sits on a throne in a 'pleasance'; next to her, a spring flows whose water tastes of nectar and within which one can see tiny fish. The 'pleasance' is surrounded by a ring of 'Wetness' in which the properly channelled waters of the Pleasance flood the whole area uncontrollably; outside this again is an area of 'Dryness' of heat and aridity. Ladies who chose their lovers wisely were admitted to the 'Pleasance'; those who loved freely were only allowed into 'Wetness', while those who refused to love anyone were confined to 'Dryness'. Beretta comments that the garden symbolism involves both sensual and Christian love (1993: 31).

Bodies of water can be argued to have more generic meanings, meanings moreover that did not depend on the possession of a specific body of knowledge confined to the religious and/or literate. At a more general level, water is also a form of ha-ha; you can see across it, but it forms a barrier. As such, it simultaneously displays the castle but denies access to lower social orders unable to gain admission to the castle. Water was certainly manipulated to produce surprises. Before the visitor mounts the crest of the slope to the south of Bodiam, he or she does not know the barrier is there. It also creates a spatial illusion: buildings reflected in water appear larger than they really are. At Donington, Cooling and Baconsthorpe, and at Tonford Manor, all structures whose walls are reflected in a moat, what appear to be towers externally are merely stair turrets internally.

Where watery landscapes act as a barrier, they constrain the movement of observers in very definite ways, as we have seen at Bodiam. They can be argued, therefore, to work in very similar ways to church architecture. Klukas (1984a, 1984b) has argued that church architecture should be seen as a frame for liturgy; the controlled manner of entry to and exit from castles, set within watery landscapes, has a definite liturgical quality to it.

Watery landscapes will also alter their meanings according to the observer or observers concerned. This is not to say that those meanings (for example, those of the swan or the rabbit within Christian theology) were restricted to a certain group, or that other groups further down the social scale did not have their own readings of the meanings of these landscapes; liturgy, after all, was experienced by the whole congregations, and its meanings meant to be communicated to all. In another context, Pam Graves has explored how ritual practices in the church would have been read differently by local congregations (Graves 1989, 2000). Leaving the church and moving around other landscapes, ordinary people would have not lost this power of rereading. Other bodies of knowledge were certainly brought to these landscapes by other groups. For example, the park or forest beyond the formal gardens was seen in quite complex ways by labouring men; as a set of resources to be illegally tapped.

47

I suggest that these watery landscapes are in part *not so much about specific meanings, but how they come to be symbolic, who gets to 'read' them and why*. In other words, they depend on the deployment of knowledge between different genders and classes. To 'read Bodiam aright', to use Charles Coulson's phrase, one needs the background knowledge of a male knight; to understand the symbolism of water, enclosed gardens, the fish and fowl one needs access to a certain set of meanings. The education or training that gave access to that system of meaning was confined to certain groups.

The estate and the hunting that went on within it was, of course, about so much more than simply keeping meat fresh on the hoof – and also so much more than simply lordly activity or conspicuous consumption. It was about what it meant to be human, and through this, what it meant to be a lord. Felicity Riddy has drawn attention to the way in which the hunted animals in *Sir Gawain and the Green Knight* are used to re-draw relations between culture and nature. She draws the implication that boundaries between male and female are redrawn in the process: I would add, boundaries between lord and peasant, master and servant (Riddy 1995). The consumption of freshwater fish was seen as an exclusively lordly activity, and as such fishponds were status symbols (Dyer 1970: 34–5).

I shall now examine some of these points with reference to two case studies – the castle of Brougham in Westmoreland, and that of Caister in Norfolk.

Brougham

Brougham is a good example of a castle built and rebuilt in piecemeal fashion over the centuries, and having little work dating to the later Middle Ages in its fabric, but where the ensemble can be seen as a fashioned landscape which would have been viewed in meaningful ways by people visiting or working in or around the castle. We often forget that where a castle remains in use, its architecture remains important: by definition, a twelfth-century castle, where it has not been destroyed, is also a thirteenth-, fourteenth- and fifteenth-century castle. The fabric of Brougham, after all, has its origins in the twelfth century when it was laid out on the location of a Roman fort, and was modified and extended in the thirteenth and fourteenth centuries, but went on to be a frame for the famous self-fashioning of Lady Ann Clifford in the seventeenth century (see Chapter 4).

Consider the approach to Brougham Castle taken by a hypothetical fifteenth-century visitor (Figure 2.12). For such a visitor, the entry to Brougham is very carefully constructed. The visitor approaches along a terrace. The ground falls away to the River Lowther on the north side, beyond which the visitor could see the old Roman road heading east towards the Pennines. The other, southern side probably had gardens at this point. (It certainly had gardens a century later; the traces of these later gardens probably mask any earlier traces that might remain; Williams 1992.) Behind

Figure 2.12 View of Brougham Castle from the east. The entrance way is on a terrace, with flood-plain below to the right and gardens above to the left. The hall is largely destroyed. Two latrine chutes can be seen at the foot of the walls of the northern range.

these gardens were the remains of the old Roman fort; the apparently deliberate placing of castles on Roman sites, and what that might have signified to the medieval visitor, are a topic for another paper.

In front of the visitor was a grand façade, which wore the marks of piecemeal accretion and alteration with pride. Though now largely destroyed, the outer walls of the kitchen, hall and great chamber could be seen from the approching terrace; the nature and function of the different buildings would be discernible to the visitor through the placing of windows. The visitor might also discern the different phases of construction of these buildings, evidence of piecemeal accretion. Behind these rose a massive *donjon*, itself visibly of two phases of construction.

Looming up directly in front of the visitor was the gatehouse; above the gate were the words 'Tys made Roger' discussed in the Introduction. However, this is not all one can see from this vantage point. To one side of the gatehouse are a series of quite prominent latrine chutes, discharging down the slope towards the river.

To the left of the gatehouse, the basic constituents of the late medieval house – service, hall and chamber, as well as tower – are visible from this critical point in front of the gatehouse, but not accessible. To gain further access, our visitor must pass through the very elaborate double suite of gatehouses separated by a court, turn left past the service range, turn left again past the lodgings and chapel before mounting the steps to the hall. At each point, the visitor might be stopped from progressing, according to social status.

Many local people may never have gained access to the castle. I suggest that they would have understood part of its message, for they would have seen its layout in their own homes; the division into service, hall with upper and lower ends, and chamber was a leitmotif of all but arguably the very lowest social level of late medieval architecture, and its corresponding values of familial and household lordship at all social levels (Gardiner 2000; Johnson 1993). Brougham displays itself and its lord to the outside world while proclaiming its inaccessibility; it sets the social order literally in stone.

Caister

Caister Castle (Figure 2.13) dates to the fifteenth century, and is associated with Sir John Falstolf. The popular guidebook loudly and indignantly protests that Shakespeare's portrayal of this individual as Falstaff is most unfair, and that Falstolf was a fine and upstanding knight and gentleman (Hill n.d.). This is certainly the ideological message of the castle that Falstolf built. The moat of the former manor house may have been retained; the historical memory of the Peasant's Revolt was clear here, as the manor had been seized and plundered at that time. The building was started in 1433; the eastern part was roofed by 1435, and the whole largely finished by 1448.

Most conventional accounts of Caister stress Falstolf's long military career in France, and go on to discuss the Continental parallels for its layout. The thin walls (less than three feet thick) are mentioned disapprovingly and the 'disgraceful' episode of the siege by the Duke of Norfolk after he had disputed the castle's succession to the Pastons is much dwelt on. Its similarity to a German *Wasserburg* is often cited, though there is no mention in the building accounts of any Germans being involved.

Internally, Caister was well appointed, with tapestries with religious subjects, hunting, and Morris dancing; the main suite of apartments had a stew or bathhouse. The windows were glazed with painted glass including the arms of Sir John and his wife. Household accounts indicate that the castle's household included paying tenants or 'sojourners', and at least one married couple among the servants (Woolgar 1999: 25, 36).

Here, however, I want to concentrate on the landscape within which Caister was set. The water level has changed since the fifteenth century. When it was built, the castle would have stood on the edge of marshy, tidal ground linked to the Yare estuary towards Yarmouth. This watery aspect was emphasised by a complex system of moats that both surrounded the castle and separated different elements of it. A visitor would have arrived by the Norwich–Yarmouth road that ran along the outer wall and moat; the

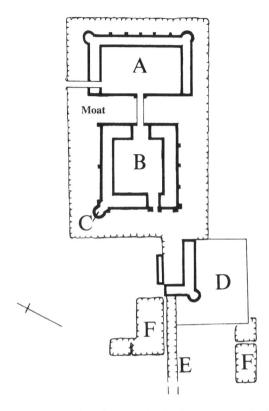

Figure 2.13 Plan of Caister Castle. A: outer court. B: inner court. C: tower. D: garden. E: canal to river. F: fish ponds. (After an unscaled 1760 drawing: Smith n.d. 1.)

entrance, however, is not set directly on to this road, but is on one side of this lower court. Falstolf planned a collegiate foundation in this lower court, which was never finished. The visitor then turns to the right before entering the inner court. Entry from the other side was along what is now a wooded valley and past a system of fishponds; it would have involved moving past an outer tower and across another body of water. Both approaches would have been dominated by the slim tower at one angle, clearly too small to act as a main residence. There are grotesque heads on the square south-west corner turret, grinning at the visitor.

For me, the key to Caister, as at Bodiam and many other late medieval buildings, is that it reveals itself to the visitor gradually. Caister is an elaborate and demonstrative building and landscape, which deliberately leads its visitors in by an indirect route made up of successive stages, so that opportunities to admire the machicolations and grotesques reflected in the

51

water are maximised. Caister is about stops and pauses, about successive staging, in both the social and theatrical sense of that term.

How much of the analysis of both Brougham and Caister is unverifiable? Have I pushed it 'too far'? I would justify what I have said in theoretical terms, and will have more to say on this subject in Chapter 5 and in the Conclusion. However, I do not think one needs to be a rampant postmodernist to claim that as we face the main façade at Brougham we face a complex accretion of buildings; history and dynasty are laid out in front of the visitor, given a social connotation, and commented upon in an complex way. At Caister, the building is gradually revealed to the visitor through twist and turns; the slim tower asserts itself as the final reference point, but the tower is always beyond the visitor, always behind the next wall or moat, or at the other end of the hall.

We will never know for certain what this or that visitor actually thought as they moved along the causeway, but we can be fairly certain that the reaction of the visitor would be as complex and as nuanced as the building itself, and that it would be expressed in partly social terms. And if we can make those claims, then we have demonstrated something of what such medieval landscapes meant, and how those meanings were drawn upon as resources of power.

Conclusion: landscapes before the English landscape garden?

To summarise, most of these castles have in common: a tight definition of staged processional routes along causeways; sheets of water manipulated through complex hydraulic systems; the manipulation of views through successive stages; often irregular boundaries of moats and park pales, and incorporation of large areas of woodland.

In these respects, such landscapes appear similar to the later eighteenth-century emparked landscapes created by the gentry and aristocracy of Georgian England. It is difficult to resist the temptation to draw parallels between the two forms of landscape. Indeed, in many cases there is direct historical and geographical continuity; many such eighteenth- and nineteenth-century landscape parks were created by gentry owners out of old medieval deerparks that had gone out of use during intervening centuries when more formal, geometrical styles of gardening had been the fashion (Bond 1994; Johnson 1996: 145–51).

Such a similarity in the physical form of medieval and eighteenth-century landscapes might be taken to indicate that one was directly descended from the other. Such a view is lent support by the writings of eighteenth-century designers and commentators, who themselves claimed that the eighteenth-century landscaping style was 'distinctively English', and had its roots in the historic and prehistoric past (Lange 1992).

Superficially, therefore, late medieval and eighteenth-century society can be seen as similar by some scholars, to the extent that one article has discussed these medieval examples as 'the English landscape garden before the "English landscape garden"' (Leslie 1993). In both cases, the elite based its power and authority on certain values perceived as 'traditional' and embedded in the land, in tradition, in past custom. In both cases that power and authority were under stress, and about to be transformed. In both cases, then, we might care to see these designed, watery landscapes as an attempt to make the social look natural, to make it appear that what was a transient social order was actually natural and beyond history (cf. Leone 1984). At Bodiam and Chatsworth, Brougham and Stowe, Caister and Rousham, the social order is laid out in the landscape and in the process naturalised. The land-owning classes of both societies were emparking like mad; Baconsthorpe was at the centre of a vast sheep run created on top of the earthworks of deserted medieval villages. At Somersham, the medieval village was removed and relocated to make way for the Bishop of Ely's park (Taylor 1998: 30). And both employed features that were used further down the social scale at socially middling levels, such as moats in the medieval period or Palladian principles in the eighteenth-century gentry park (Williamson 1993).

However, I suggest that such superficial similarities fall apart when examined in greater detail. First, eighteenth-century gardens were tied in to a quite specific set of beliefs, ideologies if you will, in which manipulation of the landscape was intimately tied in to ideologies of an emergent industrial society (Barrell 1990; Bermingham 1987; Williams 1973). These beliefs were also articulated in a very specific way. They were part of the secular realm, and articulated with reference to scientifically articulated principles of the natural world, where as we have seen much medieval design is tied in to Christian imagery. Eighteenth-century landscapes were also intended to be appreciated in the context of the printed word; their origins are related to the publication of genres such as pattern-books, a literate education involving close familiarity with certain Classical texts, and themes such as Addison's advice to owners of parks and gardens in the *The Spectator*. Equally, there is a very different use of the view in late medieval landscapes. At Bodiam, there is no classic three-quarters view of the building; rather, the perspective from the Gun Garden is very slightly off-centre. The various viewpoints of the structure are often face-on and do not appear to conform to the Cartesian logic arguably introduced by the Renaissance. Finally, 'The visitor' would be a very different person. By the eighteenth century, country house visiting was a social pursuit defined in a very particular way (Tinniswood 1989).

We must be very careful, then, about how we view these landscapes before the 'official' birth of Renaissance landscapes in England, or for that matter the period of the 'English landscape garden'. On the one hand, we now have abundant evidence to demonstrate that these were carefully designed landscapes; the archaeological evidence suggests that they were carefully thought

out and composed with reference to a very complex set of symbolic meanings. On the other hand, we cannot say that they were just like their
eighteenth-century counterparts. The eighteenth-century parallels should
alert us to the possible complexities behind the appearance of these landscapes, rather than prescribing how we should view them.

Nor can we divorce any set of meanings we might attribute to medieval
landscapes from the everyday life of the castle and its landscape. This will
become further apparent when we discuss the internal structure of the
late medieval castle, and how a visitor might experience that structure, in
Chapter 4.

3

THE ORDERING OF
THE LATE MEDIEVAL
CASTLE

Tattershall Castle stands on the edge of the Lincolnshire Fens, on the eastern side of Midland England (Figure 1.1). Today, the most striking surviving piece of fabric is the monstrous brick tower (Figures 3.1 and 3.2), that rises from this flat land as a visible marker of the wealth and power of its fifteenth-century builder and owner, Ralph, Lord Cromwell.

Cromwell (a very distant relation of the two more infamous Cromwells) was a 'new' or 'self-made man'. Although descended from a minor Lincolnshire family, Cromwell rose to the position of one of the most powerful men in the kingdom. Born in 1393, he spent his youth in the service of the dukes of Clarence and of Henry V in the French wars. According to traditional historical accounts, he owed his rapid rise to administrative ability and to marriage. Between 1433 and 1443 he was Treasurer of England before resigning; his departure was probably an outcome of defeat in the game of factional politics. Cromwell's income was substantially increased by the financial opportunities that came with this post and by his 1423 marriage to the heiress Margaret Deincourt. The Deincourt marriage brought him properties worth over £500 a year, a sizeable sum at that time.

Cromwell was, by the standards of his time and social group, an astute and ambitious member of the elite. In 1433 he was responsible for writing a statement on the state of the English economy that in the view of twentieth-century historians was 'reasonably balanced, forthright, and carefully prepared'. His strategies included creating political alliances and consolidation of landed estates through his own marriage and those of his relations; his niece and heir were married into the Yorkist faction at court. Cromwell was involved in constant litigation, for example, over the ownership of manors, but also over the culture and etiquette of social precedence. As one would expect of an elite male of the fifteenth century, 'he was extremely touchy on matters affecting his honour . . . pointing out that as he had always followed the correct procedures, he must necessarily be in the right', an attitude that was thoroughly in tune with a late medieval mentality of the importance of form and precedent to concepts of masculine honour. Goods worth over £16,000 were stolen from his estate after his death (Emery 1985: 281–2).

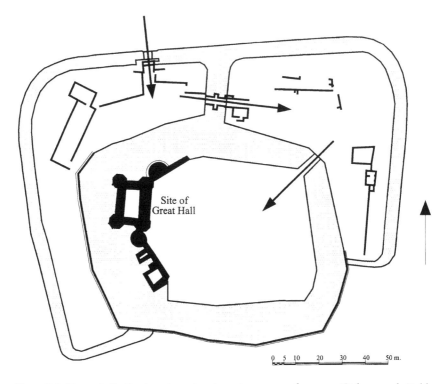

Site of
Great Hall

0 5 10   20   30   40   50 m.

Figure 3.1 Tattershall Castle: plan showing the route of entry. (Dobres and Robb 2000: 217).

Cromwell's building programme was an important arena for the negotiation of his social position. As was usual for elite households at the time, he moved seasonally between several residences, each in a different part of his scattered estates, plus a large house in London. It was clearly important to Cromwell not just that he own a series of large residences of a grand form, but that he be seen to be constantly building and rebuilding, to be following the correct feudal procedures. For many years the yearly costs of his building projects at his estates of Collyweston, Wingfield and Tattershall amounted to a third to a half of his annual income (ibid.: 330).

In contrast to many later Renaissance structures, but typically for the late medieval castle and as we have already seen at Bodiam and Caister, Tattershall Castle reveals itself gradually to the visitor. The great tower itself is visible for many miles across the fens, and acts as a landmark. As one approaches, however, one sees that this tower is merely the largest of a series of towers; as new work in brick, it is sharply differentiated from an older inner court studded with towers; this latter work is executed in stone. A fifteenth-century

Figure 3.2 Tattershall Castle: the *donjon* from the north.

visitor might note this difference in building material and note that here was a great man who did not simply wish to be seen to be following the correct procedures, but wished to be rebuilding an old and ancient pile. One gains access to the inner court circuitously, through three separate gatehouses and across two separate moats (Figure 3.1). An elite visitor arriving on horseback would enter the first gate, then leave their horse at the stables in the outer court – it being disrespectful to approach the core of the castle directly on horseback. Once within the inner court, the castle changes character; the hall being the central feature that dominates the court; the great tower rises behind the hall and is secondary to it, more 'private' and restricted in access, in terms of circulation pattern.

Cromwell's tower appears to be a relatively late addition to the scheme, possibly not planned as part of the rebuilding from the start. A combination of evidence from below- and above-ground archaeology and building accounts suggests that Cromwell took over an old site, consisting of ranges

Figure 3.3 South Kyme tower, with joist holes for
the now destroyed hall.

of buildings in a courtyard plan all built up against the stone curtain wall
and facing inwards, not dissimilar to the thirteenth-century castle of
Bolingbroke a few miles away (Beresford and Hurst 1979: 150). His first act
was to rebuild much of the fabric of the internal ranges of this structure –
though the thirteenth-century stone towers were retained and continued to
be an important part of the ensemble.

When Cromwell did build his great tower, we find that its meanings are
complex and only understood with reference to its context, in particular to
comparable structures of the period. One dimension is competition: rivalry
with the late medieval house at South Kyme (Figure 3.3). South Kyme stands
a few miles to the south-east: the two sites are intervisible across the flat
lands, at least on the rare occasion of a day clear of the prevailing Fenland
mist. South Kyme is now an isolated system of moats, within which stands
a stone tower of the mid-fourteenth century. The tower is now isolated and
even a desolate sight, with its grotesque heads projecting from the parapets

over a deserted field and a nearby church. Joist holes and other features in the tower, however, indicate that it must have functioned in a manner similar to that at Tattershall, at one end of a now vanished hall block, though the tower, hall block and whole ensemble of South Kyme is rather smaller in scale and having no heating, South Kyme is unlikely to have been a solar tower.

In 1437 South Kyme was inherited by Walter Tailboys, an old friend from a Lincolnshire family of long association with the Cromwells. In 1444 Walter died and his eponymous son Walter became Cromwell's arch-enemy. According to legal records:

> [the younger Tailboys'] seething animosity against Cromwell knew no bounds . . . [and Tailboys] decided to kill him. In 1449 he sent spies to Tattershall to see if he could be kidnapped, and when that proved impossible, Tailboys sent men to Collyweston and Wingfield manors in 1450 to murder Cromwell whilst walking with his chaplain. As that proved abortive because he was too well protected by his household staff, Tailboys laid plans to blow up the house adjacent to Cromwell's London residence. Tailboys was arrested and imprisoned.
>
> (Emery 1985: 329)

According to the recent re-analysis by Anthony Emery, the tower at Tattershall was a relative afterthought in Cromwell's rebuilding of the site. The Tattershall building accounts seem to suggest that Cromwell first rebuilt the courtyard and main domestic apartments, refashioned the moats around the dwelling, and only then turned his attention to the tower. If so, the tower dates from immediately after the first Tailboys' death. The younger Tailboys succeeded to a family home which if markedly smaller than Cromwell's Tattershall residence at least had a tower which could be seen for further around. He can therefore hardly have viewed the almost immediate start of construction of a tower that dwarfed his with equanimity – particularly in an age when a 'honour' was a central component of elite male identity. (Indeed, one might speculate whether Cromwell refrained from building the tower till after his friend's death in deference to his friend's own sense of honour, but was freed from such inhibitions once his hated and disreputable son inherited the site.)

The internal plan of the Tattershall tower (Figure 3.4) is superficially very simple but actually of critical importance. It consists of a series of rooms stacked one on top of the other. The first three, however, the basement, ground floor and first floor, are accessed independently; in other words, the tower is not self-contained; one cannot move from one floor to another without leaving the tower and re-entering via another building, one now disappeared but whose position is indicated by joist holes. To gain access to

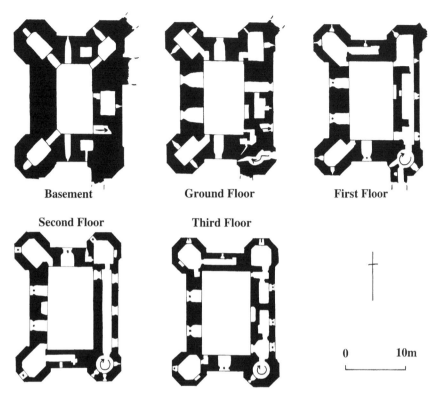

Figure 3.4 Tattershall castle: plan of *donjon*. The tower has separate entrances to basement, ground floor and stairs to first floor. Above the first floor hall, the second
floor audience chamber is accessed by a vaulted corridor with waiting chamber
at the north-east corner.

the lord at second floor level, one first mounts a stone circular stair before
turning into a long corridor that is treated with rich decoration. The corridor
takes one along the longer side of the tower to a small waiting chamber,
equipped with fireplace and latrine, where one would wait to be admitted
to the lord's presence. (Waiting, of course, is an important element of the
impression of elite identity; at other castles, such chambers have no fireplace
at all, leaving the visitor to get cold and shivering before being ushered into
the presence of the great man.)

Cromwell's building of the Tattershall tower has to be placed in two
contexts to be fully understood. First, the building of a tower to mark a
certain form of lordship is a recurrent motif of the period, part of an established symbolic vocabulary. A 'lodging tower' was added apparently as an
afterthought to one of Cromwell's other building projects at South

Wingfield; it consists of a series of lodging rooms for guests, stacked one on top of the other and with its own latrine.

Second, the rebuilding of Tattershall Castle took place in conjunction with a whole series of additions to its surrounding landscape, including an outer moat, a 'Pleasance' or garden surrounded by water, a cross placed in the market place, and most notably the establishment of a college of priests a few hundred yards away. If Tattershall tower relates to Cromwell's concern to assert his position in the present, his college on one reading is an attempt in part to assert his status after his death; the principal duty of the priests as specified in his will was to pray for his soul. A similar college of priests was a common element of later medieval castles – it was planned for the lower court at Caister, and at Warkworth; the college at Fotheringhay has also been noted. So Cromwell's identity is marked through a pairing of secular and religious institutions.

Both castle and college work in part through repetition. Motifs, emblems, 'devices' appear over and over again, around the fireplaces of the tower, in the stained glass of the college church (Marks 1984): Cromwell's insignia as Lord Treasurer (a pair of money bags), which by the rules of heraldry he could continue to use after leaving office, are surmounted with his motto 'Ney je droit' or 'Have I not the right?': other repetitive heraldry includes his personal arms and those of his wife and family. This heraldry works in a very distinctive way: it links together monuments such as church and castle, inscribes or stamps them all as the lord's own, despite their origin in very different architectural genres. The market cross itself, which the ordinary men and women of Tattershall village passed on their daily routines and which was the focus of community ceremonial as in most village communities of this period (Hutton 1994), was inscribed with Cromwell's arms. It also links together Cromwell's 'personal' identity (his own arms) with those of his office (Lord Treasurer). Similar emblems and motifs would be inscribed even on the bodies of the lord's followers, through their 'livery' or uniform.

The Tattershall gatehouses are now destroyed, but one would expect this heraldic marking of Cromwell's identity there also. With this qualification, most of this marking of identity is internal to the structure. We have already noted how the pattern of circulation at Tattershall leads the visitor to be granted access to its meanings gradually, as he or she moves inside the building. The courtyard plan is essentially one to be understood from the inside out; from the outside, ones sees only narrow windows in curtain walls. It is only when one stands within the inner courtyard, observing Cromwell's servants and retainers in livery standing to attention or bustling about taking food to and from the Great Hall that one understands the nature of this great household and thus the identity of the man who is lord over it.

Cromwell was apparently unconcerned about one thing: lack of conformity. The brick tower with ashlar plinth and limestone dressings would have contrasted markedly with its smaller circular counterparts built of light-coloured

stone. There is apparently no attempt to mask the fact that the castle is of -
several phases. There is intense concern with how one moves on a winding
path through the building, and with how rooms relate one to another, but
little sense of formal architectural composition; the tower is at one end of
the building, jutting out into the moat, again appearing through the use of
reflection to be still larger than it really is.

Understanding Tattershall

In the last chapter, we looked at how we might understand the landscapes
around castles. Now we turn to the structure of the castle itself. How do we
'understand' Tattershall? How, as students of late medieval castles, do we
classify and categorise its features, place it within a larger narrative of castle
developments? The traditional response is simple: look carefully at the dating
of the building, sort out its sequence of development, and compare it with
other examples. We can then place Tattershall in an evolutionary sequence
of development, from one 'type' to another. In a broad sense, this is what
has been done with late medieval castles as a whole, Tattershall included:
they are part of a 'transition' between the 'true castle' and the 'Renaissance
house'. In a narrower sense, Tattershall belongs to the type of 'tower-house'
versus 'courtyard house'.

It would be archaeological heresy to suggest that dating and typology are
unimportant in the understanding of castles. However, I do suggest that
they are only part of the story. At Tattershall, the division into tower versus
courtyard is perhaps unhelpful: if the tower really was only built as a late
afterthought in the overall scheme of development, the castle could easily
have remained of the courtyard 'type'. One thing is certain: Tattershall should
be understood in its own right, not simply in typological or evolutionary
terms. Tattershall was a major statement in its own right of Cromwell's identity, as were the other structures that he owned. It was as complex, and as
ambiguous, in what it meant as was Cromwell's own self-image. We should
be very reluctant to end our analysis at the point of classifying it as an
'interim stage' or typologically as a tower.

I often wonder how a man like Cromwell would have responded to the
suggestion that he was in the process of building an 'uneasy compromise'
between defence and comfort, or that he was a century 'behind' contemporary work in Italy. One does not have to be a committed student of late
medieval masculinities to predict that he would probably react in anger. And
one does not have to be a rampant cultural relativist to see that his point of
view would have some justice.

So how do we understand the layout of a late medieval castle like
Tattershall? We might start by expanding some of the comments of the
previous chapter on the social context of the period.

Power and politics in the late medieval household

As with the landscapes discussed in the last chapter, before we can approach what movement around a castle might have *meant* to participants, we have to sketch out something of its *context*. We must look at aspects of the social and cultural system of the period. Much of this system has already been hinted at in last chapter's comments on Dallyngrigge and Bodiam, and the above description of Tattershall and Cromwell. There, we sketched out some late medieval tensions in gender and in masculinity, within the social order; it is time to flesh this picture out a little more. What follows is really intended as a guide for those with little background in later medieval history.

The late Middle Ages of England, of course, have been 'studied to death' by historians. Much of their work has been from a traditional standpoint concentrating on political, legal and social dimensions. Debates continue to rage over how political systems of the period operated, the precise definitions of legal terms such as retainers and livery and maintenance, the problems of economic management of great estates. Here, I want to avoid getting into such arguments. They are important and even central issues to a major part of traditional historical study. However, the terms within which they are debated often appear legalistic and abstruse to those without a primary interest in the niceties of late medieval political, legal and administrative history. To the archaeologist, used to thinking in terms of long-term change over centuries and millennia, the historical use of material can also seem excessively fine-grained and excessively cautious in painting a wider picture. Instead, I want to concentrate on a broader, more anthropological description of some aspects of late medieval society (as some historians themselves have advocated: James 1986). Those new to this material should note that every statement made needs to be followed by a hundred qualifications from the historical literature.

Late medieval England as a whole had a population of between two and five million; the builders and owners of castles formed a very tiny fraction of this. The tax returns of 1436 list 51 lay peers, 183 greater knights, and 750 lesser knights. Most of the buildings discussed in this book were built by these social ranks, or by men of comparable rank holding offices in the Church. If we include the ranks immediately below these levels listed in 1436, we must also include 1,200 esquires, 1,600 men with between £10 and £19 a year from land, and 3,400 with £5–9 incomes; 7,184 names in total to which we must add the families (Harvey 1995: 155). As a result of these very small numbers at the apex of society, the builders and owners of castles would often know each other personally. The 1390 Council, for example, included the owners of Wardour, Penshurst, and Cooling (Coulson 1993).

The Figures above, of course, must be thought of as listing elite men; late medieval England was a patriarchal and patrilineal society. Men wielded political power, and women were expected to be subordinate to their husbands. The King ruled over all; the two major restraints on his power, the peers of the realm and Parliament, were all-male groups.

At an elite level, primogeniture was practised; that is, the landed property that was the basis of elite power generally passed to the eldest son. Such a standard practice was hedged around with qualifications (many families did not produce a male heir; property was settled on daughters and younger sons also in certain circumstances). In particular, only men were expected to own land. Movable goods were important, and the position of urban bourgeois merchants and traders could be one of great power, but the general assumption was that the basic currency of lordly authority and ultimately economic and political power was the accumulation of lands and estates. These lands and estates would often be scattered over a wide area. For example, in the fifteenth century the Percy family had clusters of estates in Nothumberland and northern Cumbria, with more scattered estates across Yorkshire. The distance between northernmost and southernmost holding was over 200 kilometres. Their rival family, the Nevilles, had clusters of estates scattered across central and north Yorkshire, southern county Durham, and northern Cumbria (Pollard 1990, Maps 3 and 4).

Elite women nevertheless occupied structurally crucial positions in this system. In the first place, they brought lands, money and property with them at the point of marriage in the form of dowry. At such elite social levels, marriages were largely arranged between the two families, with political and dynastic aims in mind. Marriage alliances cemented political friendships between the great dynasties, and could be used to build up blocks of landed estates, or to maintain and extend political power in a region. At different social levels, marriages could also be used to achieve social mobility, for example, in the case of gentry/aristocracy marriages. As a result of this and other factors, marriage contracts became steadily more complex over this period, with, for example, land being distributed via entails and feoffments (settlements of property outside female heirs: Payling 1992, 1995).

Women, however, had more active roles within this system than simply being pawns of marriage alliances. When they moved to the household of their husband, they often took their own household with them (though that household could also be predominantly male, though headed by a woman: Woolgar 1999: 8). Women could engage in gift exchange, political alliance and other activities with other female households of similar social rank (cf. Johnson 1996: 180–2). When their husbands were away at court, on military campaigns or on other business, women took over the position of head of household in their absence. (Consequently, much of our information on elite marital life in this period comes from the exchange of letters between husband and wife consulting over matters of household management.) After a husband's death, if not before by force of character, women could occupy positions of great informal political power. In many cases, contrary to the normative expectations of the time, they accumulated landed estates in their own name (Archer 1992).

Such marriages and the great families that they produced were at the core of the great households that moved between castles. Households varied in size but were often numbered in hundreds; the average size of the great household seems to have fallen after the mid-fourteenth-century Black Death and attendant economic dislocation (Woolgar 1999: 15). Such households have often been termed 'peripatetic'; that is, an elite household would have more than one castle or palace, often as many as five to ten principal residences. The household moved from one residence to another, depending on the season, the need to visit particular estates, to administer justice, or simply to satisfy the personal preference of the lord (Mertes 1988). Cromwell, as we have seen, had residences at Tattershall and South Wingfield; he also built a church and manor house at Lambley, started a new manor house at Collyweston, Nottinghamshire, and had a London residence.

We know a great deal about these households due to the records they kept. Careful accounts were kept of expenditure; where these survive, historians have used them to examine household size and composition, the changing economic fortunes of lords, and the main items of expenditure. In one outstanding case, the Household Book of the Earl of Northumberland, the daily routines and everyday ceremonies are meticulously recorded (Percy 1827; Woolgar 1999).

Power flowed from such great households in two directions. First, all members of the aristocracy owed allegiance and loyalty to the King. This allegiance and loyalty were dependent on reciprocal ties, however; the King was expected to balance the interests of ruling families against one another, not interfere with the integrity of their estates, and to respect concepts of dynastic pride and honour. Any monarch played a complex game of granting land, estates and political offices to favoured peers in such a way as to maintain a solid royal economic and political base. The King was careful not to alienate peers to the point at which a coalition of anti-royal interests built up. Arguably, it was the failure of Richard II to play this game successfully that led to his downfall.

The lifestyle and culture of the King, then, were in many ways no different from his peerage. The numbers in his household were much larger than the very largest aristocratic households, and continued to grow in the fifteenth century, but this was a difference of scale rather than of composition. A large part of the King's finances came from royal estates in which he was the feudal lord. He progressed around the country like a great baron. He patronised building and artistic projects, and endowed monastic foundations, in a similar manner to a great baron, albeit again on a much larger scale.

In the other direction, down from the great household, the lord needed to build up power, particularly in times of dynastic conflict, by the use of 'retainers'. Retainers were men from lower social levels who were granted land, a cash fee, hospitality within the castle or palace and other privileges. In return, they owed loyalty to the lord, attended him at his residence and fought for him. Such men were, of course, heads of households at lower social levels in their turn, and themselves employed servants and others. While such men were away serving their lord, their wives would run their own households in their absence. In their own business, they used the same patriarchal language as the great lord.

The Church also acted as landowner and feudal lord; kept great households of similar size to the aristocracy; had great economic power; and could act politically. Bishops and others could act as power-brokers; the Bishop of Durham, for example, often mediated in the great fifteenth-century disputes between the rival Neville and Percy dynasties in North-East England (Pollard 1990). Monasteries and others could run estates directly, or act as chief landlord. Again, these actions generated documentation that is now the *métier* of historians: much of our information on late medieval farming comes from the carefully kept records of Church bureaucrats.

The manorial lord of a given rural community could therefore be a great lord; or the King; or the Church; or a widow. Many such manors were given to religious foundations as gifts. Historians might pick apart differences in estate management between these groups, and spill much ink on the niceties of different kinds of manorial organisation. It is unlikely, however, that a fifteenth-century visitor to a peasant community could have seen much difference in terms of the appearance of the village and landscape and the everyday life of the peasants.

This political structure was articulated and represented through a series of material symbols. The burden of this book is in part an exploration of how architecture acted as a resource of power and authority in the later Middle Ages; other resources included dress and language. Architecture, dress and language were all implicated in political power; and as the nature and structure of that power evolved, so contemporaries articulated anxiety about that evolution not through direct attacks on the social order itself, but through complaints about the changing form and use of these material symbols.

To take dress as an example, particular items ranging from doublets and fur-lined robes to simple metal badges might carry the lord's symbol, or simply his colours (for example, in the 1350s the colours of the King's son, the Black Prince, were green and white, while those of the Earl of Arundel were red and white: Prestwich 1980). Such items were termed livery, which according to Nigel Saul:

> In its traditional form was a traditional symbol of patriarchal authority. Typically it was distributed twice yearly, at Christmas and Midsummer, its purpose being to impose on the members of an affinity a group identity which they would otherwise have lacked.

It served both to link them together horizontally and to focus their loyalties on the lord by whom they were retained . . . Acceptance of livery placed donor and recipient under obligation to each other. The latter was expected to serve his lord faithfully in peace and war, and to attend on him when summoned; and the former was expected to stand by his man and to support him in all causes and disputes. His 'worship' and 'good lordship' were measured by the extent to which he maintained the honour of his followers; and his ability to attract men and to retain their service depended on his continuing to be seen to be successful in this direction.

(1990: 305–6)

Different kinds of livery excited different forms of comment. Hats and hoods, and 'livery of cloth', were relatively uncontentious (in general, these were given out to men of higher social rank). Livery of signs or badges was the most controversial: the Commons demanded in 1384 and 1388 that these be abolished on the basis that those who wore them were emboldened to oppress people. Both attempts were thrown out by the Lords under the influence of the King's uncle and owner of Kenilworth, John of Gaunt, who said that every lord was capable of disciplining his own men (Given-Wilson 1986: 234–45).

Badges appeared in the late fourteenth century; metal badges could be placed on the body, or their form could be inscribed on to architecture. They could be made quickly; the Duke of Buckingham ordered 2,000 in 1454. Saul suggests that the appearance of badges was symptomatic of the breakdown of political order, and so Commons' protest against livery was a coded protest against loss of systems of personal trust and Royal authority. When Richard II resorted to producing badges he lost the moral authority of being able to represent 'one nation' (Saul 1990: 309).

Understanding a castle

We can now understand some of the elements of castles we have already looked at – the provision of lodgings, the regulation of access to the lord, the centrality of the hall – much more clearly. We can also compare late medieval English society with social systems of other periods and cultures in which factors such as faction, dynasty, and control over land and peasants played a key role.

Oversimplified as it is, archaeologists working in other areas and periods might find some of the above discussion very familiar. Recently, archaeologists working in a variety of contexts around the world have become interested in the general issues of how power is mobilised and distributed in state societies like that of medieval England. They have emphasised the role of factional conflict and competition, and have looked at the links between gender, the mobilisation of labour, the control and use of estates. This work has been placed under the umbrella terms of 'factional competition' or 'heterarchy'; these concepts have been found useful in a variety of early state societies (see for example Brumfiel 1992; Brumfiel and Earle 1987; Brumfiel and Fox 1994; Crumley 1987).

To say that late medieval England shares parallels with Aztec Mexico or with feudal Japan is not to deny its uniqueness, or to argue that cross-cultural comparisons can easily be made without careful consideration of the particular historical context. It does, however, emphasise that there were wider historical processes at work in late medieval England, processes that can be seen in other contexts and which underlie the dynastic conflicts of the period so often presented by Shakespeare and by twentieth-century scholars as an entirely contingent set of events and individual personalities.

It also means that we must understand such processes *anthropologically*, just as New Archaeology always advocated (Binford 1962; Johnson 1999: 21–2). In other words, we must develop an anthropological description of late medieval England just as we would of the people of the Trobriand Islands or of the northwest Pacific coast. These women and men were the direct ancestors of many of the scholars who study them today, but they lived six centuries ago and had a way of life utterly different from our own. They cannot be granted special privileges not accorded to other peoples whose society is different from 'our own', whether separated by time or by space.

Just as the history of the period appears superficially to be a contingent and random set of political events, but turns out to have underlying structural principles, so it is with the physical layout and organisation of castles. When we turn to the internal layout of the structures that housed these social relations, we appear at first to be confronted by a confusing labyrinth of rooms – Kafka's castle again. The modern, uninitiated visitor to the ruins is often utterly confused by the array of corridors, spaces, courts, apparently leading one off from another in quite random patterns.

This confusion is increased by the fact that late medieval castles are very different, one from another. Some are apparently 'regular', as we have seen at Bodiam and similar sites. Others are apparently 'irregular', with ovoid or polygonal outer walls and no regular spacing of towers. Some are focused on a great tower or *donjon*, others are of courtyard design without a great central tower. These variations often have no simple or obvious correlation with social status or regional tradition; often, as was the case with Cromwell at Tattershall and South Wingfield, or Yevele in south-eastern England, the same builder or owner could produce very different final building forms in different locations.

I am going to suggest, however, that underlying this apparent diversity there is a common spatial ordering to these structures. The ordering of space we find within castles is very closely linked to two other orders. The first of these is the contemporary ordering of society: the formation and structuring of different genders and social ranks. The second is the ordering of architectural detail and decoration, as well as material culture in the wider sense. So as we saw in the last chapter's comments on the ordering of landscapes, *spatial ordering goes hand in hand with the ordering of society and of material culture.*

Such an ordering meant that the visitor to a castle, of perhaps a certain social rank and gender and possessing the appropriate cultural knowledge, would not necessarily see the castle as random or labyrinth-like at all. Rather, such a person would have an implicit understanding of the arrangement of the structure in front of him or her, and with it an understanding of the appropriate behaviour expected: when to stop, when to turn, which areas were accessible to his or her rank, even demeanour and bodily position at each appropriate point in his or her progress through the castle.

Such an understanding was at least partly implicit. Just as the Commons protested against badges in a way that revealed anxiety about a breakdown of moral and political order, but would not have articulated their concerns in those terms, so a late medieval visitor would not have articulated the structuring of space in a castle in explicit terms. The Duke of Buckingham may have been charged with building too splendidly in the 1510s (Rawcliffe 1978), but his accusers did not specify what, precisely, was too grand about his new palace at Thornbury – they had no need to: it was obvious, the categories Buckingham had violated were taken for granted. The cultural anthropologist Bourdieu (1977) calls such a taken-for-granted understanding of the world *habitus*.

Such an understanding of the ordering of architecture may also have been partial – some elements may have needed explaining by a guide, in itself an action that reinforced aspects of the process of architectural framing. After all, if the castle is theatre, some productions need narrators to explain what is going on, while others encourage audience participation.

At both Warkworth and Bolton, for example, 'the visitor . . . [must enter] by choosing the correct doorway from a series of identical openings' (Dixon 1996: 53). I would draw the implication from Dixon's comment that the architectural ambiguity here is deliberate, first, in making the visitor unguided and therefore powerless in his/her approach to the hall, and second, placing power in the hands of the guide, that is either the host or the agent of the host, perhaps a man wearing on his own body the lord's livery. At Warkworth, Dixon further points out that the 'holding area' or chamber in which the guest waits before being admitted to the lord's presence also lacks orienting clues, so the visitor is kept disoriented while he or she waits. Once in the screens passage and in the sight of the lord, all is revealed. Warkworth, then, works through disorientation followed by understanding.

We might liken this understanding (or lack of understanding) of architectural space to that of language. We all possess a linguistic competence, in which once a simple set of grammatical rules are known, a range of statements can be produced. The range of statements is effectively infinite (we never run out of new sentences to speak or write). They can also be very subtle, or deliberately ambiguous, depending on the skill or intentions of the speaker or writer.

I have suggested elsewhere that castle design is like a 'grammar', and that:

> once one is aware of the main elements of castle design, one can 'read' the layouts of most such buildings quite readily . . . this ability to 'read' the layout of castle or house is true both of the contemporary historian and the medieval person.
>
> (Johnson 1996: 120 and 127)

At Warkworth and countless other examples, the architectural statements made in this manner are again quite subtle or deliberately ambiguous. However, while language is a good analogy to get the point across, it must also be stressed that understanding took place also through bodily movement and positioning – where one sat in the hall, the physical progress from lower to upper court.

The understanding of this spatial ordering is also one that needs to be appreciated on the ground. It is striking that many contemporary ideal statements of castle design such as those cited in Warnke (1994) are quite specific in terms of progress through the building, and talk at length of the experiences to be had of the views from the tower and the impressions of different rooms, but quite vague when assessed in terms of a bird's-eye view of the overall plan. What clearly interests the medieval narrator in many of these examples is not so much the bird's-eye view of the structure, what it looks like at a Cartesian or map-like, geometric level, but rather the order of rooms, the successive architectural experiences, how one progresses through the building. This movement through architectural space in terms of bodily movement rather than overall plan becomes a symbolically loaded one in all kinds of different ways; it becomes a metaphor for other kinds of movement or penetration, whether military, sexual, or social. And it is a quite different understanding from that of the traditional archaeologist, with its emphasis on dating and typology.

To explore these points further, let us take a tour around a late medieval castle. Cultural anthropologists will recognise that I do this using an anthropological method, Clifford Geertz's technique of 'thick description' (1973). What I am trying to do is develop a multi-layered, deep understanding of some of the meanings and allusions that a particular architectural feature might have had to observers, and how it might be bound up with particular sets of actions or movements; the end result is an attempt to gain a rich appreciation of the meanings of the castle and of castle life, meanings that are very different from those of the modern world. I am going to do this by completing the journey we started in the last chapter, when we moved through the watery landscapes of its surroundings: we now examine the walls and arrive at the gate.

Crossing the threshold

The moment of entry to a late medieval castle is one that involves a series of different meanings. It defines the social status of the occupant, most crudely in whether they are admitted to the building or not, but as we shall see in more subtle ways also.

Gates, to state the obvious, can be opened and closed. In other social arenas such as those of civic ritual this double-edged quality was used explicitly: in the civic receptions of monarchs at York, for example, the opening of the gates to the King carried the corollary that they could be shut again if the city authorities so desired. Civic gates were where the executed and quartered bodies of enemies of the King were set up for the benefit of the populace; some ordinary citizens of Norwich showed what they thought of such demonstration by stealing the 'rebel' Jack Cade's head off the city gate (Harvey 1995: 164). The opening of the gate thus carried the complex and double-edged message of overt welcome and covert political independence. In later periods, the shutting of the gates could become an action that could carry quite massive political and historical meaning, for example, in the seventeenth-century siege of Derry where the shutting of the gate and denial of access to the Catholic King James II was an action that is celebrated by the Protestant community to this day (McBride 1997).

But the castle gate did not carry such a simple choice. Entry to the castle was graded carefully according to social status, and might be manipulated according to the occasion. While high-status visitors might have the great doors thrown open, the battlements above lined with the bodies of retainers bearing the livery of the lord, and a fanfare of trumpets, others might enter through a wicket gate, or smaller gate set within the larger doors. Many wicket gates are so low that the lowly medieval visitor had to stoop to enter them, as well as lift their feet over the sill in rather undignified fashion. Alternatively, lesser visitors might be expected to enter via a lesser or 'postern' gate. Such a gate might be permanently or semi-permanently open, at least during the daytime; the forerunner of the nineteenth-century servants' entrance.

The simple action of entering the castle, then, was set up as a stage-setting for a very careful social grading of the visitor. As the visitor came to understand the castle by moving through it, so the castle reciprocally came to know the social status and identity of the visitor. The gate also carried a host of other connotations. In the thirteenth-century poem *Diu Crone*, entry to the gate is presented as explicitly sexual in nature.

A knight attempting to rape a lady began to search for the castle, pressing forward with great force so he could throw down as much of it as he wished. Soon the knight dismounted in front of the gate and tried to seize control of it. Luckily, the bars with which the gate was secured could not be broken by his battering ram so quickly because the lady defended herself.

(cited in Samples 1995: 198)

More generically, arrival at the castle was a recurring leitmotif in medieval romance, such as that of Weeping Castle in Malory. At Weeping Castle, the knight must fight the castellan; the loser dies and the winner becomes or continues as the castellan. Meanwhile the knight's lady must be compared in beauty with the castellan's lady, and again the loser dies. Tristram feels that the custom is discourteous, but goes along with it, killing first the castellan and then his own lady who loses out against the deceased castellan's wife (Ross 1997).

Castle gates must be seen in the context of other entrances. We have mentioned the use of gates in city walls as foci for civil ceremony: doorways of other buildings of the castle landscape are also referred to more implicitly. Most obviously, the doorway of the parish church is a focus for community memory (Douglas n.d.).

Entering a castle is the action of a guest, and as such invokes a further set of social and cultural connotations (Sinfield 1992). One trusts one's host not to abuse the rules of hospitality. The architecture of the gate acts as a series of visual reminders and frames for that trust. The first action of the guest is to walk or ride up, under the view of the battlements, arrowslits and gunports, stand under the machicolations of the gate, and wait for entry. The body of the guest is, I suggest, deliberately made vulnerable, and this vulnerability is accentuated upon entry. Most gatehouses have an inner and outer gate separated by a dark tunnel, flanked by a porter's lodge and often pierced with inward-looking arrowslits as well as in some cases the famous *meutrières* or 'murder-holes' in the vault above. At any moment during the entry of the visitor both inner and outer doors might be closed and the visitor trapped like a rat. Again, we see the hopelessness of opposing 'military' and 'social' explanations: the male knight was, we can assume, expected to show no fear under such circumstances.

Such passages with their implication of social as well as physical progress are also found in microcosm within the castle itself. This is most obvious where a castle has both an 'upper' and a 'lower' court, with a further gatehouse placed between these areas. However, staged progression can also be found in more subtle ways. The four doors opening on to the courtyard at Bolton are 'fortified' with portcullises. So the visitor at Bolton is not met by ostentation at the gate of the castle (Bolton has no gatehouse; the door is set modestly off to one side), but encounters ostentation once he or she enters

Figure 3.5 Plan of Bolton Castle. The outer gate is adjacent to the south-east tower. Four gates open off the courtyard; the north-west gate leads via turns, corridors and stairs to the lower end of the first floor hall.

the courtyard (Figure 3.5). Again, at the early fourteenth-century *donjon* of Knaresborough, Dixon (1990) has traced how it acts as a stage setting for the King's lover Piers Gaveston. It is unsurprising therefore to again find portcullises and *meutrières* at the entrance to this *donjon*.

The gate is surrounded by a series of architectural features designed to draw attention to it. On the battlements, there might be carved figures on merlons: these are found, for example, at the northern castles of Alnwick, Raby, Lumley, and Bothal, as well as the city walls of York and Newcastle. These examples all date to around *c.*1300, but later examples are found at Hylton and elsewhere (Morley 1976). On the gate tower or towers, there might be turrets; in the borders, these might take the form of bartizans. The effect of all these features is to draw the visitor's eye upwards, to be over-awed by an impressive skyline. Our visitor might then look down again, to examine the more specific meanings of the heraldry over the gate.

Heraldry at the gate

The gate, being the moment at which the outsider takes on a different social identity by being transformed into a guest, is naturally the focus of symbolic elaboration that is much more than simply being decorative. Heraldry is found above the door; as the knight waits at the gate to be admitted, he is afforded ample time to study the identity of the castle lord. Some of these symbols might be very simple: the devices found on the simple metal badges of the lord's followers might also be found inscribed on the castle fabric here. More complex messages, however, are encoded in the complex images of the painted shields above him. Perhaps the knight 'explains' how to read these devices to his companions of lower social status.

The bosses of the vault display heraldic emblems and devices. However, this elaboration is more than simply one of straightforward affirmation of status. In the first place, it reinforces the sense of the castle as social body. Just as heraldic devices were displayed on the livery worn by servants and retainers, so heraldry is found on the surface 'worn' by the castle.

It is also important to recognise that heraldry was a much more sophisticated signalling device than simply a formal patriarchal code; and it increased its complexity in the late Middle Ages (Barstow 1974). It could express marriage alliances. For example, at Hylton, dated to the end of the fourteenth century on the basis of the heraldry, the gatehouse tower has elaborate heraldry and battlements (Morley 1976). The heraldry is not simply that of the Hylton family: it includes families associated with the Hyltons through marriage. In this sense, the ties of kin and ancestry expressed by the heraldry were being creatively manipulated, as they were in other societies (Robin 2001). Again, by the sixteenth century baronial and royal devices could be paired, managing to simultaneously express baronial pride and loyalty to the Crown, for example at Ightham Mote where symbols of the local lord alternate with the rose of the royal Tudor dynasty (Starkey 1982).

The purpose of this discussion is not to present a definitive view of how the system of heraldic devices worked in all its complexity. The very fact that such an exercise would take another book tells its own story. What it does do is draw attention to part of a very complex nexus of meanings to do with the power of the past, and the education and cultural background needed to 'read' such devices. Memory, education and the ability to understand rebuses and emblems were later to be specifically and didactically linked in Renaissance emblem books (Camille 1985; Carruthers 1990: 221).

Our visitor is given the ability to understand these symbols in terms of genealogy, one of the basic organising principles of medieval elite society. Stein writes suggestively:

> In its way of creating a nexus of time, space and land based on the continuity of blood, genealogy is one of the series of strictly speaking

74

imaginary constructions that come into being [in the twelfth century] in both theological and secular realms of thought. Their common property is that they serve to provide a material embodiment for an ideal or symbolic entity . . . The family thus becomes over time an increasingly complex spatial network of alliances and land holdings . . . Far from being a mirror of social reality, genealogical narratives and origin stories are in this context strictly ideological entities: they represent the unsystematic fragmentations and reconsolidations of power and territory through the physical images of substantial identity, permanent presence, and linear succession.

(1998: 106)

The use of certain symbols, then, was a matter central to elite identities. When Lord Scrope, builder of Bolton Castle, launched his famous lawsuit against Sir Robert Grosvenor over the latter's right to the use of *azure a bend or* on his arms, it was more than some trivial matter of Scrope's being 'touchy about honour'; the issues raised struck at the very heart of medieval culture.

[T]he way the brief was presented – resting so heavily on age, on the unbroken and unquestioned chain of memory, and on collective memory and consensus – gives us a look into how the world of the written document grew from and was melded into that of social memory.

(Rosenthal 1996: 51)

And yet the gate at Bolton is not ostentatiously adorned by heraldry (Figure 3.6); its gate is hardly emphasised and, as Hislop (1997) discusses, is also not specified in the building program; there is little heraldry throughout the building. There is a similar lack of external show at Sheriff Hutton, of a similar plan to Bolton, built in 1382 by John de Nevill.

The courtyard

Our visitor now emerges from the dark tunnel of the gatehouse, blinking into the sunlight. The castle now appears revealed.

This is also, for certain social ranks, the moment of dismounting. The moment at which an elite male visitor gets off his horse is a significant one; not only is he now even more without means of defence, he gives up one more element of his identity in a society where for elite men 'learning to walk and to ride were practically simultaneous experiences' (Bennett 1999: 73). Our visitor's horse is led off to the stables.

From here, standing in the middle of the courtyard, the castle provides clear orientation for the visitor. The courtyard works, as so many late

Figure 3.6 The gate at Bolton Castle, viewed from
the village green to the east. The porter's
lodge is to the left of the gate.

medieval architectural systems work, by combining different elements
according to a common grammar. This does not mean that all courtyards
look alike. The courtyard may be square, rectangular or 'irregular', but it
will have common elements grouped around it. The hall may be placed to
the left or right of the visitor upon entry, or directly opposite, but it will
always be visible; I know of no certain example where the hall is placed
behind a visitor who has just entered the castle. Stables will always be at a
distance from the hall. Lodgings may be stacked one on top of another, or
placed in a line, but they will always have independent access.

The visitor understands the rules behind the courtyard, but not necessarily how those rules apply in the case of the specific castle he is visiting
on this occasion. Take the castle of Bolton as an example. At Bolton, the
stables and hall are accessed off the same door (Figure 3.5). These are actually some distance from one another in terms of physical movement –

corridors diverge beyond the single door off the courtyard and a further flight of stairs takes the visitor to the lower end of the hall. But the arrangement would have to be shown to the visitor by a host or guide.

The spatial and cultural logic of the courtyard is a little like the hall turned inside out. The visitor enters by definition at the lower end of the courtyard. Across from the visitor, the entrance to the hall, marked out by a porch, flight of stairs or both, defines the next step upwards in the social and spatial ladder. On the sides of the courtyard between gatehouse and entrance to the hall, doors and entrances to service areas define access to lower status areas. Just as everyone has to move through the hall, so everyone has to move through the courtyard.

The courtyard displays the household to the visitor. Stables, service, hall, 'private' apartments are ranged around it, usually with their long sides towards the courtyard. The upper and lower ends of the hall can be clearly made out from the vantage point of the courtyard by their fenestration (doors at the lower end, large oriel window at the upper). The chapel is also visible. At Chepstow, the late thirteenth-century Marten's tower, probably designed as a suite of accommodation for the lord, has a chapel window prominently placed to be viewed on entry to the castle. Where elements cannot be identified from their appearance, they are given names. Towers, for example, often not readily distinguishable one from another, acquire names ranging from the functional to the allusive (Kitchen Tower at Kenilworth; Caesar's Tower at Warwick).

This architecture frames the social activity within and around the buildings. The visitor sees bodies bustling about on everyday tasks, their clothing denoting their status and position within the household, and possibly bearing the livery or badges of the lord. Horses are led to and from the stables; dogs prowl around the kitchens. Food is brought with a clatter to the kitchens, while refuse is carted away, possibly to be dumped in the lower court as it was at Barnard Castle (Austin 1984).

Yet again, this observation is double-edged. By standing in the middle of the court, the visitor stands displayed to the household. Similarly, different members of the household can observe and monitor each other. As Alfred Hitchcock might have pointed out, there is no cover in the middle of a courtyard; it is a very lonely place. All turn to observe the visitor, maybe to greet him or her warmly as befits their social status, or perhaps to stare with cold and stony looks.

Relatively few late medieval courtyards have a central focus in the form of a well or other feature. They do not need such a central focus; the focus is provided by the people, the body of the lord or of the visitor. Courtyards are essentially frames for the social action; the bustle of household life, or for particular ceremonial moments of welcome. The royal Scottish palace of Linlithgow has the figures of the Three Estates standing above the gateway; here in a royal palace, the courtyard displays society to itself.

Of course, there is often more than one court, and the use of successive courts may be used to emphasise the experiences outlined above. For example, the visitor on horseback may ride into the lower court, but have to dismount and have his horse taken away from and led off to the stables before entering a second gatehouse to the inner court on foot.

The visitor of lower social status, people maybe supplying provisions to the castle or on business, might now be led off through the service areas of the castle. However, the framing of architectural and social identity operates at all social levels; it is not the preserve of the lord and guests of his social status. Servants, brewers, other agents observe the huge fireplaces and bread ovens of the kitchen ranges; clearly this is a castle where the appropriate hospitality can be offered to great hosts of people. This lord keeps a good house as well as a fair one (Thomson 1993: 38).

The hall

The visual focus of the courtyard, however, is the hall. And not only is it the visual focus: its spatial form is remarkably consistent. I know of no halls which are not of a rectangular form. A circular hall was probably planned at Windsor by Edward III; it was to be called the 'round table' in allusion to the Arthurian legends and to Edward's own tournaments of that name (Vale 1982), with aisles; but the plan was abandoned (Harvey 1944: 8–9).

The hall had various functions, all of which our visitor would be aware of as he passed under its tall windows and gazed up into the recesses of the roof space (Figure 3.7). Many of these functions were judiciary and ceremonial, to do with the administering of 'justice' (or more accurately, the mobilisation of feudal power) and the giving and receiving of homage. Honorial courts must have been held here; this is certainly suggested by the semantic equivalence of *curia* as place and *curia* as institution (Britnell, pers. comm). Our visitor might know that this is where knights would do homage, and men of varying social groups would receive livery, badges and other gifts. Such ceremonies would revolve around the traditional layout of the hall, with its doors at the lower end giving on to the cross-passage, service rooms and outside world, and at the other end the raised dais for the lord; lesser social orders would approach through the vast space of the hall, kneel, and then ascend the dais end before returning.

It is a mistake, however, to separate such 'ceremonial' functions from 'everyday life'. The simple act of all members of the household eating in the hall was a ceremony imbued with all kinds of meanings – if it were not important, Langland's *Piers Plowman* would not have complained about the perceived decline of the practice. Eating itself was a cultural and social set of actions as it is today. In Bertilak's castle in *Sir Gawain and the Green Knight*, knights take hunks of meat from the deer and the boar. A civilised meal, for medieval literature culture, consists of the submission of nature to

Figure 3.7 The hall at Kenilworth Castle, viewed from the lower end. The hall was re-modelled in the late fourteenth century, with the vaulted undercroft being inserted, the whole structure being raised and aisles being replaced with a vast hammerbeam roof similar to that at Westminster Hall.

culture, a submission seen also in the use of pelts of animals, and the fur of Gawain's clothing (Riddy 1995).

We are very familiar with the way space was constituted within the hall itself. Below the high table placed on the dais end, people were seated on benches in the body of the hall in order of status. The food was brought in from the kitchens through the lower end, by servants bearing the device of the lord on their bodies – the livery they were wearing.

It is striking how many late medieval halls continue with open hearths. The mid-fifteenth-century hall of Gainsborough is of a huge scale and lavish design, with an impressive oriel window lighting the upper end of the hall; yet it is heated by a hearth in the middle of the room. Clearly the cultural resonance of the smoke rising to the rafters was one that was sufficiently powerful to override the inconvenience of it.

The hall impresses through its scale, but it is also very subtle. During ceremonials the empty space between upper and lower ends created awe as those giving homage moved up and down, but as the benches and tables were moved from the sides into the centre of the space for mealtimes that space would take on very different meanings. Now to sit one or two places too far to the 'upper' end might invite insult, ridicule or even violence. To receive hospitality, then, involved submitting oneself to the social order and the lord from which that hospitality emanated. And mealtimes extended beyond the ambit of the hall itself – extended the metaphor of social order it provided into the castle and beyond. Lower social orders, the 'poor', could eat the leftovers, but these alms might be distributed either from the service end of the household or even outside the gates of the castle or house itself (Heal 1990).

Unsurprisingly, then, the hall was the focus of decoration that emphasised values of elite masculinity. As the household dined in the hall at Tamworth Castle, now destroyed but recorded by the antiquarian Dugdale, they could ponder the meanings of 'large paintings of Sir Lancelot of the Lake and Sir Tarquin' painted in the fourteenth century; other halls had scenes from Edward I's life. Heraldry was again repeated, both on walls and on floor tiles, for example, at Longthorpe Tower and at the Byward Tower, Tower of London (Tristram 1955: 31 and 36).

However, I think it is a mistake to draw too sharp a distinction between the structure and the decoration of the hall. I have argued previously (Johnson 1993: 110) that one of the central points about late medieval architecture is the way it combines technical detail with decorative effect, to the extent that we cannot draw a distinction between the two. The carpentry needed to produce hammerbeam roofs that spanned the vast spaces of Westminster and Kenilworth halls also provided a visual focus, an aesthetic effect; the upper and lower bays, the division between central space and aisles, represented both technical system and relative status.

The chamber

After a meal, the visitor of appropriate social status might be invited by the lord to go through the upper end of the hall into a suite of rooms beyond. These suites of rooms are often termed 'private', but this term needs more careful definition. Important political functions could take place in such rooms between people on a personally distant basis. In the late medieval world, personal ties and connections were central to the flow of political power. The family and household itself was a microcosm of political order. Therefore, these rooms were not private in the sense of being a domestic retreat in the modern sense. They were the room where relations of status and power could be played out at a smaller, more intimate level.

We have already seen one example of this. At Tattershall, the chamber beyond the hall is further down the line of accessibility and more socially exclusive. But its arrangements show as much concern with the regulation of access to the lord and the impression made on visitors: it has its own waiting chamber, corridor, and fireplace bearing the device of Lord Cromwell. The more intimate nature of this setting does not make it any less theatrical or intended in its effect. Chambers were carefully sited; a late fourteenth-

Figure 3.8 Window seats at Kenilworth, with a view over the mere.

century French treatise recommends that they look out on to gardens below, and naturalistic paintings of plants and animals often adorned the walls of the chambers themselves. Often the lord's '*étude*' would be linked to the garden by a private passage (Whiteley 1999: 94).

At other castles, large, apparently 'public' chambers are nevertheless provided with 'window seats'; that is, pairs of seats set into the embrasures of windows (Figure 3.8). These are generally set in pairs either side of the window, though occasionally appear on one side of the embrasure only, as at the fifteenth-century castle of Tarascon in south-east France.

Roberta Gilchrist (1999) has pointed out that 'private' chambers are often separate suites for women. In some castles, these are linked to enclosed gardens by covered walkways or cloisters, and have independent access to private chapels. She suggests that rather than these chambers simply being 'private', they represent an alternative system of moving around the castle and with it an alternative way of looking at the (gendered) systems of power that the castle represents.

Lodgings

Having eaten, and been privileged to have an audience with the lord in his chamber, our visitor might now be led to his own suite of lodgings within the castle. The mere presence of lodgings contains its own message. The visitor to Bolton, perhaps at a time when the lord was not in residence, would note the vast ranges of lodgings provided and the care taken to make these comfortable, and draw conclusions not just about the numbers and importance of Lord Scrope's followers to be accommodated, but about the importance of hospitality to Scrope's good lordship. He would further note that each lodging is itself a complete hall-and-chamber block; so each member of the lord's household had their own, smaller and socially inferior, household in turn. At Warwick, lodgings dating to the fourteenth century are stacked one on top of another in Guy's and Caesar's Towers; these two towers flank the main gate, itself elaborate but demonstrative in design, are provided with elaborate battlements, and are clearly designed to be seen; I would argue that they display the lord's provision of hospitality to the outside world.

Within each lodging, there is still no end to the repetition of spatial metaphors of social status; there is a separate service room in many cases. At South Wingfield, the lodgings are carefully graded in terms of social status, with the best accommodation in the High Tower ranging to a dormitory for servants of lower social status in the lower court. Even when asleep in his chamber, our visitor continues to be framed within spatial and social structures of power.

Common architectural principles

Our visitor has 'understood' the castle by moving through it; by performing certain rituals like dismounting, sitting, eating at different points; and by observing and decoding a series of visual cues. He has done this implicitly, using the cultural knowledge or *habitus* that he acquired in youth. Such an 'understanding' was not difficult to achieve, for it depended on a quite simple set of architectural principles or elements.

The first of these is repetition. Decorative repetition, especially that of heraldry, forms an underlying rhythm; the device or badge of the lord is repeated on every available surface. At Tattershall, the visitor sees the rebus of Lord Cromwell (the Cromwell weed, *lithospermum officionale*) everywhere, from the front gate to the fireplace spandrels of the innermost room of the tower. The visitor also sees it across classes or genres of architecture; that is, it occurs both in the castle and also in the stained glass of the collegiate church at Tattershall (Marks 1984). At Fotheringhay, there was similar repetition of the arms of the Neville family and of York in the stained glass of the Church and college (Marks 1978). The analogy with rhythm is not an idle one; Evetts (1994) has explored how decorative systems on architecture before the Renaissance follow analogous rules to those of poetry and music, and how the form and structure of all three change in analogous ways in the sixteenth century.

Repetition of decorative detail is echoed in repetition of architectural form. There may be two courtyards, one of higher social status, but each follows the same rules. Again, where there are two halls, each is nevertheless laid out with upper and lower ends, window lighting the upper end, and so on. At Warkworth and many other castles, the suite of chambers at the upper end of the 'lower' hall was used for the constable's accommodation.

The second is careful deployment of symmetry. This may sound surprising: the Romantic conception of medieval architecture as asymmetrical and 'rambling' is deeply embedded in our way of looking at things. But we have already seen that a building like Bodiam deploys symmetry very carefully. Even within apparently irregular buildings, symmetry is used carefully within particular elements. The lower end of the hall, for example, commonly has a symmetrical distribution of doorways, though the rooms beyond may not be so (cf. the lower end of the hall in Warkworth *donjon* discussed in Chapter 4). At Raby, the apparent irregularity of the castle when seen from the outside is belied when the visitor walks into a standard, rectangular inner courtyard; it is the placement of the towers on the curtain that is irregular.

The third element is that of twists and turns. Late medieval buildings almost always involve turns at critical moments, when one crosses a threshold into a space of different social status. Often the entrance to a lower court is at an angle, into a corner of the court, before a turn into the upper court. Examples are Jean de Berry's picture of Poitiers, where there is an angled entrance to the *basse cour*, then a turn to the upper court, as we have already seen at Caister. Others include Somerton, Lincolnshire, Scotney, Sussex, Cooling, Westenhanger and South Wingfield. The entrance to the hall, via a screens passage, also involves further turns. As we observed in Chapter 2, it is difficult to avoid the conclusion that the overall effect is that of a liturgical procession; religious and secular worlds are never far away in the Middle Ages. Graves (2000) has argued that ceremonies around the altar would remind the congregation of mealtimes at high table, whatever the consciously intended effect might be; conversely, the pause to enter the castle, movement across the courtyard, pause before turning into the hall to view the high table at the other end would invoke elements of religious authority for many visitors.

Whatever the case, rooms and spaces are linked very carefully. As noted above, this is not necessarily a Cartesian or geometrical layout in which rooms are at opposite ends of the building. At Hylton, for example, the hall and 'private' chambers were actually housed within the gatehouse. Again, at Old Wardour, one must enter through the gate to the inner court, turn, go up the stairs and down a screens passages before entering the hall but the hall itself has been placed directly over the gate.

The castle marks time. At a daily level, the raising and lowering of the drawbridge, and opening and closing of the gate, were performed at a regular rhythm which in some if not most cases took place at a precise moment of the day. At other times, before and after mealtimes, the benches and tables would be moved back and forth within the hall, turning it from an open administrative space to one ready for mealtimes; or the screens at the lower ends might be movable, and be moved up and down the hall to create a smaller and larger space according to whether or not the lord was in residence. Such a screen still survives at Little Moreton in Cheshire. The very occupation of the castle was part of a seasonal or yearly rhythm, in which the great household moved from place to place.

Raglan, its form and identities

The castle of Raglan (Figure 3.9) is a particularly interesting example for several reasons. First, its plan, by the late fifteenth century, combines 'courtyard' and 'tower' forms. Second, the family that built Raglan had an identity which was particularly unstable and open to negotiation.

As at Bodiam, the 'military' view of Raglan is in retreat, but has yet to be finally killed off. Kenyon has reviewed the form of the gunloops; he notes that one is blocked by the well apparatus in the ground floor of the keep, while 'those in the garderobe towers around the Fountain Court could not have been used by gunners' (1987: 164); others are positioned too high up the wall face or in the back of the fireplace in the Kitchen Tower. Kenyon, however, interprets this as due to the infancy of gunnery. I find this

Figure 3.9 View of Raglan from the east. The detached *donjon* is to the right; its face towards the approach, and the top storey, were destroyed after the Civil War.

Figure 3.10 Gunloops in the western tower of the gatehouse at Raglan Castle.

surprising. Gunnery may have been in its infancy, but five minutes' acquaintance with a fifteenth-century artillery piece would have been enough to inform a builder of the appropriate location of gunports (Figure 3.10). Either builders knew of the use of guns and simply did not care that the location of gunports was militarily inappropriate, or did not feel the need to find out how the new technology worked (and did not fear the displeasure of their masters on this point). Either way, it suggests the priority in their minds was not a purely or even partly military one.

The landscape around Raglan was certainly carefully constructed. The approach to the castle is designed to show off the great *donjon*, the Yellow Tower of Gwent, to best advantage. Beyond this, aerial photographs reveal signs of formal landscapes probably dating to the Renaissance, in particular a formal garden with diamond islands, and there are also documentary references to fishponds. These, however, together with the later Civil War entrenchments, may obscure traces of earlier medieval landscapes (Kenyon 1982).

The most interesting thing about the landscape context of Raglan has been little remarked on. Approaching the main gate from Raglan village to the south-east, the castle is hidden by a rise; one comes over the rise to see the castle laid out very suddenly. One is reminded of the sudden appearance

Figure 3.11 Entry to Raglan *donjon* from the main courtyard. The main drawbridge would only be lowered for the lord or for important guests; the smaller drawbridge on the right would be used for those of lesser status.

of the moat at Bodiam. From this vantage point, the *donjon* is both framed and rendered inaccessible by a wide moat, while the visitor continues through the main gate into the lower court. Here, inevitably, the visitor turns to the left, to access the upper court through the screens passage of the hall. A further left turn brings the visitor to the suite of lodgings and the entrance to the Yellow Tower.

The entrance to the Yellow Tower is especially elaborate (Figure 3.11). It is in the form of a bascule bridge, in which the main gate has a smaller door to one side, and both are provided with drawbridges that can be raised and lowered separately. These are common in French castles, and the traditional method of 'explaining' the Raglan bascule bridge has been to list candidates for diffusionary 'influence' from France. There are bascules for example at La Ferté-Milon (Aisne), and at Vannes (Morbihan). Curiously, however, other candidates are not mentioned. That at Tarascon in Provence, just up the road

Figure 3.12 Heraldry above the chamber windows at Raglan, as viewed from the *donjon*, featuring a device based on the bascule drawbridge and chains.

for any English noble visiting the Avignon Pope, is not considered; nor is a much earlier Scottish example at Bothwell (itself possibly linked to the great *donjon* at the French castle of Coucy).

I suggest that what is important about the Raglan bascule bridge is not where the idea came from – we can never know that. However, we can look more deeply at what it might have meant to contemporary observers, most of whom would never have been to France. The bascule bridge is portrayed in panels in the upper windows of apartments in the eastern range; thus, anyone in the tower looking out would have the image repeated for them. The bascule 'had been adopted by the Herberts as their badge by 1451' (Emery 1975: 154); the bascule is paired with shields formerly painted with Herbert impaling Devereux (Figure 3.12).

Such a bridge, together with the prominent machicolations and other features, might be seen as French, or more loosely as international in style, by elite observers. Such observers would certainly see Raglan as a palace of the very first rank, as belonging to a major peer of the realm. But the castle could be seen in other ways. It became the centre of Welsh political aspirations, the subject of Welsh verse. Hywel ap Dafydd of Glamorgan could speak of Raglan as:

> The great house with the comely roof
> The fair house with the beautiful porch;
> Curious are the ramparts
> of the palace, my great palace,
> With its towers towards the sun in the east
> And the strength of steel in the stone walls.
>   (cited in Emery 1975: 153)

I am suggesting that the great complexity of Raglan, and in particular its demonstrative use of symbols and architectural features, should not lead us into a search for diffusionary 'parallels' or for that matter particular worries about the dating of the different phases of the structure. Rather, they tell us about a particularly uncertain social identity.

Raglan is another example of a castle built by an upwardly mobile family, but in this case there is the added dimension of ethnicity. It was built by a Welsh family, who sought to present themselves both as Welsh political leaders and as English barons.

Raglan was begun by William ap Thomas. It has been argued that there was an earlier castle on the site on the basis of the irregular plan, but I do not see why an 'irregular' plan could not simply have been chosen. Ap Thomas' widow, Gwladus, ran the household in his absence; the scale of her political influence may be detected in the attendance of 3,000 people at her funeral. Ap Thomas' son was William Herbert, Earl of Pembroke, 1445–69. Herbert dropped the Welsh patronymic form of his name and attempted to play the game of national politics with some success. After supporting the future Edward IV at Mortimer's Cross, he was given land in South Wales, and a slew of honours; he was the first Welshman to be made an Earl. Herbert cemented his position by marrying into a Herefordshire family but his real break came in 1460 when he was rewarded by Henry VI for failing to support the Yorkists. From this time until 1469 he had landed interests as far away as East Anglia and a variety of trading and other interests, including the custody of minors such as the future Henry VII. Herbert even succeeded in marrying his son to the queen's sister.

Herbert's identity, however, was both 'English' and 'Welsh'. Herbert held a series of offices in Wales, and a contemporary Welsh poem asked him to become a national leader (Williams and Williams: 1965: 207). In 1462, Edward IV commanded the bards of Wales to find a suitable pedigree for him (see Bradney 1910: 224–6). Raglan's library included an extensive collection of Welsh manuscripts. I suggest therefore that Raglan castle, metaphorically as well as literally, faced two ways just as the identity of its owner did. English and Welsh visitors would see two different structures, would associate two different sets of meanings to the buildings; hence, in part, its apparently irregular appearance to our eyes. Its polygonal towers may refer to Edward I's castle at Caernarfon, associated with the Prince of

Wales. Caernarfon is not only irregular and studded with polygonal towers; it is a building carefully constructed with Imperial associations with Constantinople through the tower forms and banded masonry, and also Welsh allusions to the dream of *Macsen Wledig* which prophesies the return of a Roman emperor to Wales (Taylor 1979: 370–1). The gargoyles on the gates, machicolations and bascule bridge at Raglan may be seen as 'French'. One can argue back and forth about the specifics of the allusions but what is crucial is to note that however they are read, the allusions have a partic-ular complexity that relates, I suggest, to the complexity and ambiguity of Herbert's position.

Most writing on Raglan has focused on the chronology of building and hence the attribution of different elements to either ap Thomas or to Herbert; on the 'influences' that may be detected in the design; or on individual features such as the gunports. For me, the fascination of Raglan is in its totality, and in what the completed castle looked like, and on how its complexity related to the complex and ambiguous social identity of its owner.

Castles in fragments

Raglan is a particular example of a castle that meant different things to different people. It is a particularly interesting example in this respect, but not an exception. How, then, do castles mean things? So far, we have explored a series of possible meanings for Raglan and other castles, but the discus-sion has often been tentative. In part, this has been deliberate, in opposition to the misguided certainty of those with 'no real doubt' over a castle's func-tion and meanings. I now want to go further – I want to suggest that what a castle meant would *necessarily* have differed between observers, and that we must grasp this diversity, fragmentation even, of the meanings of castles. I suggested above that the medieval person would have an understanding of how to move around the building. Note first 'an understanding', not neces-sarily the only understanding, or a full or fully correct understanding.

In the first place, understandings varied according to social rank. Access to different elements of the structure varied in part according to social status. Thus, at mealtimes and particularly so in the case of great feasts, only those of a certain rank would be allowed into the hall; others might cluster around the screens passage doorways or external hatches waiting for the leftovers to be brought out; others still might wait at the castle gate for any further scraps (Heal 1990). In each case, the participants would have a different understanding of what space was forbidden to them and what was allowed, a different understanding therefore of what constituted 'front space' and 'back space' to use Goffman's term (1959). And with this went different under-standings of how to behave.

Second, understandings varied according to gender. We have seen that in terms of those living within the walls, castles were 'overwhelmingly masculine' (McNeill 1992: 29; he adds touchingly that 'given the crowded nature of the accommodation, it was probably best for everyone, especially the women themselves, if they kept away'; compare with McNeill 1997b). However, as Gilchrist has shown, there were castles headed or owned by women, and she has argued convincingly that they shared certain distinctive characteristics, in particular gardens, private chapels, enhanced solar blocks and private galleries or walks between these features. Solar blocks and private chapels for women might be at the most inaccessible points according to a penetration diagram, but Gilchrist argues that seen from the point of view of the inside of the castle outwards these can be understood as alternative centres of power within a wider complex (1999). In any case, even if the castle was peopled largely by men, this does not mean that the household was not gendered; masculinity was by definition just as 'gendered' and problematic a category as femininity (Hadley 1999). Many late medieval castles had a complement of religious personnel; according to some scholars the masculinities of such celibate and homosocial groups needs to be reanalysed (Swanson 1999). The image of the castle was bound up with military prowess of the knight, with chivalry, and with those values of his masculinity (Bennett 1999: 71).

Third, these understandings varied according to specific times, places and participants. In the late medieval period, people might be admitted to the hall – but only on special occasions, particular feast days. The life of the castle itself was regulated by time; the arrival and departure of a peripatetic household.

Fourth, understanding varied according to literacy. For the staff of Wressle and Leconfield, the two great East Yorkshire palaces of the Earl of Northumberland, much of the daily ordinances and rhythm was written down in the Earl of Northumberland's Household Book. Today, this book is consulted as a rich source of detail on the everyday practices of the household (Percy 1827) but also of significance is that the regulations here are *written down*. Only certain members of the household would have had access to the book, and with it access to the daily ordering of the household. Without it, a chance visitor to the castle may have only seen so much bustle, with a sense of people carrying out tightly defined roles.

One implication is that understanding of the castle's routines unfolds through time. By the end of a stay of several weeks, our visitor would 'understand' better the daily rhythm, would have learnt the names and offices of the bustling servants, gained an understanding of the daily and weekly rhythm of the household.

For one person, the castle might be 'revealed' after the outer gate had been penetrated, and the person was standing in the courtyard, observing the placement of hall, stables, kitchen range. For another, disappointed perhaps at the lord's failure to take his meals in the hall, the castle might be 'understood' after penetration of the solar tower. For a third, the experience of being flung into the castle dungeon might be 'understanding' enough of the nature and purpose of the structure. None of these understandings are 'better' or 'worse' than any other; this is not a question of higher-status people having a fuller or more accurate picture, or of lower-status people being somehow deluded or duped. It is an assertion that many different understandings were and are possible.

Deconstructing puzzles

In this chapter, I have tried to look at the different experiences of architectural and social space as one moves around a castle. This is a very different way of approaching such structures than that taken by other scholars, even those of the 'social' tradition.

From Faulkner onwards, accounts of these structures have often been couched in terms of different sequences of types. For Faulkner, any one medieval castle was a 'compromise' (1963: 215) between military and domestic functions. The evolution of thirteenth-century planning elements reached its conclusion in the late fourteenth century, when medieval planners evolved 'the ability to produce an integrated plan which solves the domestic and military problem in a single architectural conception' (ibid.: 235).

The strength of Faulkner's view has been that it has allowed scholarship to begin to consider the social aspects and functioning of castles. However, it has led scholars into thinking about late medieval castles in terms of the evolution of types, in which one evolves from another with little reference to the human agents who created and used them. In this chapter, I have tried to examine how the real human beings who visited and lived in these structures may have understood the architectural spaces they moved through on an everyday basis. Through Raglan and Tattershall, we have seen that such a perspective produces rather different understandings of castles from those of a generation of castle scholars influenced by Faulkner.

We have seen that structures may or may not conform to certain typologies, but that they are also much more complex than this and deserve to be looked at in their own right, not as interim stages. We have seen further that when we do this, we find that the understandings of the castle fragment: there is no one final solution, no single way of thinking about castles. This should not surprise us; it is where the social sciences have progressed as a general state.

However . . . They may be intellectually out of fashion, and they may moreover obscure rather than clarify our view of the real buildings on the ground, but large, all-encompassing models of castle development, and of architectural and social development generally, are still the dominant mode of thinking in both traditional and social ways of thinking about castles. They may be implicit and rarely stated overtly, but they are nevertheless there, lurking behind the descriptive tags and casual phrases – 'the decline of the castle', 'the late medieval courtyard house', 'the influx of Renaissance ideas', 'the end of feudalism'.

To follow through the points I have made above, then, we need to locate our observations on castles within a wider perspective. I suggest that 'The decline of the castle' is situated within a whole series of wider intellectual frameworks relating to architectural and art-historical classifications of Gothic to Renaissance, or historical understandings of medieval to early modern, or social theories of feudal to nascent capitalist. This is why such wider concepts are so difficult to move beyond; they are dovetailed in to very deep-seated ways and habits of thinking about historical periods.

So before we can go on to look at concrete examples of castles in the sixteenth and seventeenth centuries, we need to look more closely at the whole question of how change in this period is understood theoretically, and how the perceived 'decline of the castle' might fit into this. This is the subject of Chapter 4.

4

MEDIEVAL TO
RENAISSANCE

So far in this book, I have talked exclusively about late medieval castles. I now want to move on, and turn to the sixteenth and early seventeenth centuries. This is the period after the late Middle Ages generally referred to as 'the Renaissance' or 'the early modern period'. In the next chapter, I will look at how we can understand the late sixteenth-century additions and alterations to a major medieval castle, Kenilworth.

Before we can do this, however, I want to make some general comments on the way archaeologists and scholars in other disciplines have understood that period of time covered by the term 'the medieval/Renaissance transition'. These comments will reflect back and amplify some of the positions I have taken in the last few chapters, but also set the scene for a move forward into understanding Renaissance structures in the rest of the book.

Obviously, the way archaeologists and other scholars have understood the fifteenth to seventeenth centuries in terms of castle studies must be viewed in terms of the general context of scholarship. We must ask the more general question of how modern scholars have interpreted architectural change in England and Europe in this period. Indeed, we must look more widely still in terms of how modern scholarship has come to understand this 'transition' in aesthetic, theoretical and intellectual terms.

Clearly such a task could be conceived as a huge one. Logically, it should perhaps start with Vasari, the first historian of the Renaissance, and encompass the historiography of a series of magisterial figures in history, archaeology and related disciplines. Anyone speaking of this period does so in the shadow of past figures such as Hegel, Burckhardt (1860; 1867) and Huizinga (1924), and present figures such as Stephen Greenblatt (1980) and Lisa Jardine (1983; 1996a; 1996b). If engaging in debate with such traditions were not enough, anyone speaking of this period also does so within an early twenty-first-century intellectual environment in which the Renaissance is seen as very much tied up with nascent capitalism. It thus implicates much of social theory (in particular the sociological Holy Trinity of Marx, Durkheim and Weber, all of whom spilt much ink on the origins of capitalism and the modern world) in the argument (Johnson 1996). As a result, a thorough conceptual reassessment of the theories and methodologies used by archaeologists and historians to understand this period, if it is actually possible, really requires a further book.

Theoretical reassessment is exceptionally difficult for a second reason. In the Introduction, we noted how people's theoretical attitudes are rarely laid out neatly on a polemical platter for one to scrutinise at will, but are rather embedded deep within the texts they write. A mode of discourse, or habitual way of talking about things, reveals itself in its basic, mundane comments, made when a scholar is writing about little details, for example about how this 'type' is 'influenced' by that 'type'. Almost by definition, theoretical attitudes reside in the taken-for-granteds of interpretation, which are often taken to be so 'obvious' to the community of scholars being addressed that they do not need stating. The implication of this observation is that it is often in 'mere techniques' of definition, observation and classification of details that underlying intellectual attitudes are revealed, rather than in polemics or overt position statements.

To put it another way, Vasari, Burckhardt and Huizinga are such colossal figures that their ways of thinking have become second nature to us, obvious, accepted, part of a common vocabulary. Students today may not even be aware of their names, but the framework of their ideas is passed on every time a student writes of 'the rise of the individual' or 'the waning of the Middle Ages'. As a result, words like 'culture', 'civilisation', 'the State', 'arts', 'architecture' and even more apparently mundane terms like 'growth', 'decline' and 'type' appear to us to be obvious or self-evident in what they mean. Yet they are in fact deeply problematic terms. They all have a complex history or genealogy in modern thought that we are not always consciously aware of.

Such assumptions are particularly difficult to disentangle in areas like medieval and postmedieval archaeology. In these areas of archaeology, scholars have tended to defer to these 'senior disciplines', to work within a research framework and agenda defined by documentary historians in particular. In the process, the discursive assumptions made by these other scholars have been reinscribed into archaeological practice without being questioned or even overtly stated.

I discussed in the Introduction how such a process had led to historical definitions of castles being reinscribed into archaeological practice. Archaeologists have defined the castle as a 'private defended enclosure', but they will never be able to excavate one, because archaeologists do not dig up privacy; they dig up ditches, latrine pits, robber trenches, stretches of masonry, pieces of pottery. They might *interpret* the patterns they dig up in terms of privacy, defence or whatever, but the term 'private' has no clear or unproblematic correlates in the archaeological record. Apparently simple descriptive terms like 'growth', 'maturity' and 'decline' used habitually by historians similarly have no clear, unambiguous indices in the archaeological record. One might see how one might link one to another (for example, multiplication of settlement sites indicates population rise indicates 'growth'), but such links are generally assumed rather than argued through, so, in this example, how many more settlement sites? Are they defined through documentary references? How are they dated? And so on. As a result, archaeology will always be judged and found wanting in many respects while it sets itself the task of addressing questions defined in advance by documentary history. Dave Austin has explored this problem with respect to historically defined 'origins of the manor', where archaeologists have attempted to 'dig up' correlates of a process of 'manorialisation' which is defined in documentary terms (1990: 19–23).

Further, as Hayden White (1973; 1978; 1987) has observed, a way of understanding the past characteristically resides not in a formal set of theoretical statements, but in a narrative, a story. Such a story is apparently factual, and often claims to reside outside theory – it presents itself simply as an account of 'what really happened'. However, White argues that if it is deconstructed it can be shown to actually encompass a specific theoretical position. What I want to do, therefore, is to start with one version of the Story as it is told about the end of castles, and continue by looking at its underlying assumptions.

The Story

There is a story about castle design that goes something like this.

Once upon a time, there was a thing called the castle. The castle existed in its classic form in eleventh- to thirteenth-century England, at the same time as 'feudalism' or the 'high Middle Ages'. Indeed, the castle is in a sense coterminous with feudalism.

The design of castles evolved, as techniques of attack and defence progressed. Early castles were of earthwork form, and when of stone, were dominated by a great tower, keep or *donjon*. However, the keep was shown to be weak, not strong; so forms other than the square keep – circular and polygonal keeps – became more popular. At the same time, systems of defence moved away from the use of stone keep as strongpoint towards stress on a curtain wall studded with flanking towers; water defences were elaborated; entry to castles was protected in increasingly sophisticated ways, through barbicans and elaboration of gatehouses; 'concentric' systems were evolved, first falteringly at castles like Dover and later more confidently.

By the late thirteenth century, castles had reached their apogee, a state of 'perfection' if you will. In England, this perfection is seen in the Welsh castles of Edward I, who in many historical accounts is also the greatest English king of the Plantagenet dynasty. Edward's last great castle, Beaumaris, is the geometrically perfect application of concentric design to a flat site (Figure 4.1).

Thereafter castles took on a rather different form. Many were abandoned. In others, outer courtyards were lost. The new castles that were built were

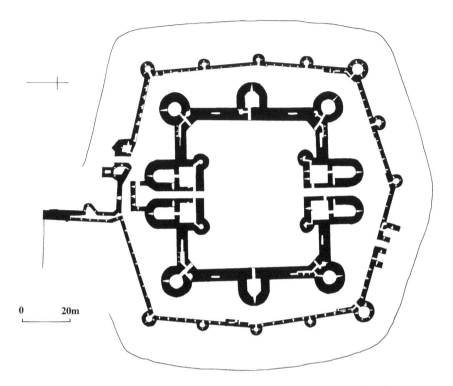

0   20m

Figure 4.1 Beaumaris Castle. The Friary Gate to the north was never completed; nor were the tower summits, the gatehouses, and internal domestic ranges.

often smaller, of tighter design, with thinner walls more frequently pierced by larger windows. In older versions of the story, these new forms of castles are explained in terms of 'bastard feudalism', or specifically the fear of mercenary retainers according to Douglas Simpson (1946); the lord locked himself up in his gatehouse or *donjon*, almost as afraid of his own paid mercenaries as he was of any enemy outside. Simpson's arguments have been largely discredited, but other factors that might be cited are the crisis of the feudal aristocracy; the changed nature of late medieval warfare with a preference for fighting in the field; and of course, the introduction of gunpowder and the cannon.

Whatever the case, late medieval castles take the form either of tower houses or of courtyard houses, lightly fortified to protect against the endemic 'casual violence' of the later Middle Ages, in particular the Wars of the Roses, rather than a formal, full-scale siege. (The siege of Caister by the Duke of Norfolk is often cited at this point as an example of the general lawlessness of the times.)

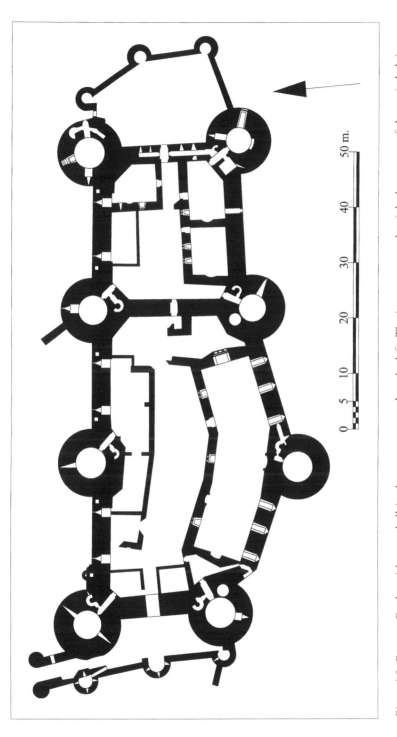

0 5 10   20   30   40   50 m.

Figure 4.2 Conway Castle, with great hall in the outer courtyard to the left. The inner court to the right has ranges of domestic lodgings to south and east, and has been interpreted as a 'courtyard house'.

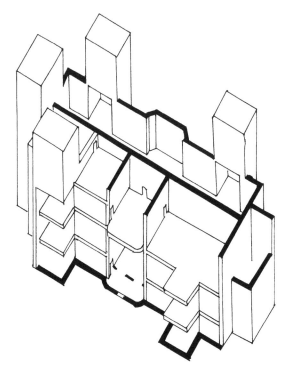

Figure 4.3 Isometric cutaway of Hardwick Hall. (Dobres and Robb 2000: 227).

One form in particular evolved: the courtyard house, in which the elements of the late medieval household are arranged around the four curtain walls of the castle. The courtyard house is present in 'nascent form' at thirteenth-century castles such as Goodrich and Conway (Figure 4.2). However, it reaches its 'maturity' in the late fourteenth and fifteenth centuries when curtain and towers are integrated with the internal disposition of rooms as at Bolton (Figure 3.5). As such, the courtyard house is a transitional form: it looks back to the quadrangular castle, and forward to the Renaissance country house.

In the sixteenth century, we see the arrival of 'the Renaissance' in England. This pivotal event happens 'off-stage', in Italy; its 'influence' arrives in England in successive waves. At first, attempts by English builders to embrace principles of Renaissance art and architecture are mainly superficial and seen in elements of decorative detail applied to buildings rather than the underlying structural and aesthetic principles as well as the new values of the individual that go with them. As generations pass, however, Renaissance principles become more fully integrated. Late sixteenth-century buildings like Hardwick Hall (Figure 4.3) reflect a perfect synthesis of late medieval English and Italian Renaissance design.

In the early seventeenth century, Inigo Jones produces the first perfect examples of Classical design; being a 'genius', he is the first to fully grasp the nature of what he is looking at when he travels to Italy and makes notes on what he sees. However, others are slow to adopt Jones' new designs, and it takes another several generations for the full acceptance of Classical principles and the final rejection of medieval models.

It is essential to note right at the start that *much existing 'debate' over the nature of castles, and about the nature of the medieval/Renaissance transition in general, takes place within the parameters of this story, rather than questioning the story itself*. For example, different national traditions can claim priority in castle innovation: was it Edward I of England and his employee Master James of St George who produced the greatest thirteenth-century castles, or was it the French king Phillippe-Auguste? I don't know, but the existence of an 'issue' of priority between France and England masks the underlying acceptance of certain models of innovation and design in which changing design is attributed to the genius of individuals, 'great men', and in which the existence of 'national traditions' is assumed rather than explored. Again, to what extent were changing forms dependent on ideas stemming from France, or from the Crusades? I don't know, but the existence of an 'issue' masks the underlying acceptance of certain models of diffusionary explanation. Was the 'decline of the castle' due to the military impact of the cannon, or the changing domestic requirements of the late medieval household? I don't know, but the existence of the 'issue' masks the underlying acceptance of organic models derived in part from traditional art history in which an 'ideal type' experiences periods of growth, maturity and decline, in which the 'castle' develops, has an apogee and then fades away.

In particular, the existence of the Story enables a particularly unfortunate piece of interpretive doublethink to arise within which alternative approaches to castle studies and to the period in general can be resisted. New ideas about castles, suggest adherents to the Story, are not really new; we already know that the militaristic interpretations of an earlier generation are now out-of-date. One senior scholar in castle studies said to me the year before this book was published that all this fuss about new approaches was misconceived, as 'none of us have believed in Douglas Simpson and Cathcart King for some time now'.

The problem is that substitution of 'the social' for 'the military' merely replicates rather than transforms the basic structures of the Story. Its underlying assumptions, in which castle forms are explained using a vocabulary of evolution in which one 'type' gives way to another, or change in response to changing balances of untheorised 'needs', remain unchanged, unquestioned.

Now these assumptions may be correct ones. It may be the case that we can fit different castles into a vocabulary of types, or that the 'needs' of the late medieval household changed. However, this should be the start of the analysis, not the end. Why did those needs change? What vocabulary of types would the medieval mason or his master have used? How and why did the Renaissance lead to a transformation of these needs and types? Unless one believes that such 'why?' questions should be left to the superior intellects of people in disciplines other than archaeology, we have to try to address these issues.

And although in most of its versions no explicit reference to theory is included, the Story is hardly factual or self-evident. After all, Beaumaris, a structure which in many ways represents the absolutely central point of the Story, was never finished; it never had a postern gate or gatehouses in their full form. The final, crystalline form of Beaumaris was *actually never built*; its postern gate, the summits of its towers, and its gatehouses were never finished. Yet despite its non-existence it is possibly the most central piece of evidence in the whole Story. The majority of Edward's 'great' Welsh castles either do not have a gatehouse or in some way do not conform to the model (Caernarfon has a Great Tower, Conway lacks a gatehouse, Beaumaris was never finished). Others are defined out of the Story or given marginal positions within it (Flint has a *donjon*, but of course, Flint is not really one of Edward's 'great' castles – why not? According to Emery (1996: 25) the great baronial castles of the later medieval North-East deserve an equal place in the Story but are little mentioned – why not?). Different structures can be classified as courtyard or as tower houses in different accounts.

Previous chapters have already started to chip away at the foundations of the Story. In the Introduction, we noted how the Story was anecdotal and unverifiable, without a rigorous sample of structures being identified. In Chapter 3, we asked how Ralph Lord Cromwell might have reacted to the suggestion that either Wingfield or Tattershall was a 'transitional' type.

However, the theoretical attitudes and assumptions implicit in the Story are best confronted not with a set of formal counter-arguments but a concrete example of a piece of architecture. I shall look at one such example and discuss how attempts to fit it into the Story reveal the underlying discursive structures of traditional explanation. It is often when the mode of discourse is made to confront something that does not fall into one of its easy classifications that we see its underlying geology exposed.

Warkworth

The *donjon* or keep of the Northumberland castle of Warkworth (Figures 4.4 and 4.5) is quite an unusual piece of domestic architecture whose form does not fall into easy classification. So how do established ways of talking about the architecture of this period deal with this building?

Let us take as a starting point the comments of that famous architectural historian, Nikolaus Pevsner. These comments are taken not from his more

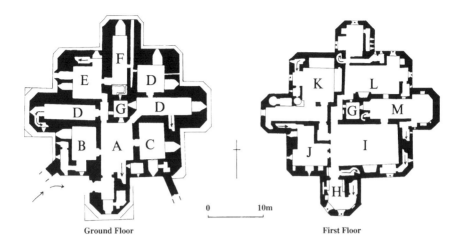

Ground Floor   **First Floor**

0   10m

Figure 4.4 Plan of Warkworth *donjon.* The reconstructed ramp up to the entrance can be seen in Figure 4.5. The various cellars and service rooms on the ground floor (left) have independent stairs up to the rooms above. Note the slight asymmetry in the plan. Water from the rooms drains via the light well into the tank room and thence to flush the latrines. A: entrance hall; B: guard room; C: pages' room; D: cellars; E: goods hall; F: larder and tank room; G: light well; H: ante-room with benches; I: great hall; J: buttery and pantry; K: kitchen; L: chamber; M: chapel.

consciously discursive works (1956 and 1976), but from that work of description and classification *par excellence,* his monumental *Buildings of England*:

Now for the KEEP. It is placed on the base of the higher and more pointed Norman mount. Here is one of the rare cases where the military engineer happened to be a great architect. The design of castles and bastions as a rule has nothing to do with the art of architecture. Shapes are devised for utilitarian purposes exclusively, openings are made, whether doors or windows, as safety permits. Considerations of aesthetics are as a rule completely absent. But the Warkworth Keep is a work of architecture in the sense that both its mass and its inner spaces are beautiful as well as useful. It was the Edwardian engineers of the late 13th century who for the first time in England had raised castle building to an art capable of aesthetic effects as intense as those of churches. Harlech and Beaumaris in their crystalline shapes are as much art as the Westminster Chapter-House. The fourteenth century, then, thanks to internal peace on the island, saw a great increase in comfort within the castle – at the expense of formality.* . . . Warkworth is the apogee of formal design, and it

Figure 4.5 Warkworth *donjon,* viewed from the south.

proves the genius of its designer that it is at the same time a residence of considerable comfort.

Note: *Let nobody argue that informal architecture can also be
architecture. Of course it can, but one has little reason to assume
that the designer of a fortified manor house arranged rooms, ranges
of rooms and towers for reasons of aesthetic effect.

(Pevsner 1957: 315–16)

Pevsner here is driven to philosophical excursus on the nature of aesthetics
and the history of medieval architecture because Warkworth *donjon* is a
building that breaks the rules. Not only is it a building of exceptional fascination, but it is the last thing that someone of Pevsner's outlook would
expect to find on top of a motte outside a small town at the northern edges
of the English kingdom.

Warkworth *donjon* probably dates to the late fourteenth century or slightly
later (lack of precision is due to the absence of extant building accounts). Its
plan form is that of a Greek cross. At basement level there are a series of
cellars, each linked to rooms upstairs by separate stairs. Above this level, we
find a hall, lobby, kitchens, solar and chapel. In a further storey above, part
of this area contains a series of private apartments. All these rooms are traditional elements of the late medieval plan, and all are linked one to another
in a largely traditional way. However, the overall plan is quite novel – the

rooms are stacked and laid out within the parameters of the Greek cross in an exceptionally skilful way (Figure 4.4).

A progress through the building conforms to many of the elements discussed in the last chapter. A visitor has first to pass through an elaborate arrangement of buildings in the lower courtyard, featuring many twists and turns. A ramp leads around the side of the building to the gate, which is placed so as not to be visible from a visitor approaching directly. Once inside, a stair leads up from a spacious lobby to a waiting area with bench and fireplace, beyond which is the hall (Dixon 1996).

This careful laying-out of the plan within a geometric figure is one aspect of a design that might suggest 'Renaissance influence'. Other elements also suggest this. Running down the centre of the building is a light well. From the inside, this light well appears to be central to the building; from the outside, however, a central turret appears to dominate the building. On the plan, they are adjacent, and neither is central. The light well, moreover, is carefully laid out to catch rainwater, which is then carefully guided into a basement cistern and thence to help flush out the latrines.

Wider implications

Faced with such a building, commentators scatter in different directions. Pevsner reacts in the passage cited above by reasserting a whole series of divides which the Warkworth *donjon* leads us to question – between military and domestic, aesthetic and functional, medieval and Renaissance. It is almost as if, faced with such an elaborate, demonstrative piece of architecture right on the northern fringes of his beloved England, Pevsner needs to reassert his own identity, the intellectual foundations of his own position, in response. In this way what he writes is very revealing, although in this context it is assertion rather than argument.

Others react, as often happens with 'unusual' buildings of any kind, with a search for parallels, with the implication that once we have found a parallel we can then look for a diffusionary link between these different examples in which one is explained by reference to 'influence' from the other. Such examples, however, are hard to find. One candidate is Trim Castle, in County Meath in Ireland (McNeill 1990; 1997a: 20–4). Trim *donjon* is over two centuries earlier, but its form appears to be that of a Greek cross. However, the arms are not part of the original plan, and the internal layout of Trim is quite different.

The one most striking parallel for Warkworth is rarely mentioned in the literature, perhaps because instead of being a grand structure at some other pivotal point in the kingdom, it is a modest building on a forgotten and rather bleak and windswept hill above the Coquet valley, tucked away behind a modern farm. Cartington Castle, 20 kilometres east of Warkworth, is a much smaller house apparently consisting of a rectangular residential block forming one side of a small courtyard. Cartington is a much smaller house and is of lower social status; it was built by John Cartington, who obtained a licence to crenellate in 1442. The similarity here is in the series of independent stairs that, again, lead up from a series of interconnected vaulted cellars to a first-floor suite of rooms. Interpretation is hampered by later alterations, and by the destruction of much of the upper floors (Emery 1996: 63–5).

Another possible parallel for Warkworth is two centuries later, at Lulworth; here, the distance of two centuries has been explained by classifying Lulworth as 'an essentially medieval plan' (Goodall 2000: 34). We might make similar claims for the early seventeenth-century Little Castle at Bolsover, which also sits on an earlier mound and has a small lantern. However, though they are similar in *form* and the similarity is significant, I view Lulworth and Bolsover as fundamentally different in terms of what they *mean*, for reasons which will become clear below.

A second common strategy for explaining away buildings that do not conform to the Story is to point to the constraints of an earlier building. The apparent slight irregularity of the layout has been attributed to the presence of earlier stone foundations on the site. However, Milner (1990) cannot identify such traces, and neither can I.

A third strategy is to try to fit the building in to a different point in the Story. At Warkworth, at least one commentator has suggested a redating of the keep to the early sixteenth century, on the grounds of the wide plinth, the geometry of the design and other features; parallels with early sixteenth-century Italian design are noted (Milner 1990). Warkworth is thus in this view a first-generation example of 'Renaissance influence'. Milner's views have been rebutted in detail (Hislop 1991) and the earlier date for Warkworth is almost certainly correct, but what is striking in this context is what this suggestion reveals about the nature of late medieval architectural studies.

A fourth strategy is to claim that Warkworth is not really that unusual at all. Douglas Simpson himself (1938; 1941) saw the structure as a miniature manor house, with the light well being a courtyard in miniature; Warkworth thus becomes a standard late medieval courtyard house similar in its basic elements to Bodiam, Bolton and others, with the elements 'ingeniously' arranged in a compact plan. Parallels can then be drawn with structures such as the polygonal *donjon* at Durham Castle with its now vanished internal courtyard, largely rebuilt in the nineteenth century (Emery 1996: 77).

Many of these comments contain a lot of truth, but is seems to me that all of them skirt around the central questions posed by Warkworth rather than tackling them head on. Rather than allow the contrary evidence to provoke questions about the Story itself, they try to make Warkworth fit the Story. For me, the central point is that Warkworth breaks the rules. It contradicts long-held notions of architectural narratives embodied in the Story. We should turn, then, to look more directly at Warkworth *donjon* itself, setting aside narrative accounts that have been shown above to be highly theoretical in nature.

In some ways, the most revealing statement I have read about Warkworth, the comment that has helped me understand it most, has been an early seventeenth-century comment on the structure. In 1603 King James VI of Scotland was riding south, on his way to claim the throne of England as Queen Elizabeth's successor. James knew all about the instability of identities and structures of power; he was fond of remarking that he had been threatened even before birth, with a dagger pointed at his mother's womb (Fraser 1995: 67). Looking up at the *donjon*, and pointing to the symbol of the Percy dynasty placed upon it at the end of the high street of the town (Figure 4.6), he remarked: 'The lion holds up this castle.'

Viewed on one level, such a statement is clearly ridiculous. The lion is a decorative device, heraldic symbol of the Percy family. But what James meant, of course, was that the castle was held up by what the lion symbolised. The lion, particularly in its rampant form on the north side of the keep, is a metonym of the prestige and honour of the Percy family; it refers back to countless Percies, most famously the son of the late fourteenth-century Earl of Northumberland, Harry Hotspur. Hotspur's exploits were chronicled in Holinshed and other works, and had been brought to the stage in 1597 in Shakespeare's *Henry IV* (where Hotspur is paired figuratively with the future Henry V and where in Part II the castle is called 'this worm-eaten hole of ragged stone').

But James may have had more contemporary and pressing matters in mind also. He had engaged in secret correspondence with the present Percy Earl of Northumberland, a Catholic, prior to Elizabeth's death, in efforts to secure his hold on the succession; reference to the lion was in part a reference to contemporary political events.

Reference to the lion holding up the castle, then, is reference to a complex world of border politics and in particular to the place of the Percy Earls of Northumberland within it. It places the *donjon* and its owners in the context of the values and symbols of a masculine honour code, and of royal and baronial dynastic politics. The real parallel to be drawn is not with other buildings of the same architectural form, but with other statements of the same social form – most notably 'Tys made Roger' at Brougham (see Chapter 2).

What Warkworth shows us, then, is that the familiar story is not necessarily completely wrong, but that it needs to be *deconstructed*. That is, we need to take its different elements apart, look at each of them critically. For Roland Barthes, the nineteenth-century historian Michelet produced a Middle Ages that was smooth and seamless; much of what Barthes identified in Michelet went on to structure intellectual enquiry into the Middle Ages and Renaissance, just as the work of Burckhardt and others did (Barthes

Figure 4.6 The Percy lion on the north side of
Warkworth *donjon.*

1987). The smoothness of its edges, its seamless fabric, needs to be roughed
up and pulled apart.

There are several dimensions to such a deconstruction. We can critique
its periodisation: Early, High, Late Medieval and Renaissance. We can question its use of a stylistic or aesthetic model of change, and assumptions of
diffusion and organic evolution that are linked to this. We can look at the
social categories that are assumed by the Story, and finally identify elements
that rely on essentialist arguments. In what follows, I shall try to prise these
assumptions away from the smooth surface of the narrative and examine each
in turn.

Medieval to Renaissance

Part of the underlying problem is that the Story is embedded in a very deep
context. It is told in different ways in different disciplines, with different

106

bodies of evidence. Art and architectural history move from Romanesque to Early to High to Late Gothic to Renaissance; the apogee or highest point in Gothic is around c.1300, with the construction of the French cathedrals of Reims and Amiens. Rural settlement studies see the period up to the late thirteenth century as one of expansion: the high-water mark of c.1300 is followed by demographic and settlement contraction (Aston *et al.* 1989). That all these stories revolve around the same pivotal 'high-water mark' is not just coincidence; it suggests that they are different versions of the same basic story. And it further suggests that even the most atheoretical scholar who continues to use this terminology is working within an overarching theoretical framework; the claim to be 'atheoretical', to be able to write from outside theory, is disingenuous (Johnson 1999: 6).

And if the Story frames our view of the later Middle Ages, it also does of the transition to the Renaissance. From Burckhardt onwards, the divide between the medieval and Renaissance worlds has been seen as a very basic split. The precise date may vary (1465, the fall of Constantinople; 1485, the battle of Bosworth; 1500, a nice round number; 1536–8, my own favourite, the dissolution of the monasteries) but the basic split remains the same.

It is obvious enough that such a categorisation exists in traditional practice, but I want to make the point that more recent and radical scholarly traditions have tended to reinforce rather than subvert these categories. For example, I have explored elsewhere how influential traditions of Marxist historiography have also perpetuated this split. They have done so by seeking to analyse the 'feudal/capitalist transition'. They have taken a synthetic picture from each side of this 'transition' gleaned from secondary writings of documentary historians and attempted to glue them together. Unfortunately the two synthetic pictures have been compiled from very different source material and the final synthesis is unsatisfactory (Johnson 1996: 37–42).

More recently, apparently subversive approaches have also reinscribed this division in the apparent act of questioning it. In historical geography, the work of Denis Cosgrove and Stephen Daniels and others (Cosgrove and Daniels 1988; Cosgrove 1984; 1993) has been central in opening up new ways of thinking about Renaissance landscapes. It has tended, however, to posit 'the Renaissance' at the point of origin for a genealogy of practices and buzz-words (Palladianism, the gaze, Cartesian ways of figuring the landscape) that lead directly to modernity. Though it is not a necessary corollary of their arguments, the implication has tended to be that what happened before the Renaissance, the later Middle Ages, did not have these features or characteristics. On a vulgar reading, the Middle Ages becomes implicitly caricatured as a kind of 'mush' in which nothing very much happened of any interest to the student of modernity. In Chapter 2 I suggested that this was one underlying reason why we have been slow to recognise formal landscapes in the Middle Ages.

The subversive approach to the Renaissance *par excellence*, literary New Historicism or its counterpart of Cultural Materialism on this side of the Atlantic (Greenblatt 1985; 1994; Dollimore and Sinfield 1985), has similarly bypassed the late Middle Ages. Here, practices such as emergent colonialism, 'self-fashioning', the constitution of modern notions of gender, and the construction of the modern nation-state are sought for (together with their subversions) within Renaissance literature. Again, though it is not a necessary corollary of their arguments, the implication has been that if the location of these practices is found in the Renaissance, the late Middle Ages therefore did not have these tensions, these areas of interest. David Aers (1992a) has rightly condemned New Historicists for failing to take the late Middle Ages seriously.

We might also note archaeological work on the 'Georgian Order' in this context. James Deetz's hugely influential book *In Small Things Forgotten* (1977) discussed the Georgian Order as a series of structural principles of order, symmetry and segregation underlying many aspects of material life. Deetz located the origins of the Georgian Order in the values of 'the Renaissance'. The implication was that 'pre-Georgian' or 'medieval' ways of life (terms which Deetz and others tended to use interchangeably) did *not* have these structuring principles. However, we have seen at Bodiam and many other castles that space is often carefully ordered and segregated in the later medieval period, often moreover with deliberate deployment of symmetry (for example, in the layout and placement of doors in the hall and service areas, a symmetry seen also at vernacular social levels; Johnson 1993: 55–8).

As a result, a spectacular paradox has arisen within recent scholarship on this period. The more exciting and entertaining work on the Renaissance has become, the duller the later Middle Ages has become by implication. And the more a basic tenet of traditional scholarship – that of the medieval/Renaissance divide – has been reinscribed, even as every other tenet has been questioned. In short, new ways of talking about our period have ensured that the Story is reinscribed in the very act of questioning it.

The ideology of the aesthetic

> We cannot separate literature and art from other kinds of social practice, in such a way as to make them subject to quite special and distinct laws ... [The arts] may have quite specific features as practices, but they cannot be separated from the general social process.
>
> (Williams 1980: 44)

Raymond Williams' point goes for architecture as well. His basic point, that the split between social and aesthetic life is at heart an ideological one, has been elaborated by Eagleton (1976) and is now very familiar to students of cultural studies.

If we accept this split between social and aesthetic values, as most tradi-tional art and architectural history does (cf. Fernie 1989; 1995), its implications are that the aesthetic impact of our castles cannot necessarily tell us about the workings of society. This assumption lurks behind many of the accounts of castle architecture. It is certainly there in Pevsner's assertion that insofar as the castle is 'utilitarian', it cannot be 'aesthetic' and is therefore not 'architecture', or in Fernie's opposition between 'archaeology versus cultural iconography' which he equates with 'quantification versus architectural analysis'; for Fernie, archaeologists explain things in terms of mundane changes of the builder's mind, whereas architectural analysis deals with the subtleties of meaning (1989: 20). It is also there in accounts in which entire aesthetic systems are explained in very totalised ways, even when this is done in relation to a total humanistic/philosophical systems. Such a totalised explanation is most obvious with Burckhardt's explanation of the Italian Renaissance in terms of 'the individual', but following him are more recent scholars like Cooper (1999). It is there most deeply when we talk of one type of architecture evolving into another ('the hall gradually declined in importance') without reference to the builders of the different types.

The intellectual defences which the traditional scholar erects to stop the 'social' penetrating and intermingling with the 'aesthetic' have a double purpose; they are also the prison walls which stop the aesthetic/material from engaging with the social. We see this in implicit assumptions that fashion does not tell us very much. Somehow, whenever the word 'fashion' crops up in studies of buildings, one knows that it will be preceded by words like 'whims and vagaries'. Ironically, archaeologists have continued to resort to such tenets of traditional art history at the same time as art history itself has moved on to more exciting territory (Wicker 1999).

Issues of aesthetic interpretation, the meanings we place on fashion or artistic or architectural style, are also clouded by an ambiguity in definitions of culture between different disciplinary traditions. It can mean

> enlightenment and excellence of taste in the arts and humanities among those who through interest, experience, observation and commitment had learned to value and promote beauty and distinc-tion. But the word culture can also be used in the broader sense of a society's pattern of behaviour in thought, speech and actions.
>
> (Sherborne 1994: 171)

It is the latter definition that is the only one that can have any meaning for the serious student, since it is difficult to see how 'enlightenment and excel-lence of taste', not to mention 'beauty and distinction', are in any way definable or measurable; it is difficult therefore to see what their place might be in a modern social science committed to any kind of rigorous objectivity.

Ripples from Italy

Whatever the transition from medieval to Renaissance was, traditional scholars agree that it came from somewhere else. It was, in some versions, the result of diffusion – the spread of ideas, or more specifically the 'impact of the Italian Renaissance'. Innovations that started in Italy in the late fourteenth and fifteenth centuries, in this view, spread like ripples across Europe; they arrived in England in successive waves in the sixteenth century, at first affecting only decorative detail, later producing very new forms of building.

It may be worth rehearsing the basic criticisms of diffusion developed by prehistoric archaeologists many years ago (Binford 1972; Renfrew 1973). To say that this or that style or feature is the result of 'influence' is to explain nothing at all. It begs the question of why the influence was adopted by that culture, individual or social group at that time, which in turn raises the question of why, socially, intellectually or aesthetically, the group was 'ready' to 'receive' the influence. So to be a full and intellectually coherent explanation, ascription of 'influence' must at the very least be accompanied by a full social analysis of the culture being influenced, rather than being an alternative to it.

Take, for example, the castle of Nunney, a rectangular block surrounded by a moat where the form of the towers has been held to represent 'French influence'. Allen Brown for example cites the Bastille, Pierrefonds and Tarascon as parallels without citing any evidence (1970: 137). But Nunney is hardly unique in England. Dudley with a much earlier date of *c.*1320 and with four corner towers is one possibility; and a little-known parallel exists at Mulgrave, between the North York Moors and the coast. This was surveyed by the Royal Commission in the spring of 1990 partly for the purposes of monitoring the decay of the site (ref GCE NZ83951168). Mulgrave now stands in a wood, on a promontory cut off by a ditch. Traces of its landscape context have been erased by late eighteenth-century carriageways and drives and rendered difficult to observe by thick undergrowth. A wall encloses the site, within which material has built up; the wall is in fact little more than a thin revetment, held back by buttresses. Small towers stud this wall at various points. Within this wall are indistinct earthworks and other traces of buildings; unpublished excavations revealed various blocks of buildings. Most notably, Mulgrave centres on a tower with four corner turrets. The tower is much smaller than that at Nunney; its internal arrangement is uncertain and its internal arrangements masked by later alterations, though a gallery, fireplace and windows survive. Repton's rather unreliable account refers to fragments of machicolations though there is no evidence of these today.

My point here is not that there is any necessary link between Nunney and Mulgrave but that first, we should be careful about asserting a structure's uniqueness and, second, the search for 'parallels' rather misses the point. Any late medieval structure will be unique – outside Roman forts and Georgian houses, few buildings replicate each other exactly. An explanation of any castle, as with any building, has to be in terms that refer to those human beings who built it and lived in it. 'Parallels' are interesting but are not a substitute for explanation in human terms.

Similar statements have been made about Old Wardour (Figure 2.6). Saunders and Pugh write (1968: 3): 'The inspiration for Old Wardour clearly came from France, perhaps as a result of Lord Lovel's campaigning there during the Hundred Year's War.' They turn to the Château de Concressault (Cher), which has a hexagonal courtyard with angles with turrets on corbels. However, the Cher is well south of Orleans, and therefore unlikely to have been visited by Lord Lovel; English depredations destroyed an earlier castle on the site, not the hexagonal structure cited by Saunders and Pugh (Tealdi n.d.: 214–16). And most fundamentally, why should Lord Lovel choose to imitate Concressault when an earlier generation of Dallyngrigge and his contemporaries chose English models? What does that choice tell us about contemporary identities and social systems?

The selection of France as the constant candidate for parallels in late medieval architecture is I think revealing. There was plenty of late medieval contact with Spain, most obviously through the Black Prince and John of Gaunt's military campaigns there. There was also plenty of obvious contact, both friendly and hostile, with Scotland. Yet the diffusionary arrows always seem to point in the same direction: from south and east to north and west. French culture and civilisation seem to be perceived as inherently 'superior' in the past just as French food and wine are in the present. There is nothing wrong in this as a personal judgment of taste, and it does mean that the search for parallels to English castles and the predilection of the academic middle classes for pleasant summer holidays in France can be happily combined, a combination which this author has indulged in as enthusiastically as anyone else. However, it cannot on its own make for a serious analysis of past societies.

Turning to the Renaissance specifically, how did it actually arrive in England in the diffusionary model? Clearly not wholesale. There is an assumption implicit in the 'waves of influence' model that each generation of native builders was only mentally prepared to accept a limited amount of Classical influence. Thus, the first wave has only a superficial effect; builders can mentally take on board a certain element of decorative detail, but cannot digest the whole thing. Fifty years later, Inigo Jones, being a 'peculiar genius', can grasp the total model, but his lesser contemporaries are more limited and can only take on a bit more; thus the full impact of Classical design has to wait for another few generations. Biddle *et al.* write:

> The 16th century saw an awkward transition in English architec-
> ture, from the perfection of medieval Perpendicular to a clumsy use

of the ill-understood forms of the Renaissance. Ever since Henry VIII had become interested in the new style, it had increasingly ousted native architectural traditions based on the use of the pointed arch. But it was only in the early years of the next century that Renaissance models were finally accepted and fully understood.

(2000: 80)

Quite apart from being massively patronising towards people who because they are dead cannot answer back, the problem with these kinds of assumptions is that, like those made about parallels, both 'peculiar genius' and 'natural conservatism' should be starting points for a serious analysis, not factors cited in explanation that need no further exposition. Why were builders not mentally prepared to accept new models? What was it, specifically, about their world-view that led to them taking this attitude, and why, specifically, had this changed several generations later? Jones himself, after all, changed his own style after 1630 (Worsley 1993); did he become a different person, abandon his earlier 'peculiar genius'?

Thus, for example, Chettle and Leach (1984) write of the sixteenth-century decoration at Kirby Hall that the central arch of the loggia flanked by pilasters

> adorned with compositions of arabesque, candelabra and *putti* which are taken from . . . John Shute's *The First and Chief Groundes of Architecture*, of 1563; this is a particularly good example of the untutored methods of the Kirby mason, for the design comes not from any of the architectural plates in the book but from the title page.

I suggest that it is revealing that two modern architectural historians cannot allow the Kirby mason to use the title page. On whose authority is the mason forbidden to do so? How do we know that the Kirby mason was not in fact making a very witty statement about the use of pattern-books, a wit that would be very 'Renaissance' in character? The implication of such comments is one of regret – that if only the Kirby mason had had the benefit of the 'correctly tutored' insights of modern architectural historians, how much more 'properly' could he have deployed the designs! In this view, there is only one 'right' way to read a book like Shute, and to use a design from the title page rather than the designated plates is the ultimate *faux pas*, rather akin to calling lunch dinner. Howard's (1990) cautions against such readings notwithstanding, other English Renaissance builders have been characterised as being on a 'long steep learning curve' and their carvings 'crude' (Cooper 1999: 20 and 21). Rather than being crude, they might be seen as merely assertively vernacular.

It is worth asking what an audience might make of such comments if directed towards a piece of non-Western art or architecture. We have been quite properly warned by anthropologists of art that it is ethnocentric to apply Western critical standards to 'primitive' and non-western art. Where artists from non-Western societies use motifs or images from the West, such a use is deliberate 'appropriation' (Ashcroft *et al.* 1998: 19–20); it would be ethnocentric or worse for critics to imply that creative use of Western images in ways other than those prescribed by Western methods was somehow 'crude' or 'untutored'. If such an observation holds for interpreting art and architecture produced by modern non-Western societies, it must hold also for interpreting art and architecture in sixteenth-century England. In both cases, it is the first principle of any kind of objective enquiry that the ways of life and modes of artistic expression being studied are simply different, not better or worse, than our own, and cannot be judged by an ethnocentric yardstick.

There are other problems with the 'ripples from Italy' model. Ripples can come from other places than Italy. There is a tendency to identify 'Renaissance influence' with classical features; however:

> Renaissance work does not have to be mediated by Italian art . . . Other options were open to Northern artists and the heroic, ideal and mythological were not the only 'antique' models available. The northerners would be equally indebted to the classical past even though they favoured the underside of classical art, the ungainly and grotesque, the imagery of daily life, and ancient genres such as satire and comedy.
>
> (Sullivan 1994)

Such figures as 'grotteschi' could even be emblematic of the process of invention (Farago 1995: 10).

Most fundamentally of all, why accept Renaissance ideas? Many English builders did without them quite happily for over a century, and selected buildings were constructed in late English Gothic style all the way through the late sixteenth, seventeenth and eighteenth centuries. Buildings are, among other things, choices. The overall scale and workmanship might be constrained by economic factors or the availability of labour, but the decision to build in Gothic or Renaissance was exactly that, a decision. The gradual nature of the acceptance of Renaissance principles suggests that builders made different decisions at different times. Any explanation which approves of certain designs as 'correctly tutored' or forward-looking, and conversely denigrates others as 'crude', 'conservative' or backward-looking, runs the danger of a Whiggishness of architectural interpretation.

If the Renaissance was an 'advance' or if its eventual victory was part of an internal aesthetic or social logic, then it has to be explained why it was not adopted immediately and wholesale. One way to do this is to make reference, either explicit to implicit, to evolutionary ideas.

Gradual evolution

A different way of explaining the gradualness of the acceptance of Renaissance ideas is to make reference to the slow pace of change. Architectural forms in this view have their own logic: they rise, have periods of maturity, decline, die out. It is immediately apparent that such models are closely linked, first, to notions of the aesthetic as a discrete category discussed above, second, to ideas of organic evolution on which building types are like species and rise and fall according to their adaptation to their environment, and, third, to archaeological methods of typology and seriation. Architectural forms in this view are just like animal species, better or worse adapted to their environment.

The first problem is that the evidence does not back up ideas of gradual change as clearly as it might. Take, for example, a classic evolutionary idea, the 'decline of the open hall', in which the hall declines as its environment – the needs of the great household it serves, or 'competing' forms of houses with ceilings throughout – change (cf. Thompson 1995). Jane Grenville has made the point that contrary to the generally accepted model of the decline of the open hall, halls do *not* diminish in size towards the end of the fifteenth century and that some major examples are known from the following century, most notably that of Henry VIII at Hampton Court Palace (Grenville 1997: 108–9). In parallel to Grenville, at least one formal landscape was laid out in fifteenth-century England using a series of ideas current in Italian Renaissance gardens – at Bassingbourn in Cambridgeshire (Oosthuizen and Taylor 2000). It was nevertheless over a century before landscape design 'evolved' into general acceptance of such forms.

Evolution can be presented as a steady story, in which any reference to human beings is rendered quite redundant. Consider the following account of late medieval architectural development, revealingly couched in narrative form, by Douglas Simpson:

> The introduction of groined vaulting led to the strengthening of the sides of the buttresses and the casing of the angles by square or circular clasping projections, often capped by or rising into turrets. The architectonic need for these consolidations impeded the growing desire for spacious windows to light the hall, hence a tendency to concentrate these openings in one wall, usually a narrow one; and from this tendency, again, with the increasing sense of the decorative value of large traceried windows in the later phases of Gothic art, came the development of one side of the building as a 'show-front'. At the same time, the growing power of the means of attack led to the heightening of the building and to crowning it with an oversailing defensive parapet. With this added height the interior

is divided into several storeys, forming a series of great halls, one above the other, each devoted to a special purpose.

(1960: xx)

One does not have to be a rampant postmodernist to see that human beings have been entirely erased from such an account – or that there is something awry about this. We should therefore turn to attempts to write the human beings back into the Renaissance – to look at ways of understanding architectural change in terms of changing social requirements.

Public and private

A more sophisticated set of propositions concerning the influence of the Renaissance is that these different aesthetic qualities were symptomatic of, or tied in with, a new set of values relating to 'the individual'. Again, this assertion derives strength from being implicit within different forms of discourse apparently at odds with one another. It is certainly there in Burckhardt, where the emergence of new forms of art and architecture and of the (elite, male) individual were implicated one with another; but it also appears in the New Historicist emphasis on 'self-fashioning' (Greenblatt 1980). My own work can be linked to this model also, seeing the loss of the open hall in vernacular buildings after *c.*1500 as related to changing cultural ideas of privacy and segregation (Johnson 1993).

I am uncertain about the proposition, however, that public and private is a valid distinction for the period before 1600. My lack of certainty increases the further back one goes. Cultures can only draw a sharp divide between the public and the private if they have a strong sense of the individual in the first place. Such a strong sense did not necessarily exist during the fourteenth to seventeenth centuries, and, if it did, any such statement needs to be severely qualified with respect to class and gender. Further, if such a sense of the individual is part of 'Renaissance culture' and specifically linked to literacy, then there is every reason to question its existence as part of the medieval or pre-Renaissance mentality. Brück (1999), indeed, has argued that such a distinction had a specific historical genesis in the Enlightenment and cannot be indiscriminately applied to past societies.

Many of the artefacts that are commonly interpreted in terms of 'the private' actually have quite other meanings. These other meanings repeatedly revolve around gender and sexuality. The classic recent example is the redefinition of the word closet as it is applied to polite architecture. The closet is generally seen as a 'private room', but Stewart's re-analysis of the term concludes that 'the male closet is not designed to function as a place of individual withdrawal, but as a secret non-public transactive space between two men behind a locked door', most notable for its inaccessibility to women (Stewart 1995). In other words, what we see as a 'natural' desire for privacy

115

is actually all about the location of power within the house and the exclusion of women from that power. I would argue in parallel that our designation of particular areas of fifteenth- and sixteenth-century life as 'private' need similar rethinking. Italian Renaissance studies, far from being 'private' spaces, were stuffed full of display objects (Thornton 1997).

Gendered spaces

'Privacy', then, and with it our idea of the individual, needs to be unpacked. It is about power, gender, and other variables, not just about a disembodied rise of the individual. Mark Breitenberg writes:

> Older accounts of the emergence of a distinctly modern identity in the Renaissance have been decidedly masculine without saying so, as if to ask questions about identity were by definition to ask them about men. It is not surprising to find such an assumption in Jacob Burckhardt's celebration of the 'perfecting of the individual' in Renaissance Italy, nor in Tillyard's pronouncement that in Elizabethan England 'Not only did Man, as man, live with uncommon intensity at that time, but he was never removed from his cosmic setting.'
>
> (1996, 7)

For all the feminist writing of the past twenty years, the dominant frame of discourse in architectural history remains 'decidedly masculine' in Breitenberg's terms just as it remains decidedly Burckhardtian. The smooth flow of much writing on the Renaissance continues unperturbed, as if the feminist or New Historicist critique had never happened. Girouard (1981; 2000), Thurley (1993), and Cooper (1997; 1999) all account for changes in the form of elite houses in terms of a generalised account of what the changing requirements of a 'gentlemanly' lifestyle were. There is little room for exploration of different gendered attitudes to space, or for that matter of the attitudes and actions of different social classes (see Chapter Six).

Castles and architectural types generally are a unified story. As such, they fall victim to Lisa Jardine's critique (1996a, Chapter 8) about how to write a different history that takes the actions and experiences of women seriously. Jardine points out that women are left out of most unifying discourses about the past, to the extent that when traditional scholars try to 'put them back in' they are beset by apparent methodological problems. She suggests that to take women's history seriously, we have to pick apart the generalised assumptions made about Renaissance societies and about the nature of history as it is traditionally written in general.

A good example of the way women have been assimilated into a 'wider picture' and in the process subsumed and ultimately ignored is the treatment of Lady Anne Clifford, a major castle-builder of the north-west in the seventeenth century. Lady Anne was aware of Classical models; she spent much of her youth at Renaissance palaces in southern England. After the political defeat of the English Revolution, she retired to her estates in Westmoreland, where she proceeded to rebuild a series of castles at Brough, Brougham and Appleby, as well as erect a series of other monuments including her own tomb. Tradition states that when Cromwell threatened to destroy her castles, she insisted that she would rebuild them just as quickly (Charlton 1977).

The style in which the castles were rebuilt is not a Classical one; it is, rather, on 'traditional' lines, albeit with windows in the new style. Even her own tomb erased the marks of her own gender – it has no effigy, only an elaborate heraldic portrayal of her lineage. So Lady Anne 'fails to have an impact' on castle design, just as she 'replicates' the feudal North, just as women are 'seen as scolds' (Friedman 1997). The celebration of her eccentricity is, by definition, a celebration of the patriarchal social system that defined her as eccentric and thus marginalized her (Barthes 1977).

If some women become 'eccentric', others become 'mundane'. Elizabeth I has traditionally been praised for her spendthrift nature: unlike her father, Henry VIII, and the son of her successor James, Charles I, Elizabeth never built a major palace in her life. A prudent policy of a prudent stateswoman, no doubt, particularly considering the fate of Charles who fifty years later walked to his death from the window of one of the expensive and unpopular creations of himself and his father (Whitehall Palace). It has also been suggested that rebuilding in the Elizabethan period was unnecessary given the broad continuity of practices of access to the monarch and provision of other accommodation at Court (Thurley 1993), though other architectural historians have drawn attention to striking aspects of change in the way Elizabeth used these rooms; where she chose to eat, for example (Girouard 1978: 110).

But this, I suggest, is only part of the story. Elizabeth was a female monarch in a patriarchal society, a society moreover where masculine and feminine identities were changing as they were elsewhere in Europe (Stafford 1995). In 1558, just before her accession to the throne, John Knox expressed the patriarchal attitudes of his time when he wrote:

> to promote a woman to bear rule, superiority, dominion or empire above any realm, nation, or city is repugnant to nature, contumely to God, a thing most contrarious to his revealed will and approved ordinance, and finally it is the subversion of good order, and all equity and justice.
>
> (Aughterson 1995: 138)

As such, Elizabeth's fashioning by herself and others was both complex and unstable (Levin 1994; Berry 1995). One stable element derived from the past was the memory of her father, Henry VIII, perceived by many as the saviour of the nation from Catholicism, the last great king, and prodigious builder of the palaces Elizabeth was brought up and lived in.

Elizabeth used this stable element as a political resource. She famously negotiated her own identity at a moment of supreme threat to her monarchy, the prospect of invasion by the Spanish Armada, when she remarked that though she was a weak and feeble woman she had the heart and stomach of a king, and a king of England too. Listeners would have understood the indirect reference to Henry. A portrait of Henry VIII hung at the centre of political power, the Privy Chamber, at Whitehall; one visitor commented that 'The King as he stood there, majestic in his splendour, was so lifelike that the spectator felt abashed, annihilated in his presence.' Elizabeth may well have explicitly identified her own physical body with that of Henry, and her physical body became a metaphor for the Tudor State and the source of male fantasy and anxiety (Levin 1994: 142–3; Loomis 1996). As young Elizabethans walked through Henry's galleries and apartments that were also Elizabeth's, stood before Henry's tapestries that were also Elizabeth's, knelt before a female king in a royal setting that was Henry's and Elizabeth's, the message would have been clear.

Elizabeth's most sophisticated tactic in marking her own identity was to refrain from rebuilding and erasing the marks of her own parentage. Such absences are often difficult to analyse, but in the study of architecture and identity they are often the most subtle – and effective – marks of all.

Part of the problem is an unwitting empathy with the lack of representation of women within dominant sixteenth-century male discourse; writers on Renaissance architecture have identified too closely with the male architects, just as the historian Elton, the expert on Tudor administration, identified too closely with the world-view of Tudor bureaucrats. For castle buffs as much as for Shakespeare, 'their non-existence is assumed as part of the unspoken structure of the world' (Greenblatt 1994: 105).

I am suggesting, then, that accounts of the 'rise of the individual' mark an advance on previous work in that they place social developments at centre stage of our understanding of this period. However, these accounts need in turn to be unpacked, particularly with reference to the unstable and contested nature of gender in this period.

Essentialism

Underlying this series of conceptual problems is an idea that is so natural to us that it is rarely expressed in explicit terms: that of essentialism. Essentialism is 'the assumption that groups, categories of classes of objects have one or several defining features exclusive to all members of that category' (Ashcroft *et al.* 1998: 77). As such, it appears a fairly harmless and obvious proposition. It is certainly taken for granted in the main sweep of castle studies. However, when examined more deeply, it can be shown to have a series of profound problems.

One of the key assumptions made in the Story is that castles are in some sense 'distinctively feudal'. Cathcart King makes this quite explicit when he lays stress on the castle being a *private* defended enclosure, that is, one that is not part of State or public power. The castle is thus tied in with the nature of power in the feudal world. Such power has been seen by students of feudalism as being tied in with the baronial use of armed retainers. Allen Brown points out that the concept of the 'private fortress' was a key component of Stenton's definition of feudalism, and continues:

> Fortification, like all warfare on the one hand and all architecture on the other, directly reflects the society responsible for it and is an integral part of the social complex . . . If one enquires what it is that distinguishes the castle from other types of fortification both earlier and later, and wherein lies its uniqueness and its feudality, the answer lies in its definition: for the castle is a fortified residence, uniquely combining the dual role, and moreover it is the private, as opposed to public, and the residential fortress of a lord, who may or may not be the King or Prince.
>
> (1973: 19 and 30)

David Sweetman binds all these assumptions together into a potent cocktail when he writes:

> The expression 'An Englishman's home is his castle' may have some truth but what makes a true castle is its defences. Many so-called castles for instance in Scotland are merely 'chateaux' or grand houses of the late 16th and early 17th centuries and are not true castles because they do not have the defensive features of the medieval fortress. The castle is essentially feudal and is the fortified residence of a lord in a society dominated by the military.
>
> (1999: 41)

Such an assumption immediately links the 'essential nature' of the castle to the 'essential nature' of feudalism, and in turn to some reference to the castle's essentially military nature. Now feudalism is a dangerous word to bandy about casually. Traditionally, it refers to a certain set of legal conditions to do with tenure, knighthood, service and the unfree peasant, most classically articulated by Maitland (1897). In Marxist terminology, it refers to a specific mode of production in which the key division of labour is between feudal lord and unfree peasant; feudalism in this view arises out of the ruins of the ancient mode of production, and gives way to nascent capitalism (Cohen 1978). Feudalism can also be fitted in to certain forms of colonial understanding. When Tom McNeill wrote his recent book on castles in Ireland (1997a), he subtitled it *Feudal Power in a Gaelic World*; the implication being that 'feudal power' was something distinctive; that it was brought over by the Anglo-Normans; and that it was to be imposed on a non- or pre-feudal population.

Again, however much these views are different one from another in their language and indeed their political implications, I would argue that they are all part of the Story – they share certain characteristics in common. They all identify a 'central' period of feudalism, somewhere between the eleventh and the thirteenth centuries. This, of course, corresponds to the 'apogee' of castles. And they all have difficulties dealing with the protracted period of 'transition', after this apogee but before the Renaissance.

For those in the tradition of Maitland, this is the period when one argues about the existence of 'bastard feudalism', and consequently gets lost in interminable debates over the existence of certain forms of tenure and authority that the outsider sees as quite irrelevant and frankly tedious until their historiographical context is pointed out. For Marxists, debates over the 'feudal/capitalist transition' are fraught with difficulty (I have summarised these in Johnson 1996: 37–43). The postcolonial debate has only just started in castle studies, but its implications are instructive. Tadhg O'Keeffe has argued that Irish castles and tower houses should not be seen as reflective of a certain level of 'Anglicisation', or as the imposition of a feudal power on a pre-feudal world, but rather as active statements of diverse and contested identities (cf. O'Keeffe 1998; 2000; forthcoming).

When, therefore, we see a High Medieval 'ideal type' of the castle being created, to which later medieval examples are held to approximate to a greater or lesser extent, we are seeing essentialist assumptions being pursued to their practical end. They were certainly deeply embedded in the history of castle studies. Late medieval architecture was ignored by Clark (1884), and dealt with incompletely by A.H. Thompson (1912) and Braun (1936). Emery comments that 'the character and importance of keeps and tower-houses were not appreciated' (1975: 180). Charles Coulson states that much analysis of Bodiam was prefigured by GT Clark's analysis (1884: 239–47), but points out that: 'Clark's 101 other monographs nearly all deal with much earlier and major castles, to which he tried to assimilate Bodiam . . . Subsequent general surveys of castles have discarded his careful case-study method and popular synthesis has . . . been repetitively superficial' (1993: 59). Similarly, A.H. Thompson (1912) also moved from a military view centred on the twelfth century to a consideration of Bodiam. Even Gilchrist does this, referring to 'the true castle' (1999: 234).

Coulson's sustained attack on the meaning of licences to crenellate that we looked at in Chapter 2 can be set in its broader context here. Traditional accounts of feudalism have centred on the tension between royal and baronial power. If baronial power was reflected in the number of private or baronial castles, it stands to reason that the King would resist issuing licences to crenellate. By demonstrating that such licences were not at all to do with a weakening of royal authority, Coulson has knocked one of the supports away from under the definition of castles as 'essentially feudal'.

Any search for the 'essential features' or the 'distinguishing characteristics' of 'the castle' or the human groups associated with the castle runs the danger of descent into essentialist argument. Hence my stress on the fact that the castle was *not* a stable or obvious category, in the Middle Ages or in the present, developed in the Introduction. In a sense, I am suggesting a New Historicist analysis of castles here, but in reverse. New Historicism looked to question apparently stable categories of the modern world such as the individual or the nation-state by looking at their contingent historical 'origins' in the Renaissance. Here, I am questioning the existence of the 'castle' as a stable medieval category by tracing it *forwards* to the point of its dissolution in the late Middle Ages and Renaissance.

Towards an alternative understanding

It is tempting to stand back from all of this and throw one's hands up in despair. Any general accounts of castles or of architecture in general are doomed; even worse, they are complicit in unifying and essentialist ways of thinking. We can do nothing, then, except produce individual accounts of castles, an endless parade of particularities.

Indeed, some archaeologists come close to such a position, in rejecting a whole range of possible models of long-term change on offer, in rejecting the notion that in their field any pivotal changes can be seen, or in preferring detailed exposition of individual castles and the short, pithy paper to the synthetic monograph. At the risk of personalising the issue, I find it revealing that the writers on castles I most admire have tended to put their key insights into papers characteristically focusing on particular castles rather than producing synthetic monographs giving a more general view. Richard Bradley (1993) has written of archaeology's 'loss of nerve' as a discipline, a loss of nerve I have identified also in studies of vernacular architecture (Johnson 1997); the more perceptive writers on castles have perhaps lost their nerve also.

Forsaking any kind of larger picture, in my view, is tempting but ultimately untenable as an approach. In the first place, it carries the danger of inconsistency. All writing cannot avoid being situated within assumptions about larger stories, just as there is no such thing as a theory-free account of the evidence. Second, there clearly were larger-scale and deeper forces at work during this period; the view that fourteenth- to seventeenth-century England was fundamentally about continuity rather than change is, I think, mistaken. I have discussed what I view as a series of ruptures in other books (Johnson 1993; 1996) under the umbrella term 'closure'.

My aim in coining this term was twofold. First, I wanted to get away from the crude Marxian connotations of terms like 'the feudal/capitalist transition'. Marxism has contributed more than possibly any other body of thought to our understanding of this period, and anyone writing of this period does so against an intellectual horizon defined by Marx, whether they like it or not. Nevertheless, it is not the only model of large-scale underlying change. Second, I wanted to get away from an idea of a single set of underlying factors (fruitless questions like 'Was it, at heart, all about economics? Or was it, at heart, all about class conflict?) without sacrificing the notion that there are underlying deep structures in this period, and that this period was a particularly critical one.

I do think that there were a series of critical changes in sixteenth-century England, changes that mark it off, culturally and architecturally, from the late Middle Ages. However, I do not necessarily see these changes straightforwardly reflected in the specifics of architectural forms, with this form being characteristic of this period and that form of that period. As we have noted, examples of towers with hall complexes inside them can be lined up from both sides of the medieval/Renaissance 'divide', from Warkworth to Lulworth and Bolsover. Also, I do not think we necessarily see these changes straightforwardly reflected in terms of what those architectural forms meant. Late medieval castles clearly referred to values of 'chivalry'; the great Renaissance palaces of Wollaton and Burghley House clearly referred to 'chivalry' also.

I suggest that the mid- to late sixteenth century saw the *construction* (no pun intended) of *elite domestic architecture as a discursive object*. More precisely, this period saw the application of new discursive rules to the inscription of architectural forms on the physical and cultural landscape. Having been reconstructed through new discourses in this way, old buildings such as medieval castles came to carry very different meanings. Such new meanings in turn were actively deployed in the construction of the identities of sixteenth-century elites. Again, the identities of these elites might refer to words like honour, nobility, chivalry, but these again were constructed as discursive objects in very new ways. My conclusion therefore is that sixteenth-century social identities are constructed around *the way buildings are viewed*, rather than simply changing architectural styles (Perpendicular, Renaissance). Such a conclusion, is, of course, a starting point in its turn.

We can explore these propositions in more detail by looking at things which did change in the sixteenth century, and how these affected the perception of old castles. We can start by asking new questions about the oldest 'prime suspect' for the death of the castle – gunpowder.

Castles and cannon

Gunpowder was invented in China in the thirteenth century. It reached western Europe in the fourteenth century; cannon were used at the Siege of Calais in 1347 (O'Neill 1960: xiv). By the end of the fifteenth century, gunpowder artillery had supplanted other forms of siege engine, and by the late sixteenth century the musket had replaced the longbow and crossbow.

New forms of military architecture developed alongside these new forms of weapon. Being vastly more powerful, the cannon required defences of much greater scale; the perimeter of the artillery fortress was much greater than that of the castle. It was difficult to mount a cannon facing downwards, for obvious reasons; so developed artillery defences were low, enabling artillery to fire along extended stretches of wall. The walls themselves were low, and revetted with earth to absorb the impact of the shot. Cannon were protected by bastions. Where medieval towers were circular, the sides of these bastions were angled to sharp points, so that raking fire from one bastion could perfectly flank its neighbour (Figure 4.7).

I do not want to explore these developments in any detail, or to delve into their underlying logic. Arguably, the principles of artillery defence and attack developed during the course of the fifteenth and sixteenth centuries in the wars between competing city-states in Renaissance Italy. Here, scholars have seen a steady evolution between the high round towers and curtain walls of the medieval castle, through a succession of intermediate forms that were developed as military architects came to terms with the new technology and as that technology itself evolved and improved (Duffy 1979). We should note, however, that these new developments went hand-in-hand with the Renaissance. Often the same individuals were involved with the new art and the new fortification. These new developments also went hand-in-hand with the use of systematic geometry and an 'organic' plan, in which the angles of the sides of one bastion were determined by the angles of the cannon fire from its neighbouring bastion. The regularity of such a system invited regularity within the circuit, for example in the radial street plan of many fortified cities (Lewis 1994).

I suggest that the importance of these new forms for sixteenth-century understandings of castle architecture in England was that, put simply, they contributed to a separation between the categories of 'military' and 'social'. To repeat the arguments of earlier chapters, Bodiam and other late medieval castles used a common vocabulary of building where elements of 'defence' and 'residence' are not easily separated. By the end of the sixteenth century, this situation had changed radically. It would be impossible to confuse the new fortifications of Berwick on the Scottish border or Upnor on the Thames with residential palaces.

The converse – that 'chivalric' decorative elaboration on a building like Wollaton or Bolsover or Burghley would no longer be associated with military intent – is also true. The fourteenth-century knight would gain a whole series of impressions from Bodiam that alluded to military strength. However, the seventeenth-century gentleman with military training might observe the battlements of Lulworth without for a moment thinking of the building in the same bracket as that of a military fort.

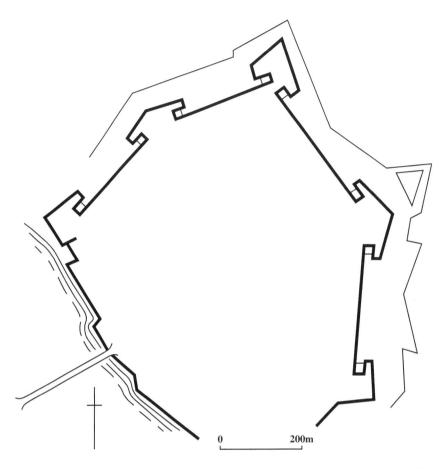

Figure 4.7 Late sixteenth-century artillery fortifications at the Anglo-Scottish border town of Berwick.

In short, therefore, the development of forms of military architecture that looked and operated very differently from the late medieval castle led to *a loss of architectural cross-referencing*. It led to the development of two classes or genres of structure where previously there had been one, and the loss of a common vocabulary between the two.

The exceptions to this rule are revealing ones. The obvious exception is the northern borders of England and indeed beyond into Scotland and Ireland, where a range of architectural forms included both military features such as gunports and often well-appointed residential accommodation. These forms run across a range of social levels, from the relatively humble bastle, through tower-houses and peles of various forms, to refitted castles and even royal residences.

At Norham, towers were remodelled into bastions at a critical border location; at the Scottish castle of Stirling, even a royal castle has a great artillery bastion thrown out in front of the main residence. Stirling, however, contains the distinction in microcosm: the bastion is of severe geometrical design, whereas the Renaissance apartments within the King's and Queen's Chambers have no military pretensions about them. The Queen's Chambers in particular are, viewed in isolation, a Renaissance courtyard house. Craignethan is another complex example of the combination of military and palace. The gun-ports of its lower courtyard are completely useless; a gun pointed through them could shoot straight into the rise of the hill a few metres away. Again, the caponnier placed in the inner ditch would fill with smoke and be uninhabitable after a few minutes of action (MacIvor 1977).

I am not suggesting that southern England was 'leading the way' in terms of architectural fashion and the North was taking a little time to follow. After all, there are architectural examples of sophisticated Renaissance design to equal anything south of the border, for example the King's and Queen's Lodgings at Stirling; the later sixteenth-century loggia and rusticated façade added to the medieval castle of Crichton; and elements of the later phases at the royal palace of Linlithgow. However, certain forms of community and social identity based around the raiding and reiving of the borders continued here till the beginning of the seventeenth century, and I am suggesting that the architectural links and metaphors that went with this therefore persisted also.

Castles and the Reformation

At the same time that the English elite was learning to distinguish the military from the social, they were learning to distinguish the religious from the domestic. Heslop (1991) points out that modern scholars have separated religious from domestic architecture, a distinction that did not necessarily apply in its modern form before the Renaissance. The majority of parish church towers were crenellated. There are many examples of the church and defence being combined, most obviously in the thirteenth-century fortress-churches of the Languedoc but examples closer to home can be found of the combination of church and castle, for instance, at Durham where the cathedral is incorporated into the outer wall of the castle (Bonde 1994).

Centuries earlier, a ruling class of men sent their younger brothers into the monasteries: the Church was the other side of the coin from the secular realm. As a result, 'alongside the *castella*, symbolically linked, were the *castra Deï*' (Nelson 1999: 141). It should not surprise us therefore to find that just as architecture held a common vocabulary between defence and luxury, so it had a common vocabulary between the religious and the domestic.

Again, around 1400 a common vocabulary of architecture could be said to exist. Coulson has explored one aspect of this in 'conventual crenellation';

Figure 4.8 The fourteenth-century abbey gatehouse at Bury St Edmunds, constructed in the years after the townspeople rioted against the abbey.

he suggests that the dummy battlements and arrowslits of buildings such as Bury St Edmunds gatehouse (Figure 4.8) carried an ideological and moral message to the townspeople who a few years earlier had risen up against the abbey. Cruciform arrowslits have their own ideological message also (Coulson 1982). Many castles had collegiate foundations in their lower courts.

However, by 1600, the monasteries had been dissolved. Many of them now stood in ruins in the landscape, visible testaments of political and religious transformation (Knowles 1974). Others had been converted into domestic residences, though the marks of their origins were there for all to see. Across the country reused monastic stone could be seen in countless buildings. A familiar and customary aspect of the landscape had been destroyed, and marks of its destruction made a great impression on contemporaries.

It went along, of course, with the abandonment and ruination of many castles themselves. As the early sixteenth-century commentator Leland

126

Figure 4.9 Rushton Triangular Lodge,
Northamptonshire.

travelled across England, he noted countless ruined or derelict castles. Ruins of both castles and monasteries rapidly became objects of antiquarian discourse. The stone from such structures could be reused in meaningful ways: the stone from the castle at Cambridge, in ruins by the fifteenth century, was used for King's College from 1441 onwards, and later for Emmanuel and Magdalen colleges (Brown 1989). At the same time, much of the traditional imagery and iconography of ordinary churches had been destroyed (Philips 1973). This does not mean that sixteenth-century people failed to understand such imagery; the Octagon at Ely, for example, was spared from iconoclasm because the images depicted royal foundation (Lindley 1995: 145–6).

The most famous secular building with religious cross-referencing proves the rule in that it was of course Catholic and therefore no longer allusive to the established religion of the Church of England: Sir Thomas Tresham's Rushton Triangular Lodge where the grouping of architectural features in threes right down the lengths of the three sides and the 99-letter inscription (Figure 4.9). However, this building is first of all isolated and unusual; like Lyveden New Build and a few other structures, it is a piece of self-consciously 'witty' architecture. Second, it no longer expresses a religious system that carries State and social authority with it – indeed, it can be seen in subversive ways; popular tradition states that the Gunpowder Plot was hatched in this building (Barnes 1997). So where there was a system of architectural cross-referencing that was implicit, customary, taken-for-granted, now such cross-referencing was witty, allusive, a riddle to be discussed and commented upon.

Castles and royalty

The third loss of architectural cross-referencing is between the power of the monarch and the power of the aristocracy. Around 1400, a visitor to the majority of royal palaces would have noted little difference between their layout and those of a great baron. The size and scale of the very largest would have been beyond even the greatest duke, but the standard late medieval arrangement of rooms around the great hall was at the core of all these palaces. Many late medieval buildings passed from royal to baronial hands and back again with little obvious change in the architectural arrangements of the great household. Edward III built or rebuilt Queenborough, Windsor, Isleworth, Sheen/Richmond, Westminster Palace, the Tower of London, Gravesend, Rotherhithe, and Hadleigh, all around the Thames Estuary; he moved between them in later years, taking his chivalric court with him (Steane 1993). Of these, only Queenborough with its circular form is a building that might be readily distinguished from a 'private' or baronial castle; the scale of the work at Windsor, where Edward spent £51,000, should not make us forget that this was mainly on collegiate buildings for the Order of the Garter, plus a palace in the upper bailey – the same combination of collegiate church and residence that we find at so many baronial sites. The hall at Westminster Palace dwarfs its nearest rival, Kenilworth, in terms of size, but its form is customary and familiar.

By the middle of the seventeenth century, royal palaces were very different not just in their scale, but in their arrangement, decoration and fittings, to the extent that historians talk of an emergent split between court and country. Elizabeth set a new pattern in royal building by *not* building; I argued above that in so doing she was referring indirectly to her father Henry.

Henry's palaces, most notably Hampton Court and Nonsuch, are buildings that in many respects follow traditional layouts; the hall at Hampton Court, for example, is the largest – and one of the last – of its kind. However, they possess very new features alongside more traditional elements, and were perceived by contemporaries as something very different (Figure 4.10). William Harrison (1587) wrote less than fifty years later:

Figure 4.10 Roundel bearing the head of a Roman
emperor at Henry's palace of Hampton Court.

Those [palaces] that were builded before the time of Henry the eight,
reteine to these daies the shew and image of the ancient worke-
manship vsed in this land: but such as he erected (after his owne
deuise (for he was nothing inferiour in this trade to Adrian the
emperour and Justinian the lawgiuer)) doo represent another maner
of paterne, which, as they are supposed to excel all the rest that he
found standing in this realme, so they are and shall be a perpetuall
president vnto those that doo come after, to follow in their workes
and buildings of importance. Certes masonarie did neuer better
flourish in England than in his time.

(cited in Edelen 1968: 225)

Henry also exemplified this 'maner of paterne' in other areas: he designed
jewellery, armour, siege engines, and a tiltyard; he kept plans and drawing instruments in his studies. At the same time as he was creating a new

landscape by the dissolution of one of its most ancient components, namely the monasteries, he was changing the domestic landscape by ensuring that never again could a baronial palace be mistaken for a royal one.

I am arguing, then, that the creation of a 'court style' by King James, King Charles and their architect Inigo Jones was prefigured by the building of Henry a century earlier. I am also arguing that behind the emergent 'court' and 'country' styles of the early seventeenth century was a much more complex configuration of power and the way power was mobilised ideologically.

Castles and the State

And while Henry was dissolving the monasteries and building royal palaces, he was creating a new kind of State out of the ruins of the old. Deal castle, one of Henry's new artillery forts, is of Caen stone, possibly from the fabric of a dissolved monastery.

Henry's forts along the south coast are usually seen as an interim stage between the medieval castle and the developed artillery fort: they feature low bastions and casemates for guns, but the bastions are circular rather than angled (Figure 4.11). I suggest, however, that Henry's forts faced inwards to the nation as well as outwards across the Channel. They did not simply act as protection: they asserted a new kind of State.

Henry's artillery forts were the first scheme of comprehensive, planned system of national coastal defence since the Saxon shore forts, and the last till the eighteenth century. Other schemes were planned at Berwick, where

Figure 4.11 Low bastions for artillery at Henry's fort of Camber Castle, Sussex.

similar arrangements to those proposed for Norham were planned but never carried out (O'Neill 1960: 70); fifty years later Elizabethans planned artillery lines along the Scottish border, plans that were abandoned after the accesion of James VI and I to the thrones of both Scotland and England. Buildings like Camber, Deal, and Upnor were not merely different from late medieval palaces; these new defences were physical embodiments of the defence of the Commonwealth. On the Continent, the new styles of artillery fortification were explicitly linked to State power and to that of absolute monarchy in particular (Duffy 1979).

Castles and theatre

One of the most obvious ways in which self-consciousness affects architecture and culture is in the development of the metaphor of the stage itself. Mystery plays and other such productions were a familiar part of medieval life, though they were usually associated in one way or another with the Church. Castle imagery was routinely bound up in such performances; it was one image, along with 'genealogical trees, tabernacles, fountains and gardens', that was used in festivals and civic welcomes to present ideals of good governance to the king or lord being welcomed (Strong 1984: 8).

We have seen that much of the way medieval castles landscapes carried meaning was via the medium of bodily movement – progress in and out of castles, twists and turns along causeways. The metaphor here was in part that of liturgy, so important to the late medieval Church. The sixteenth century saw meanings being conveyed in a rather different way. The English stage marked a radical shift in the nature and manner of staging, and became a source of tension and anxiety, to the extent that modern scholarship about it has become a growth industry (Breitenberg 1996; Newman 1991; Jardine 1991; Zimmerman 1992).

The Elizabethan theatre displayed society to itself. It was, after all, arranged in the form of a circle or globe, an architectural form which referred back to the medieval tower and has been taken as referring forward to the Enlightenment panopticon (Belsey 1985: 19–27). The theatre was placed in a liminal zone, on the city boundaries (Mullaney 1991). Within this structure, seats were arranged in tiers that corresponded to social status, just as seating in church marked out rank (Johnson 1996). And on the stage, Elizabethans ranging from the common folk in the pits to the more civilised gentry in the upper tiers saw the social order simultaneously affirmed and subverted. On stage, women spoke of the husband's mastery of his wife, and yet the part of the wife was played by a young boy (Jardine 1991). Kings were presented as divinely ordained, and yet were summarily deposed and even murdered by usurpers.

So the very metaphor of staging that has guided our understanding of castles was itself transformed in the Renaissance. It became secularised; it became associated with both authority and subversion; and most centrally, it showed how the social order was based on *performance*, both inside and outside the theatre.

Castles and elite values

The great household was changing. Its numbers had declined through the late medieval period, though they rose again just before the end of the fifteenth century (Woolgar 1999: 15). At the same time, its gender composition was shifting. There were, proportionally, many more women at all levels of the great household in 1600 than there were in 1400.

All these changes were partly bound up with the introduction of Protestantism and the rise of a 'secular culture' commented on by historians. Henry's Reformation of the 1530s and Edward's of the 1560s led to the upbringing of an aristocratic and gentry class whose religious beliefs were at some distance from traditional medieval Catholicism, whether or not they were committed Puritans or for that matter recusants influenced by the Counter-Reformation. As a result, I suggest that as they travelled around monastic landscapes or attended old churches, their experience of historical disassociation with what they saw would be heightened. This sense of distance from religious forms was heightened by the secularisation of education and literacy. Where great men had been educated by priests, now many went to grammar school or had secular tutors.

This change is also involved with the rise of literacy and of the printing press. The values of late medieval architecture had to be experienced or were commented on obliquely in romances. What explicit comment there was on architecture was largely religious rather than secular architecture, the most famous example being Abbot Suger's writings on the structure and aesthetics of the early Gothic church. Late medieval masons worked in guilds whose organisation and training were customary. The systems of mason's marks inscribed on the surface of castles are testament to this organisation and the shadowy identities embedded within it.

Cooper has drawn attention to subtle shifts in the way ideas like honour and display were articulated among members of the gentry classes. Sixteenth-century literate thought drew on Aristotle, Vitruvius and Castiglione to construct a new picture of how a 'gentleman' should live. Magnificence and display were still there, but should be deployed with 'taste', and was an ornament to the 'commonwealth'. Such subtle shifts also marked a change in attitude towards the process of architectural design. By 1600 a distinct idea of 'architecture' had emerged that was held to be distinct from the practical skills of the artisan. The distinction between architectural knowledge and that of the craftsman had an explicitly social dimension; architectural knowledge was the preserve of the gentleman, and should be deployed quite explicitly to control and delimit the activities of the artisan. John Dee wrote:

'the true Architect is [able] to teach, Demonstrate, distribute, describe, and Judge all workes wrought, And he, onely, searches out the causes and reasons of all things'. Henry Wotton added for good measure that 'speculation [on rules of proportion] may appear to vulgar Artizans . . . too subtile, and too sublime' (cited in Cooper 1999: 13–14, 27).

By 1600, whatever was being drawn from written sources, the everyday experience of architecture had changed. When the local lord went to church on Sunday, he no longer saw an interior filled with colour and paintings depicting biblical scenes. These had been whitewashed over and covered with texts from the Bible, most obviously the Ten Commandments. When he returned home, he might sit in solitude in a newly constructed study and could look over a new printed book just imported from France or Italy. Such a book might give patterns or designs for Renaissance architecture and fittings, and explain something of the system of proportion behind them, and the values to which they alluded; Lucy Gent (1981: 71) has shown that such treatises were both present in gentlemen's libraries and lent to others by 1620. Our lord might never have thought about these things before. He might pick up such a book after reading the Bible for a time, and before consulting a work on civility (Bryson 1998). He might then move on to a book on devices and emblems, and ponder the question set by such a book, of how symbols come to have meanings (Bath 1994).

When a Renaissance lord left his study, he might look up at the towers and battlements of his old pile and think about whether they wanted to rebuild all or part of this ancient edifice. He might well decide not. After all, such an old and ancient building reflected values of hospitality and good lordship, just as that poet had declaimed to much applause after dinner in so-and-so's house the other day. And if the monarch visited next year, they could point out the historical events associated with this or that chamber, maybe even put on an Arthurian romance.

So the old castle in which a sixteenth-century lord lives had hardly been changed physically; maybe a small study added, the domestic ranges refitted. And yet the way it carried social status has changed utterly. This is why structures like Lulworth and Bolsover are very different from buildings like Warkworth and Tattershall. Their physical form might have similarities, and some of the meanings those forms had carried (hospitality, lordly authority) were comparable but one was a living system, largely implicit; the other was a conscious attempt to invoke values seen as being under threat.

Conclusion

In the latter half of this chapter, I have tried to sketch out some very broad ways in which I think we can talk about long-term transformation centred on the sixteenth century. Rather than talk of the rise and decline of partic-ular architectural forms such as the castle as if it were a species of animal,

Figure 4.12 Burghley House, built by Lord Burghley in the late sixteenth century: a 'courtier house' using elaborate late Gothic forms.

I have focused on context – how one building related to another within a physical and cultural landscape, and how all fitted with a genealogy of changing social practices linked to the emergence of a new kind of State and a new kind of ideology to go with that State.

Specifically, I am suggesting that whatever were the changes in particular form, and whatever the changes in what the forms meant, one of the key transformations was that of how the forms came to carry meaning. Let me clarify with an example. Bodiam clearly, at some level of interpretation, referred to 'chivalric values' in its layout, form and landscape context. So, too, did the late sixteenth-century Burghley House (Figure 4.12) but the way in which they did so had changed radically. At Bodiam, the references are implicit, hardly overtly commented on; at Burghley, they are self-conscious, overtly allusive. At Bodiam, the meanings are experienced by moving around and through the monument; at Burghley, they can be taken in from a single vantage point. At Bodiam, the meanings are by their very nature taken for granted and not written down, which is why they are so difficult for us to disentangle; at Burghley, the building is the subject of contemporary commentaries.

The sixteenth century opened up discursive spaces between objects. Between military and domestic objects; between religious and secular objects;

between the body of the monarch and the State; between present and past, the present no longer being one of custom and tradition since time out of mind; between an idealised view of the landscape and the reality of that landscape. These spaces thus became problems. Connections now had to be explicitly argued between things that before were customary and taken-for-granted. Emblems had been a standard practice for centuries, Renaissance emblem books agonised over what emblems really represent and put these anxieties on to the printed page where they could be studied by new audiences (Bath 1994). Late sixteenth-century poetry constructs idealised images of a female king, agonising over gender and monarchy in the process. Pattern books define correct and incorrect ways of representing social values through building. Histories become more than mere narratives, and confront the problem of anachronism (Burke 1969). Nation-states such as England are no longer embodied in the monarch, so they have to be defined and re-defined through maps (Helgerson 1992) and 'descriptions' (Edelen 1968). Even anxieties about the individual are worked through in new discourses of the body (Sawday 1995).

However, such comments are suggestions for a broader picture; just as interesting are particular examples where general patterns were *not* followed. When today we visit a castle or Renaissance palace, what excites our interest are the differences – this one did it this way for this reason, that one did it that way for that reason. What I think we need to do then is look at particular examples where new ideas were deployed in old contexts by knowledgeable social agents. Only when these have been understood in their own terms can we go on to make broader and deeper statements – but we can, indeed must, go on to do this. I will attempt to do this in the next chapter, in an analysis of the ancient pile of Kenilworth.

5

KENILWORTH

The evidence house

One of the most revealing statements any castle buff can make is to name his or her favourite castle – the one they most enjoy wandering around, talking and writing about; the one that always has something new to offer on each fresh visit in different light and weather conditions or simply the different mood of the scholar. For this writer, there is only one candidate: the shattered red sandstone ruins of Kenilworth.

The 'evidence house' was a room or building at Kenilworth. It is recorded in accounts of the late sixteenth century; it has left no archaeological trace or, to put it more accurately, none of the buildings still standing on the site can be positively identified as such with any degree of certitude. This building held an archive of documents, accounts and other papers relating to the estate; in 1590 the previous owner's widow was accused of removing papers from it after his death (Adams 1995: 3).

In this chapter, I want to discuss the archaeology of Kenilworth castle and landscape as a whole as an 'evidence house', a vast store of archival material to illustrate more general points about castle interpretation. First, I look at the medieval development of Kenilworth in the light of some of the points I have made about late medieval castles in earlier chapters and, second, I use Kenilworth to illustrate the more theoretical discussion of how to begin to understand the 'medieval to Renaissance transition' developed in the last chapter.

An old castle

The castle of Kenilworth stands in the county of Warwickshire, almost perfectly set in the middle of England (Figure 1.1), now an island of peace set within criss-crossing motorways. Its history up to the late sixteenth century can serve as a recapitulation of points made in earlier chapters.

The castle was first built in the twelfth century by the local baron, Geoffrey de Clinton. Its precise initial form is uncertain, though it may well have been of ovoid motte-and-bailey form, with an earthen motte in the position of what is now the stone *donjon*. However, as was usual with such castle

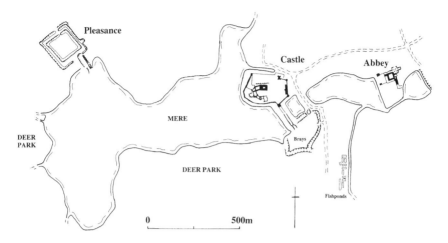

Figure 5.1 Kenilworth: general plan of context.

foundations, the castle was only one part of the twelfth-century transformation of the landscape (Figure 5.1). A monastery was founded on a site adjacent to that of the castle, and the settlement of Kenilworth grew up around the crossroads in front of the monastery. The town of Kenilworth was granted borough rights allowing it to hold a market in 1125.

In the thirteenth century, the castle of Kenilworth and its associated elite landscape were expanded. The castle itself had inner and outer courts rebuilt in stone on a huge scale (Figure 5.2). The inner court's ovoid form suggests that it may be a rebuild of an earlier earthen form; it includes a massive rectangular *donjon* with corner turrets. The outer courtyard wall was studded with circular towers with elaborate cruciform arrowslits. Around these outer walls, a system of artificial lakes or meres was created by throwing a dam up to the south of the castle. This earthen dam also functioned as a causeway leading south from the main gate. Water thus completely enveloped the castle, in particular, stretching away for some distance to the south and west, and continuing into a system of leats and dams associated with the monastery to the east.

Beyond this body of water again were further outworks, usually interpreted as thirteenth-century defences of the dam and causeway. The southern end of the dam was protected by a semicircular area called the Brays; by the end of the thirteenth century, the semi-circular earthwork was surmounted by a stone wall studded with circular towers or bastions. Today the Brays serves as the visitors' car park. Beyond the Brays again, and to the west of the Castle and mere, were several deerparks enclosed by park pales and at least one set of fishponds.

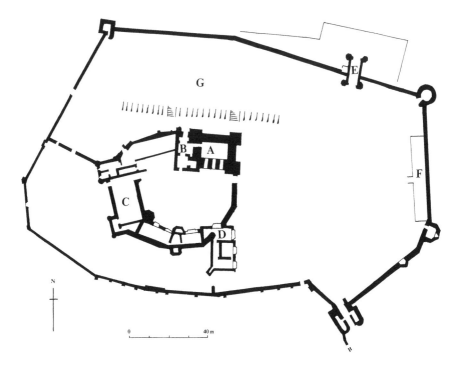

Figure 5.2 Kenilworth: the inner buildings. A: Caesar's Tower; B: the loggia; C: the hall; D: the visitors' block; E: the northern gatehouse; F: the stable block; G: the garden.

In the mid-thirteenth century, Kenilworth was owned by the (in)famous Simon de Montfort. The de Montfort family had been prominent across Europe, in part for their crusades and persecution of Jews and heretics such as the Cathars of southern France; school texts now gloss over this insalubrious past and concentrate on de Montfort's role in the Whiggish political narrative in which de Montfort figures prominently in the events that led to the setting up of the first English Parliament. After de Montfort's political defeat and death at the battle of Evesham in 1265, the castle became the refuge for his defeated followers and was besieged by the King. It is at this point that the castle becomes directly relevant to points made in previous chapters.

This siege became a landmark in narratives of castle development, often substituting for that of Edward's Welsh castles as the central moment in the development of attack and defence. For some, the successful siege and capture of the immensely strong Kenilworth, despite many difficulties, demonstrated to medieval defenders the ultimate futility of locking oneself up in a fortress and passively resisting. From that date onwards, it is alleged,

138

military commanders preferred engagement in the field however strong the defences of neighbouring castles (Stocker 1992). However, it is often forgotten that the thirteenth-century castle had other dimensions. In 1279 a tournament was held at Kenilworth involving 100 knights and their ladies (Taylor 1998).

Watery landscapes revisited

Whatever its character in the thirteenth century, by the late Middle Ages Kenilworth became a site for another watery landscape of the type discussed in Chapters 2 and 3. In the process, earlier features which may or may not have been 'defensive' in their original character became transformed – their physical form remained the same, but they acted as a frame for a great later medieval, and subsequently Renaissance, palace. This palace could be either baronial or royal at one time or another, as it was first forfeited to the King, then given to a King's younger son John of Gaunt, Duke of Lancaster, and then passed back through the sons of Gaunt into the hands of the Lancastrian Kings of England.

By the early fifteenth century, the mere was a vast pleasure lake. This can be seen by the addition of a quadrangular structure at its north-western end, the Pleasance or 'Pleasauns en Marys' (Taylor 1998; Thompson 1964). Today, the visitor to Kenilworth can walk across the fields to the Pleasance where the site is marked by the usual lumps and bumps in a field full of cows. Viewed from the air, these lumps and bumps indicate two rectangular moats, one inside the other and separated by a raised terrace. This arrangement is similar to that at Somersham (Taylor 1989) and probably indicated a walkway with water on both sides. There are also clear indications of a canal and dock for approach to the site across the mere by boat or barge. Documents and excavations (Morley *et al.* 1995) indicate that the interior had a stone building still visible as an earthwork, timber buildings, and corner turrets. The Pleasance could be used as a residence in its own right. For example, in 1421 'Henry . . . rode to Kenilworth, where he rested at his manor of Pleasant Marys. There he was joined on 15 March by the queen . . . On the same day, the royal couple rode to Coventry' (Doig 1996: 169).

What is particularly interesting about the Pleasance is its location, around a corner of the mere. Between it and the castle there is a low rise, so the site is 'tucked away'. Its roofs would have been intervisible with those of the castle, but the turn away from the castle into a secluded spot is again emphasised.

John of Gaunt

A generation before the creation of the Pleasance, the range's domestic accommodation around the inner court had been largely rebuilt by John of Gaunt,

Duke of Lancaster. Gaunt, a younger son of Edward III, later uncle to King Richard II, is representative of a social level little seen in England: a great duke second only in power and status to the King, like a great European duke. He could even aspire to royal status – he was king of Castile for a short period (Prestwich 1980).

It is important to remember this social position when we consider Gaunt's alterations to the castle. Gaunt rebuilt the hall and its kitchens on the west side of the inner courtyard, and the 'private' range to the south. The range of private apartments in particular is now severely damaged but enough remains to make some observations.

The hall is huge (Figure 3.7). Its roof may have been a predecessor of the hammer-beamed roof built a little later and surviving at Westminster Hall (Colvin 1983; Thompson 1977), though Emery argues it could equally have been of arch-braced form (2000: 404). It stands on the site on the earlier great hall of the castle, and is usually considered to be a remodelling and extension of an earlier ground floor hall.

Figure 5.3 Two of the Perpendicular windows on the east side of the great hall at Kenilworth.

Most discussions of the hall centre on its architectural position: its windows and wall panelling comprise an early example of the style of Perpendicular Gothic (Figure 5.3). Discussions then go on to discuss the 'genesis' of this style in the royal courts of late fourteenth-century England. The panelling of the hall walls and windows is quite stunning, but here I want to look in more detail at the archaeology of the hall – its form, the way it controlled movement and access, its context within the Kenilworth landscape. By so doing, apparently 'odd' or 'anachronistic' features of the hall's layout make sense in terms of the human actions it delimited and controlled.

In the first place, the hall was raised – instead of entering at ground floor level, the new hall was raised over a vaulted undercroft. This is the reverse of the usual typology of hall forms for the period, in which 'early' first floor halls are supposed to give way to 'later' ground floor forms (Grenville 1997: 86). This raising must be understood in the context of the mere and deer-parks beyond the walls. The window seats of the hall now had a view over this landscape, a view that would have been barred by the outer walls of the castle had the hall floor been at ground level.

It may also have been possible to view the mere from a platform outside. An irregular earthwork abutting the west side of the hall (Figure 5.4) has traditionally been interpreted as a later, Civil War gun emplacement. A plausible alternative, however, is that it is a later medieval viewing platform of the sort we have seen at other sites (Chapter 2), directly accessible from the cross-passage at the lower end of the undercroft. The position of this 'gun emplacement' makes little sense in terms of Civil War military tactics, as attack from this direction would have been hindered by the mere. Additionally, it is striking that the east side of the undercroft has narrow slit windows; these are not provided on the west side, implying that the earthwork was already there, or was planned, when the undercroft walls were constructed.

The raising of the hall also had the effect of creating a more defined and impressive entrance at its lower end. The cross-passage was now approached by an extended stair from a point directly outside the now ancient keep, with the vast kitchen range to the right. The kitchen range is again badly damaged, but a system of huge fireplaces and ovens remains. The ramp led up to an ornate doorway with vaulted porch in front.

Over all of this new building, the new decorative scheme was applied in the form of panelling. This effect of this Perpendicular style (Figure 5.3) on the visitor would have been to act as a kind of surface wallpaper covering the façades. A common decorative pattern thus unified all the buildings from the south-east corner of the inner courtyard round the southern and western ranges in a single sweep. This would have continued round beyond the kitchens to the junction with the *donjon*. A little-known architectural frag-ment survives at first floor level at this junction, just enough to indicate a

Figure 5.4 General view of Kenilworth from the south, in the middle of the now drained mere. The 'viewing platform' is to the left of the main buildings, within the outer walls.

complex panelling system in the Perpendicular style of the rest of Gaunt's buildings dating from this period (Johnson 1999; Figure 5.5; see also below).

If these buildings are viewed from the outside of the castle from the west, whether from the borders of the mere or from a boat upon it, a distinctive and regular rhythm is also provided by the overall form of Gaunt's building. The hall has been cleverly fitted between two towers in such a way as to give the whole block an element of external symmetry, though this symmetry is not reflected in the internal arrangements. Kenilworth, then, is another example of regular and even symmetrical planning being fitted into irregular forms.

The medieval development of Kenilworth, then, reflects many of the points we have made in earlier chapters about watery landscapes, the arrangement of internal spaces, and the relation between architecture and social identity. However, the central phase of interest to us here opens in the late sixteenth century.

The Renaissance palace

By the 1570s, Kenilworth had been transformed once more. Not only were structural changes made to its fabric, but changes in the context of the castle

Figure 5.5 Fragment of decoration above loggia. The stone panelling formerly flanked a Perpendicular window, probably a smaller version of those of the Great Hall.

marked a transformation in its meanings even where that fabric remained the same.

In the first place, there was the loss of familiar and traditional elements around the castle. The monastery had been dissolved in the 1530s. Today, there is little left of the monastery; only a rather forlorn gatehouse and a few other buildings now set in a small park. Many nearby buildings, however, are constructed of reused stone from the monastery, an active process of rebuilding and reuse that probably started soon after dissolution in the mid-sixteenth century. The parish church stands a little to the north of the monastic site and incorporates monastic details; its form was altered in the late sixteenth century when the chancel was rebuilt.

The erasure of the monastery from the landscape must have been rapid, and by the 1560s the younger people of Kenilworth would not have remembered the presence of the monastery as a functioning institution; they might have had the ruins that remained and the reused stone pointed out to them by older people as emblems of an age that had passed, for better or worse. The traditional medieval pairing of secular and religious authority in the form of castle-and-monastery was now lost to this new generation.

On the other side of the castle and its mere, the Pleasance had been abandoned. Its timber-framed buildings had been dismantled and re-erected within the outer walls of the castle in the early sixteenth century by Henry VIII (Morley *et al.* 1995). Again, however, the lumps and bumps of the field next to the mere marking its site were visible evidences of its passing.

Other buildings in the castle were added to or transformed in the late sixteenth century. A new stable block, visitors' block and gatehouse were added; the ancient *donjon* was given a clock on one corner and a loggia to one side; and a formal garden was inserted to the north of the *donjon*. However, rather than look at these buildings as species of architectural styles, in isolation from the medieval structure of which they were a part, I want to look contextually at their archaeology, at the interrelationships between them – how some new buildings were viewed in the context of the old, how others served to frame certain perspectives. To do this, I will take a tour of the castle as it might have been seen by a male visitor towards the end of the sixteenth century.

Outer court

The visitor approaches the castle from the south, as, he is maybe aware, countless generations of medieval visitors have before him. He passes one of the several vast deerparks surrounding the castle, possibly spotting the deer moving dimly within the trees, on the other side of a huge earthen bank surmounted by the park pale. He may also pass a group of fishponds, and see scores of fat carp below the surface of the pools (these fishponds are extant but may have been abandoned by the late sixteenth century). He arrives outside the Brays, walking along the side of an even larger earthwork surmounted by stone wall studded with towers before turning left to face a gate, clearly ancient, flanked by twin circular towers (Figure 5.6).

Having had his identity challenged and having negotiated access through the gate, the visitor moves ahead through the open space of the Brays. After a few yards he turns right to face a second ancient gate. It is only at this point, well after his initial entry to the castle, that the full scale and nature of the castle are first revealed (Figure 5.7). To the left of the gate our visitor looks across the vastness of the mere. The water appears limitless from this viewpoint as its borders cannot be clearly discerned; it stretches off to the left, with more vast deerparks on either side. Above the mere rise the outer walls of the castle. These blank walls punctuated with buttresses are reflected in the water, making them appear even larger than they really are. Above the outer walls again rise the buildings of the inner court, which in contrast to

Figure 5.6 The largely destroyed outer gate to the Brays, now the entrance to the visitors' car park. The earthen banks were capped by a stone curtain wall studded with towers.

the severe appearance of the outer circuit are studded with vast windows glittering in the sunlight. From this distance there is perhaps nothing to distinguish the windows to the west from those to the east, though as he gets closer those to the east will be seen as stylistically different, part of a new visitors' block. Above all rises an even larger rectangular mass, that of the *donjon*. The light also accentuates the distinctive colour of the red sandstone with which the castle is built.

After again negotiating access, the visitor moves through the second gate. As he emerges from the darkness of this gate chamber, he moves on to a long causeway with two bodies of water on either side. It is not immediately apparent that the water level on either side of the causeway is different, and therefore that what appears as a long bridge across the water is actually a dam between two levels. (When the same feature reappears as Audley End in Essex it is hailed as an example of the genius of eighteenth-century landscape gardening.) Perhaps a guide identifies for the visitor this long, enclosed area as a tiltyard used for tournaments. The visitor walks down this causeway for what seems like an infinity, the buildings of the inner court looming gradually ever larger. As he does so, he notes the expanse of the mere to the left with the distant trees of yet more deerparks beyond it, and to the right a fine circular flanking tower with ancient cruciform arrowslits; further still

145

Figure 5.7 View of Kenilworth from the Brays.

to the right, the ruins of the old monastery may appear through the trees. Straight ahead, he is faced with a further gate with its own twin towers.

Passing perhaps with yet further ceremony through this inner gate, the visitor arrives in the outer courtyard of the castle. From this point it is necessary to pause, as the gaze of the visitor takes in a range of buildings both old and new: from left to right, a visitors' block and a *donjon*, at either end of the range defining the inner court; straight ahead, a gatehouse giving access to the castle from the north; and to the right, a stable block. I want to stress that these four buildings are all seen in the one sweep of the view as he emerges from the gatehouse. The meanings our visitor attributes to these buildings, and the identities he ascribes to their builder and owner, must be seen simultaneously, as a synchronic moment. Our visitor then looks more closely at each in turn.

First, the large, tower-like residential block to the left (Figure 5.8). Its position opposite the *donjon* suggests that it is intended as an apartment block for visitors. Sited at the other end of one range of the inner court, its large mass balances that of the *donjon* at the other end. Its architectural style, our visitor notes, is up-to-date, in conscious touch with the very latest in architectural fashion. The ashlar blocks have an exceptionally fine finish. It has huge, tall windows stacked one above the other in several storeys; the overall effect is very like Hardwick Hall, mocked in local rhymes as 'more glass than wall', and built in the 1590s by the formidable widow Bess of

146

Figure 5.8 The visitors' block, as seen after entry through the southern gatehouse.

Hardwick. However, the Kenilworth visitors' block is not immediately accessible by any visible gate or door; clearly, one has to enter by a door or gate (now destroyed) further up the inner courtyard wall to its right and then double back. This is a building not only of architectural fashion, but also of some social status, judging by its difficulty of access.

Straight ahead is a large and impressive gatehouse (Figure 5.9). In some respects, it is like the other gatehouses already encountered; it has the flanking towers the visitor has already seen at Kenilworth, but here there are four of them, and they are polygonal, taller and slimmer and arranged in two pairs at the back and two in front. The form of the gatehouse appears ancient; our visitor might recognise such a form from buildings centuries old, or from Oxford and Cambridge colleges. The style of the windows, however, suggests it has been recently built. The battlements on its walls and turrets are highly visible, but clearly too small to be used in any serious manner. They are clearly demonstrative. They suggest that the builder of the gatehouse knows how to self-consciously project values of chivalry and martial valour.

To the right of the visitor, there is a stable block, running along the line of the curtain wall (Figure 5.10). The stable block is flanked by two circular stone towers of old and ancient form; that to the right is the circular tower so prominent when our visitor crossed the causeway. But this block is not

Figure 5.9 The northern gatehouse. The former
gate passage has been blocked.

like other buildings in the castle. The lower parts are of the same distinctive red sandstone, but it is half-timbered in its upper storey. Half-timbering
was a form of building with social connotations: it occupied the lowest rung
in a hierarchy of building materials of stone, brick, and timber (Howard
1987). Timber-framing was ideally reserved for lower social orders; at palaces
such as the royal residence at Eltham, timber-framed structures are found in
the lower courts if at all. In this case the stables house the lowest social order
of all, that of animals (Thomas 1983: 29).

It is clear to the visitor or to any contemporary observer, however, that
this is not some building shoddily put up, for the timber-framing is of the
very highest quality. The timbers used are of generous dimensions, with
elaborate use of middle rails and passing-braces. The form of the passing-
braces resembles that of the owner's 'device', a ragged staff, seen elsewhere
in the castle. If this building is vernacular in some sense, it wears its
vernacular badge with style and pride. It is deliberately, assertively 'rustic'.

Figure 5.10 The stable block.

Figure 5.11 Caesar's Tower, as seen from the inner courtyard. The loggia entrance is to the left.

The final building visible from this point is a large rectangular mass framed between the visitors' block and the gatehouse. It is an ancient *donjon*, whose antiquity is reinforced when it is pointed out to the visitor as 'Caesar's Tower' (Figure 5.11). On its south-eastern corner, at a point most visible to our visitor entering from the southern gatehouse, there is a large clock on the south and east faces (the mortises for the fittings of this clock are still visible).

The inner court

Our visitor dismounts, and has his horse led off to the stables to the right. He turns, again, this time to the left, through a gate by the side of Caesar's Tower. He emerges into the final, inner courtyard. Rising in front of him is the great hall, with vast, tall windows not so dissimilar to those of the visitors' block. To the left of the visitor is that block, next to the private apartments of the lord, clearly indicated by the windows at first floor level. To the right is Caesar's Tower. Caesar's Tower has large windows of similar design to those of the visitors' block, and an entrance to a loggia to its left (Figure 5.12).

The loggia is plain, even severe in its design. If our visitor had seen a pattern-book from Italy, he might well recognise the loggia as a near-perfect copy of a piece of Italian architecture. And looking more closely at Caesar's Tower and walking through the loggia, the allusions to Renaissance design in Italy are reinforced. On the other side of the loggia, the visitor looks down on an Italian Renaissance formal garden, fitted between Caesar's Tower and the outer wall of the castle (Figure 5.13). However, the meanings of Caesar's Tower, loggia and garden are more complex than just the latest style.

In the first place, Caesar's Tower is clearly old and ancient; its name indicates that. It also has prominent and archaic 'fishtail' arrowslits near its summit, of a visibly different design to those on the towers in the outer courtyard. Yet also and at the same time it resembles a very contemporary piece of architecture. It has large windows, round arched openings and an ordered appearance, not unlike contemporary Renaissance buildings; and unlike other buildings at Kenilworth, it does not have battlements. Its overall form suggests an Italian Renaissance *palazzo* (Figure 5.14). This impression is best seen now from across the inner courtyard, though the northern façade must have been given an even more effective impression when viewed from the Italian garden (that side of the tower is now largely destroyed). Caesar's Tower, then, does not have a single identity or message. It reveals itself to the visitor as simultaneously old and new, both ancient and up-to-date.

This impression of different identities is reinforced by the immediate context of the loggia. Just before the visitor enters the loggia, he looks up, and sees a Perpendicular window and surrounding panels above it. This is quite different in style to the severe and Classical style of the arch before him; it is ornate, with very detailed panelling covering the surface of the

Figure 5.12 The southern entrance to the loggia.

walls and linking the façade with those to the visitor's left. It is not easily appreciated today, as only a tiny fragment of the window and panelling survives (Figure 5.5; Johnson 1999).

The garden below the other end of the loggia also carries different meanings. The steps down from the loggia into the garden are very carefully constructed. Rather than going straight down, they turn left, then pause, then turn right (Figure 5.15). The steps pause at a point where the garden can be viewed to best effect, with the castle wall beyond. The steps also descend on to a raised terrace running right and left between Caesar's Tower and the garden, along which visitors can walk under the shadow of the *donjon/palazzo* and gain different perspectives on the garden below.

The garden was described in a 1569 letter as follows:

> In which by sundry equal instances, with obelisks, and spheres, and white bears, all of stone upon their curious bases, by goodly show

151

Figure 5.13 View from the loggia steps of the reconstructed Italian garden; green and houses are visible beyond the outer walls.

were set; To these, two fine arbours . . . at each end one, the garden plot under that, with fair alleys, green with grass, even voided from the borders on both sides . . . And unto these, in the midst, against the terrace: a square cage, sumptuous and beautiful, joined hard to the north wall (that on that side guards the garden, as the garden the castle) of a rare form and excellency were raised . . . In the centre, as it were, of this goodly garden, was there placed a very fair fountain, cast into an eight-square, reared four feet high, from the midst whereof, a column upright . . . upholding a fair-formed bowl . . . from which sundry pipes did lively instil continual streams into the reservoir of the fountain . . . Here were things, ye see, might inflame any mind after looking . . .

(cited in Morley *et al.* 1995: 90)

The stone balls or spheres found in various small-scale excavations around the castle may be relics of this garden, rather than missiles hurled by engines from the de Montfort siege, as is generally supposed.

However, the view or 'prospect' is not so simple. Both steps and terrace look out not just on the garden, but on the castle's outer wall, and the view beyond. And this view is also carefully constructed. The visitor sees a village

152

Figure 5.14 Elevation of Italian Renaissance
house (After Burckhardt, 1867: Figure 326).

green, with vernacular houses dotted around that green – another careful construction of the 'rustic' viewed from above, framed and kept at a suitable distance by the outer wall of the castle (Figure 5.13). As such, our visitor might be reminded of other, artistic portrayals of the vernacular, for example, in wall paintings (Starn and Partridge 1992: 33–8).

The visitor returns to the inner court through the loggia and walks up the long stairway to the great hall, passing the heat and noise of the kitchens and the servants' hall on his right. The loggia might be a new architectural form to him, but he is now on familiar ground – kitchens and service area, the bustle and activity of a great household, the entrance and screens passage, the turn, to the left this time, into the great hall. And the hall itself is familiar, even if it is on a scale unparalleled outside royal structures such as Westminster Palace and Hampton Court (our visitor is reminded of both by the Perpendicular stylistic detail and the possible hammer-beam form of the roof, shared by those other structures).

Figure 5.15 The slighted north front of Caesar's Tower. The two figures on the right are standing on the stairs down from the loggia, at the point where these stop and form a 'landing' before changing direction.

We can trace the rest of our visitor's progress with less confidence. The private apartments beyond the upper end of the hall are now largely destroyed; they were largely on first floor level, and what remains is largely the foundations of the cellars and rooms below. They have been reconstructed as a private hall and series of chambers by Emery (2000). However, there would certainly have been more tall windows and Perpendicular detail, and suites of well-appointed rooms.

Understanding Kenilworth

How does Kenilworth work? To 'understand' Kenilworth, its features have to be placed next to each other, and considered as elements of a whole. We have to forsake the methods of traditional architectural history in which buildings are treated as species or as exemplars of styles, and value judgments made on that basis (Brown, for example, describes the windows in Caesar's Tower as 'dreadfully inappropriate': 1989: 134). Instead, we must embrace archaeological concerns of a careful, material, embodied consideration of context, informed by close examination of detail and of landscape context (the mortises for the clock on the south-west corner of Caesar's Tower and the fragment of architectural detail above the loggia have not been noted in any discussion of the castle I have read; the gatehouse has been carefully positioned so as to be of maximum visibility to the south rather than to outsiders approaching from the north). Otherwise the northern gatehouse becomes merely an example of 'architectural conservatism', and the great tower one of 'piecemeal accretion'.

Instead, we have to empathise with the visitor as he moves through the structure, do our best to understand what expectations and associations might have been made with each new twist and turn. For example, we have seen views of the 'rustic' or 'vernacular' set up at several points in the building. Kenilworth is an elite building, but this does not mean that vernacular traditions and the social elements they are associated with are simply ignored or absent. Rather, they are *framed* – that is, they are present, but delimited and acknowledged, I suggest, in part as an act of control. The stable block is a 'play' on the vernacular, but it is the *stable block*, fit for horses and other animals: in an age when common men were akin to the oxen and horses of their master (Hill 1964: 453), this was, an elite visitor might conclude, only appropriate. Similarly, the village green is made part of the view from the loggia steps, but it is placed beyond the garden, visibly on the outside of the castle wall.

Stephen Greenblatt and others have argued that late sixteenth-century literature works in much the same way, acknowledging the dark underside of society and its discontents while delimiting its presence, for example, assigning it to genres of 'the comic' or 'the pastoral'. They suggest that Renaissance texts thus endlessly defer its challenge to the established order: thus inequality is legitimated and the threat of its presence deferred endlessly in the very act of being acknowledged (Greenblatt 1985; Dollimore and Sinfield 1985). I am suggesting here that a large and complex piece of Renaissance architecture works in a parallel manner to such texts.

Leicester and Elizabeth

I have reached this point purely by considering the archaeology of the building – its physical structure, the spatial relationships it embodies, its landscape context – and what ideas and assumptions a contemporary visitor might bring to its fabric. I now want to turn to the documentary associations that we can build up with Kenilworth.

In most cases, we find that these associations add depth and richness to the picture I have painted. In particular, they make some of the associations I have argued for less fanciful and the interpretive leaps less wide, for example, on the question of 'rustic' style and the framing of the vernacular. In particular, they allow the way in which the meanings of the castle are gendered to be explored more fully.

Critics might suggest that what has been written above is all a parlour game, for it is impossible for anyone familiar with late sixteenth-century politics and culture to write of Kenilworth without having a specific visitor and host in mind. The host, the owner of Kenilworth and builder of the recent work, was Robert Dudley, Earl of Leicester, a man of high but precarious social status. Dudley's father had been executed in disgrace but he had been raised to his present position, and granted the castle of Kenilworth, by his visitor. Leicester acquired the property in 1563 but only visited once (1566) before 1568; from 1570 onwards he visited more or less annually (Adams 1995: 26).

And the most famous and celebrated visitor to Kenilworth was not the *he* described above but a *she*. Elizabeth I was a female king, who in her person and body embodied the instability of political and social identities in the Renaissance. Elizabeth represented and embodied both changing attitudes to gender and patriarchy and through her actions consciously manipulated those attitudes; I have already suggested that Elizabeth's 'failure' to build any great palaces of her own was in part a conscious strategy (see Chapter 4).

Elizabeth made several visits to Kenilworth. Documented accounts of her visits add depth and detail to the archaeological description but do not, I think, change it substantially. They do give a clearer hint of Elizabeth's view on her own gender and agency and how we can situate the meanings of the castle within the self-fashioning of both Elizabeth and Leicester. The ceremonies and 'entertainments' were organised by Leicester, and accounts subsequently published as early forms of propaganda.

Elizabeth arrived on the most famous occasion in the early evening of 9 July 1575. She was welcomed by Hercules, complete with club and keys to the gate. As Elizabeth crossed the causeway the Lady of the Lake emerged from the mere. The Lady gave a potted history of the Castle and emphasised its ancient origins in the process of declaring that this is the first time since the days of Arthur that she had chosen to emerge from the lake. (In one account the Lady starts by describing herself as the mistress of the lake. Elizabeth interrupts, remarking dryly that as Queen she was actually the mistress of the lake, whereupon the Lady, probably being played by a boy or young man, retreats in some confusion.) Gifts for Elizabeth were placed along the sides of the Causeway, each alluding to a different Classical deity. As Elizabeth entered the Castle, the blue and gilt clock that stood on the corner of Caesar's Tower was stopped – during her visit, Leicester had decreed that time was to stand still. During the rest of her visit, Elizabeth stayed indoors till five in the afternoon. An account given by a male author remarks that this was due to her frail nature and the extreme heat of the summer, but goes on to mention that she was strong enough to get through enough administrative business to necessitate the arrival and departure of twenty horses a day carrying paperwork to and from her secretariat.

We also perceive Leicester's fashioning of himself and his ancient castle in more detail through the documents, though again the documents amplify rather than alter the archaeology. At a literal level, the language of much of the Kenilworth festivities is one of courtship – Leicester urging Elizabeth to marry; implicitly he is urging his own hand in marriage. Leicester was, however, already married, and the subsequent mystery surrounding the death of his wife Amy Robsart only served to render such a match an impossibility. In any case, at least one of Gascoigne's homilies on the virtues of marriage was never performed, possibly due to the displeasure of the Queen who a few years later was to issue a 'Statute of Silence' forbidding public discussion of her possible marriage (Wall 1995: 134). The cultural resonances of the festivities and the architecture can be traced more widely, however. Leicester was a committed Protestant, anxious to aggressively pursue a new culture and set of political and cultural interests. He did so at home through association with a court culture that included the Protestant poet Philip Sidney. Sidney was himself an owner of the medieval pile of Penshurst Place, recently extended and altered. Sidney's writings express in nascent form the more fully developed colonial themes of the Anglo-Irish poet Spenser – they certainly supported an active, militant Protestantism which re-cast values of chivalry in the service of a Protestant state and queen (Skretowicz 1990). Elizabeth herself rejected much of this militant self-fashioning (Sinfield 1992: 184–5). Leicester translated his Protestantism into foreign policy, leading military ventures against Spain into the Low Countries in the 1580s; here, he was met with civic and other ceremonies every bit as complex as those he had already provided for Elizabeth, though the expedition led to ultimate political failure (Strong and van Dorsten 1964).

Leicester's gatehouse, in its conscious archaism and use of battlements alluded in part to this cluster of elite male self-images of Protestant chivalry. In contemporary paintings and literature articulating this set of values, the figure of Elizabeth took over the symbolic position of the Catholic image of the Virgin Mary. These self-images were to be developed further in succeeding decades, most obviously in Spenser's *Faerie Queen* (Hackett 1994). At the same time, Elizabeth also takes the position of another medieval and chivalric image – the female, passive, unattainable object of courtly love, desired yet never attained by the male knight stricken with desire. Contemporary fashions in literature suggest that the vernacular style of the stable block is a deliberate play on these values through a parallel construction of 'the rustic'; the elaborate braces (Figure 5.11) may be a representation of Leicester's emblem of the 'ragged staff', as the white bears in the garden were another of his devices (Morley *et al.* 1995).

Kenilworth, then, acts as a stage setting. Popular tradition has it that the Kenilworth festivities inspired much of the imagery and allusion of Shakespeare's *A Midsummer Night's Dream*. This is unlikely, given that Shakespeare would have been eleven in 1575 and there is no evidence of him being present at Kenilworth (Fenton 1999: 59), but the tradition conceals a deeper truth. Kenilworth stages Elizabeth's identity as a female king; it creates a complex image of its owner, Leicester, as simultaneously old and ancient and new and modern; it alludes to a series of symbols and images connected with the development of the Tudor State, a Protestant 'national' religion, and even to nascent colonialism. Gascoigne's poems for the festivities were published and used as Tudor propaganda. The production of this propaganda was itself shot through with tension (Wall 1995).

The analysis of Kenilworth could be extended for many pages. A full analysis would have to examine the portrayal of Elizabeth as a specifically Protestant queen, and the role of Protestantism in the self-fashioning of the male knights implicated in the gatehouse; the political career of Leicester, who had possibly been Elizabeth's lover, and was now still seeking her hand in marriage though married himself (Doran 1996: 40–72). However, I want to conclude my analysis of Kenilworth by looking at one particular aspect – the (re)construction of the deerparks, and the social construction of the 'wild man' who dwelt in them.

Taming wildness

The landscape beyond and around the castle was one of deerparks, vast hunting grounds. They were full of trees, but were hardly natural; enclosed by park pales and backed up by a judicial apparatus that handed down the most severe retribution to ordinary folk found within their boundaries. A sixteenth-century Warwickshire survey referred to the trees not as elements of a 'natural' landscape, but in terms of their human use, as building members for houses (rafters, joists, purlins: Smith 1980). Like everything else at Kenilworth, then, the natural or pastoral world the deerparks alluded to, was in fact carefully constructed with reference to contemporary social and political themes.

Contemporary pageants and iconography portrayed Elizabeth (among many other images) as Diana, goddess of hunting. This association was rendered all the more powerful by its play on Elizabeth's gender, and could even have nationalistic overtones as well. Philippa Berry comments:

> In the literary discourse of French Renaissance absolutism, Diana, as an idealised representation of the French nation, was subordinated (at least in theory) to the authority of the male monarch as her lover/consort. But as is clear from her developing association with nature in courtly literature, Elizabeth emblematised the state which she also ruled. Her role as an earthly incarnation of the immortal body politic of England was used to emphasise the corporate identity of the state ... This political metaphor was given a specific application within the discourse of Elizabethan courtiership, where representations of the queen as the centre and source of an evergreen pastoral world were used to affirm the existence of a 'natural' order.
>
> (1995: 84)

Gascoigne's accounts of Elizabeth's time in the deerparks of Kenilworth makes some of these associations clear (Cunliffe 1910: 96–101). At one point, Elizabeth is met by a Green, Wild or Savage Man, a familiar and traditional figure from medieval imagery; he is often depicted in images found in churches and other structures across Europe as covered with hair, as well as moss or ivy. In medieval texts, the Wild Man often represents the base inner instincts that the chivalrous knight strives to keep under control. By the late sixteenth century, however, the image of the Savage Man had become associated with the Classical tradition of pastoral, and also with that of emergent colonialism (natives both of Ireland and of North America were seen as wild, untamed, in need of order and control). Elizabeth's 'Hombre Salvagio' presents himself as a wanderer; he pledges the loyalty of himself and men like him to the Queen.

The deerparks of Kenilworth were of medieval origin. Fragments of their boundaries, and of the earthworks associated with the mere, remain at various points around the landscape to the west of the castle; though largely destroyed, enough remains to indicate their massive nature. There is also a house destroyed in the last war attributed to Leicester and identified as a hunting lodge (OS records, SP27 SE5). Before it was pulled down, the initials RL (Robert Earl of Leicester) were identified over the doorway.

Yet these ancient deerparks came to act as backdrop and stage setting for the formation of distinctly modern identities – discourses of gender, of colonialism, of an idealised version of the countryside, of the threat of a rootless lower social order, 'masterless men'. And the architecture of the castle, the experiences of space which it set up and framed, the combination of ancient and modern, the careful construction of views, played a central role in this construction. If we want to understand the archaeology of Kenilworth, we need to look at the social identities of its inhabitants; but if we want to understand those social identities, we must inevitably return to the archaeology of the buildings and the landscape beyond.

Conclusion

Every generation gets the Kenilworth it deserves. Fifty years after our imaginary and Elizabeth's real visits to the castle, Kenilworth had a less welcome set of visitors; Oliver Cromwell's army. The north side of Caesar's Tower was blown up by Parliamentary gunpowder (Figure 5.15). The view from the terrace north of Caesar's Tower may have 'framed' the village beyond, but the gunpowder wielded to such effect by Cromwellian troops, themselves in the main hailing from socially middling backgrounds, certainly did more than merely 'frame' Kenilworth; it destroyed it as a residence, rendered it uninhabitable. In 1649 the mere was drained, leaving the castle as it is now, high and dry amidst an unspectacular Midlands landscape of fields and hedges.

The red ruins, of course, live on; Sir Walter Scott's eponymous Romantic novel *Kenilworth* retold much of the story of Amy Robsart and the rest, albeit in the spirit of impenetrable Victorian sentimentality (I have tried several times to read this book, but have never been able to get farther than the first few pages of stolid yeomen). Impenetrable to us it may be, but it is Scott's *Kenilworth* that inflamed the minds of Victorian visitors, as Oakley's guide, dated 1886 and priced 6d, testifies:

> This lordly place, where princes feasted and heroes fought – now in the bloody earnest of storm and siege and now in the games of chivalry, where beauty dealt the prize which valour won – all is now desolate. The bed of the lake is now verdant meadows, and the massive ruins of the castle only serve to show what their splendour once was, and to impress on the musing visitor the transitory value of human possessions. Seldom did a fabric of such unequalled strength and splendour perish so ingloriously. From the time of Cromwell its history is that of gradual decay and final ruin . . . Desolation would probably have gone on for ages; the stones of Kenilworth would still have mended roads and been built into the cowshed and the cottage; and the ploughshare might have passed through the grassy courts; but, some seventy years ago, a man of middle age, with lofty forehead and a keen grey eye, slightly lame but withal active, entered its gatehouse and passed many silent hours within its walls. That man was 'Walter Scott'. Then was the ruined place henceforward to be sanctified. The progress of desolation was to be arrested; the torch of genius again lighted up the spacious pile; visions of sorrow and suffering, of woman's weakness and man's treachery, all were to be for ever after associated with recollections of ancient splendour.
>
> (Oakley 1886: 8)

This century, intermittent attempts have been made to re-flood the mere. On film, the Hollywood blockbuster, swashbuckler and love story *Elizabeth and Leicester* has been succeeded by the post-feminist (and arguably post-colonial) *Elizabeth*; the castle features in both as a backdrop, in the latter film being represented by a digitally enhanced Alnwick.

Last year I took a public tour of the castle; the English Heritage-sponsored guide informed us that if we wanted to understand what we were looking at, we had to think of it as the medieval counterpart of the burnt-out shell of an Iraqi tank. Myths can be comprehensively academically discredited yet still live on, not only in Hollywood.

6

BEYOND THE PALE

So far, this book has dealt with a very small section of late medieval and Renaissance society, namely the elite: barely more than 7,000 families even if the most all-inclusive definition of the higher status levels is taken (see Chapter 3). If, however, we are to give a full answer to the questions 'What did these buildings mean? And how did those meanings change over time?' we must obviously address those outside these 7,000 families – those who lived outside the park pale, who in the main, save on specific ceremonial occasions, were denied access to the castle and its estates.

What did buildings such as castles mean to people of the middling and lower sort? And further, since we have argued that castles were about culture and power, how were their reactions bound up with changing patterns of culture and power in the late medieval and Renaissance periods?

'Resistance' has become a fashionable concept in historical archaeology (cf. Frazer 1999; Johnson 1999). It has been pointed out that archaeologists have become very good at finding patterns of domination in material artefacts and buildings: how this castle or that Georgian house represented and reinforced dominant values. It has been stressed, however, that this is only one side of the picture. Only the most reactionary scholar would argue that ordinary people in the past were mute, passive objects incapable of articulating or acting on their own views of the world. People were active agents, even if the forces of domination they encountered were exceptionally powerful. They may not have written their views down directly for the benefit of documentary historians, and resistance may have been at the level of everyday activity rather than consciously articulated, but they had their own views nevertheless.

We have a variety of different sources of evidence to bear on the ideas and attitudes of ordinary people towards castles, palaces and the elites who lived in them. We have some indirect evidence through textual records compiled by the literate elite, both of people's attitudes and also records of the actions they took to express their attitudes. More fundamentally, we have the things these ordinary people created, in part as expressions of their view of the world and their place in it. In other words, we have the buildings they lived in themselves – excavated and standing peasant houses – as well as the surrounding landscapes that they in part created, and the artefacts they made, used and threw away as they inhabited those buildings and landscapes. There is, then, no shortage of evidence.

And yet, the examination of the ideas and attitudes of ordinary people is often thought to be fraught with difficulty. The methodological problems of the documents are stressed – how can we rely on biased, second-hand accounts written by members of the literate elite as authentic evidence? How can a medieval peasant house, the name of whose owner we do not even know, be taken as evidence of a particular mentality or world-view? Aren't ways of peasant building 'just traditional' or heavily constrained by the region and environment – how can such simple, apparently functional actions as a yeoman building a new dairy on the end of his house possibly be interpreted as an act of resistance, a subversive commentary on the great house down the road? Isn't it fanciful, even tendentious, to read expressions of a world-view into a landscape when 'fields are primarily about farming' (Williamson 2000: 58)?

I am going to suggest in this chapter that the difficulty in piecing together non-literate attitudes and actions towards elite buildings and people lies not in the evidence, but in the restrictive ideas and attitudes that we as modern scholars bring to that evidence. Looking for resistance is only a 'problem' while we regard certain other models as *not* a problem, much as feminist historians have argued that the task of looking for women's attitudes in the past is only a 'problem' while we take androcentric attitudes for granted (Jardine 1996a; Johnson 1999: 119–21).

Breaking down fences

There is, in fact, an abundance of documentary evidence for the attitudes of ordinary people to castles and the estates surrounding them. Isobel Harvey has identified four factors in popular attitudes in the late Middle Ages, which she identifies as a period of rising self-confidence among the peasant classes. First, ordinary men were needed to fight. Since the late thirteenth century, all men below the rank of knight or esquire had to be armed, and trained in the use of arms. Most famously, men were required to practise archery on Sundays. Second, they were all taxed. Third, they remembered the precedent of the 1381 protests, which started as a protest against the hated Poll Tax, whose principle of all men paying the same tax was manifestly unfair. The 1381 protests

> established a blueprint for the conduct of a regional uprising. The procedure was to rouse the counties of the South-East to ride upon London, pitch camp at Blackheath and then enter London where the king was to be petitioned and his evil counsellors slaughtered.
>
> (Harvey 1995: 166)

Fourth, ordinary people were conscious of bitter dynastic conflict at the apex of society. This visible conflict between different elements of the ruling classes loosened vertical bonds of loyalty between servant and master, tenant and lord. As a result, during the fifteenth-century Wars of the Roses, popular support had to be actively wooed by the elite protagonists, not expected as a concomitant of feudal ties.

And ordinary people were capable of a range of political actions that ranged from quite drastic forms to petty vandalism and poaching. This frequently took the form of opposition to the elite landscapes so frequently mentioned in previous pages. In 1447 the bishop of Chichester gained a royal licence to impark 12,000 acres of land, wood, meadow, heath and furze in Sussex. Three years later he was killed by the mob, an action which suggests that Thompson's (1998: 8) view of bishops as respected figures akin to senior civil servants today is rather over-generalised. More everyday resistance included the destruction of fences, poaching and trespass, and assaults on park keepers. The park at Somersham featured in Chapter 3 had its hay burnt in 1301, and its fences burnt in 1306; this did not stop the bishop from enlarging the park in 1390 (Way 1997: 154).

The boundary between illegal poaching and hunting by night, and popular protest and sedition on the other, was impossible to draw. The 1485 Act of Parliament noted 'how persons in great number had often times hunted by night as by day in divers forests, parks and warrens by colour whereof rebellions, insurrections, riots, robberies and murders ensued' (cited in Harvey 1995: 163). The mob routinely intervened in politics, leading to the death of unpopular leaders such as the bishops of Chichester and Salisbury, Lord Scales, and the Earl of Salisbury. Parliament was repeatedly petitioned; the way these petitions were drawn up reveals a degree of political sophistication, using the language of tradition to the king in an effort to redress grievances.

Given all this evidence, the attitude of traditional historians is somewhat surprising. Harvey (1995) states with absolute confidence that 'there was no popular politics in 15th-century England', though she qualifies this by stating that 'popular politics is not understood to mean popular political goals or a set of agenda distinct from those of the ruling class'. This is a revealing statement of traditional historical method.

I suggest that it is not surprising that 'popular political goals or set of agenda' were so *little* articulated. It is rather surprising how *much* evidence there is for political thinking and action at middling and lower social levels. First, much of the documentary evidence habitually used by historians is based on court records. The late medieval and early modern periods were ages when subversive attitudes attracted the unfavourable attention of the authorities. Unfavourable reference to the monarchy, to the established Church, to the local lord, even in the most casual conversation, could land one in front of the magistrates facing the prospect of legal and physical sanctions. By the early seventeenth century a young woman's derisive but apparently casual statement that her minister's sermons were 'such a deale of bibble babble that I am weary to heare yt and I can then sitt downe in my seat and take a good nap' led to her appearance in court and hence the documentary record of her comment (cited in Wrightson 1982). Christopher Hill has shown how when sanctions were removed, during the brief break in censorship of the English Revolution, all sorts of radical and subversive ideas bubbled to the surface; Hill (1972) argues that many of these mid-seventeenth-century ideas represent continuity from ideas articulated in the late fourteenth-century peasant revolts. Chris Evans has explored in detail how oral traditions and stories did articulate resistance to enclosure and drainage of the Fenland. That we know of these stories is, however, a geographical accident, namely the proximity of the Fens to the University of Cambridge and hence academic interest in recording and publishing these stories (Evans 1997).

The absence of anything that might qualify on the historical definition as 'popular politics', then, is merely testament to the fact that court inquisitions could not find witnesses to such attitudes. This proves only that peasants and other ordinary people sensibly kept their attitudes to themselves, whatever they were, or that what was said in the alehouse was not repeated in the courts.

Second, it is difficult to point to a formalised political code at the top of society in late medieval England. In contrast to later periods, there is little overt discourse beyond a world-view implicit in values of chivalry, advice to lords and comments on what constitutes 'good lordship' and loyalty, and entreaties to high standards of honour and personal conduct, for example, in didactic 'courtesy books'. These do not add up to a formal political position such as those articulated by Machiavelli or later Renaissance writers. In asking for written evidence of such a formal, overtly stated position from the peasantry, then, we are asking for something historians have not required from their late medieval social superiors.

This second point leads us to revisit an argument developed in Chapter 4: a fundamental division between the medieval and Renaissance worlds. The Renaissance sees the production of printed maps, of ideas of the nation-state, and secularised ideas of political discourse. At the risk of over-generalization, these are largely absent from the medieval way of doing things. But as Helgerson has pointed out, once the map and the idea of the nation-state have been produced, this technological apparatus can become double-edged, and work against the monarchy and nobility. The map makes an idea of 'the nation' separate and independent from the individuals and dynasties at its apex possible. People of all social levels, then, can see their loyalty as being to a nation, rather than to a particular individual or family. In Helgerson's view, this division comes to structure the battle lines of the English Revolution. A king can be beheaded for disloyalty to a 'nation' conceived of as over and above the body of the monarch (Helgerson 1992).

Generations before and after the late Middle Ages, popular protest was formally articulated into alternative ways of organising society. The 1381 risings did see an alternative political vision being articulated (Hilton 1973). Elite fear of this vision casts a long and dark shadow over the fifteenth century, even if it was rarely overtly mentioned. The demonstrative nature of Caister Castle must be set against the backdrop of folk memories of the destruction of the manor house there during the troubles of the 1380s (see Chapter 2). And of course, towards the end of our period of interest, we see all sorts of radical ideas surfacing in the 1640s (Hill 1972). That there is little evidence of it having happened between these two dates is simply testament to the implicit nature of much political discourse and the (short-term) effectiveness of mechanisms of repression.

Social emulation

If ordinary people were not necessarily following the accepted political order, with no clearly articulated world-view of their own, neither were they necessarily trying to 'ape', copy or emulate their social betters.

The idea that much of architecture and material culture in this period is the result of attempted emulation of the elite is a popular one, particularly when applied to the socially middling classes. Archaeologists have used such terms to explain changes in houses, artefacts used in dining, and patterns of dress. Ideas of emulation are often expressed implicitly in reference to features of architecture and material culture 'filtering down' the social scale.

Such a view has a number of strengths. First, it resonates with much of what we know of late medieval and Renaissance England. England between 1400 and 1700 was indeed a very status-conscious society, and physical forms such as dress, furnishings and architecture played a pivotal role in defining that status. Second, there are undeniable features of architecture and material culture that do indeed appear first at the apex of society, and only appear at middling and lower social levels much later. Third, there is clear documentary evidence of contemporary concern about the social status of certain goods in the form of sumptuary legislation. Sumptuary laws were a series of statutes enacted from the late fourteenth century onwards that laid down prescriptive rules for a wide range of material culture, most obviously dress. The fact that sumptuary legislation almost never worked (few people were prosecuted and most laws seem to have been largely ignored) also suggests that people strove hard against the conventional rules of status and its expressions in dress and mode of life. Concern about the breaking of codes and social status is clearly manifested in the fifteenth and sixteenth centuries. Social commentators complained of ordinary people 'aping' their social superiors (Hinton 1999: 177). Fourth, the idea that there was a degree of social mobility in England, in particular an 'open elite', was one that was extensively discussed by contemporary commentators (Stone and Stone 1984).

However, I think that there are a series of problems with the idea of social emulation that archaeologists should consider very carefully before applying the concept to this period. In parallel to criticisms of geographical diffusion, stress on emulation tends to relegate the action to the wings rather than place it at centre stage. In other words, instead of archaeologists explaining the adoption of new goods and lifestyles in terms of people thinking and acting in their own world, we simply see the borrowing of traits from their social betters. Even if people did this, it begs the question of choice – why did ordinary people choose to do so? Why did they choose certain traits and ignore others? If 'fashion' is not trivial, as we argued in Chapter 4, then the decision to follow certain trends rather than others is itself not trivial.

For if some elements were clearly borrowed from the higher social orders, others were resolutely ignored. Vernacular architectural style remains resolutely vernacular up till the early eighteenth century. This preference on the part of the middling sort for vernacular design is not a matter of lack of knowledge of other architectural models or of the assumed 'innate conservatism' of craft tradition. The peasants of Kenilworth had a series of up-to-date Classical models of architecture on their doorstep, and their houses displayed innovative features of their own. Yet they chose to adopt none of the Classical features of Leicester's additions. Instead, their houses remain relentlessly 'vernacular', with exposed square framing and cruck construction (Figure 5.13). When the craft tradition could change, it often did so very quickly and introduced innovations before parallel developments at higher social levels. For example, Sarah Pearson (1994) has pointed out that the open hall was abandoned and new house forms adopted more quickly at middling than at upper social levels in rural Kent, possibly because groups of lesser social status did not need the hall for formal ceremonial purposes.

Colin Campbell has subjected notions of social emulation, as deployed in eighteenth-century studies, to a pithy critique which in my view is equally applicable to earlier periods. He writes:

> The prevailing assumption has been that particular sections of the population of England revised their consumption patterns at this time as a consequence of a new willingness to give expression to their desire to be regarded as equal in social standing to those who were their acknowledged social superiors.

However, 'the mistake made is the failure to recognise that any one observed pattern of conduct is actually consistent with a variety of subjective meanings', a comment we could extend to the practice of non-elite building also (Campbell 1993: 40, 41). The social 'trickle-down' of goods or of architectural ideas does not necessarily imply imitative behaviour; the new pottery forms or window styles could be desired for their own sake. Even if it was imitative, this does not imply it was emulative. As we suggested for the meanings of castles and houses in earlier chapters, there may be a diversity of meanings behind the one pattern.

That the upper classes assumed that adoption of elite forms of material culture was emulative and therefore threatening, and legislated against it or mocked it as 'aping', only tells us about elite attitudes. When Thomas Starkey and others complained about men building above their 'state condition and degree' (cited in Howard 1990: 213), these complaints tell us only of the feelings of anxiety of those at the top of the social scale. This anxiety is interesting in itself, but it tells us nothing about what the motivations were of those lower down the social scale.

More fundamentally, 'emulation' is itself an interpretation of an activity that, like the use of the terms 'conspicuous consumption' or 'display', appears familiar and obvious to the modern scholar but actually conceals hidden depths. Apparent emulation could be a desire to rival in fashion, to impress social peers, to dupe social superiors, or because the adoption of an upper-class way of life is an ideal in its own right. Campbell cites the eighteenth-century ideal of gentility in this regard, but we could as easily cite that of late medieval 'gentilesse' or that of chivalry. In this respect, the easy familiarity of ideas of competitive emulation and conspicuous consumption are a weakness, since they encourage us to elide these different factors.

If the social emulation model worked, we would expect Sir Thomas Hungerford, Speaker of the House of Commons in 1377 and attendant on John of Gaunt at Kenilworth, to build in emulation of his master, especially as Gaunt had just refitted his castle with a magnificent suite of apartments. But he did not. Sir Thomas chose a quadrangular plan for his castle at Farleigh Hungerford in Somerset, more like Cooling at least in external appearance with four angle towers. Each tower was too small to have a parapet of its own. The outer walls encased an earlier manor house of traditional plan centred on a hall and cross-passage.

What we are really looking at, then, is a very complex pattern of changes in material culture and architecture between the fourteenth and the seventeenth centuries. One possible explanation of some of this pattern is emulation, but it is not the only one. And if the architecture and material items that ordinary people bought and chose are not evidence of a mad rush to emulate social betters, it might tell us about other things, such as their own view of their own world.

Building up houses

Peasant housing of the late medieval and Renaissance periods in England is now very well known. We have thousands of standing structures, still inhabited, that have been well studied by a generation of scholars of vernacular architecture; indeed, one commentator has recently suggested that the study of 'polite' buildings such as castles have been neglected as a result of this

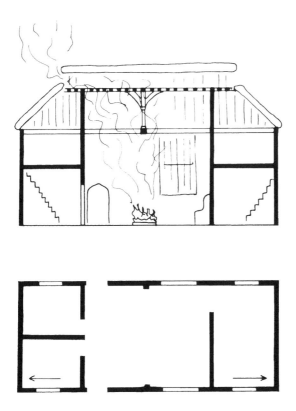

Figure 6.1 The late medieval vernacular hall: compare with the layout of high status halls
(cf. Figures 2.2, 3.5, 4.4). (After Johnson 1993: 43.)

concentration on the vernacular (Emery 1996: 2). There are continuing questions concerning which social levels inhabited these houses, in particular
whether they represent dwellings of the middling sort or a broader span of
the peasant population. A related question is to what extent the houses that
survive comprise a representative sample of those that originally stood (Currie
1988; Johnson 1997: 146). In particular, standing peasant houses dating
from before 1500 are rare outside the south and east of England; there is a
particular concentration in Suffolk, Essex, the Home Counties, Kent, Sussex
and the West Country. Interestingly, it is these areas that were the home-
lands of fifteenth-century peasant protest.

The form of these houses bears striking parallels to the form of the late
medieval hall discussed in Chapter 3 (Figure 6.1). In almost all cases the
familiar elements of opposed doors or screens passage at the lower end of the
hall, window lighting the upper end, door to chamber beyond the upper
end, doors to service areas at the lower end, are here also. We might infer

therefore that elements of the same system of social and cultural meaning are here also. Certainly, features replicating the same effects are found here. For example, though there may not be a raised dais end, peg-holes in the timber framing of the upper end of the hall often reveal that a bench for the master of the house was fixed against the wall here; and timbers are routinely 'faced in' as they are in higher-status structures.

Does this therefore mean that the hall is an example of social emulation? I suggest that it does not. Following Campbell, there is plenty of evidence to suggest a common pattern, but the culture and motivations behind this common pattern have a number of explanations. I suggest that rather what we see in these common architectural forms is an expression of common principles of power and authority running up and down the social scale. Walking in to the lower end of John of Gaunt's hall at Kenilworth, Thomas Hungerford knew how to behave through the familiar visual cues. His own hall contained these cues and his own house was arranged on the same pattern, albeit on a much smaller scale and within an *enceinte* of different form. He expected his 'men' – servants, retainers, local tenants – to show the same deference to him in his hall as he did to Gaunt at Kenilworth. And his retainers and local tenants, walking in to the hall at Farleigh Hungerford, recognised the pattern also, for it was the same as in their own smaller halls scattered across the Somerset countryside. The hall, then, and the arrangement of rooms off it, acted as a leitmotif for late medieval society, running across social levels from royalty to gentry and socially middling groups; even the excavated remains of quite humble peasant dwellings on the heathlands of Dartmoor exhibit the same elements (Austin and Thomas 1990: 54).

I suggest, then, that the power of the hall lay in its context. It acted as a system of cultural cross-referencing. In this sense the form of the hall goes alongside other systems of architectural cross-referencing we noted in Chapter 4, those of crenellation or military cross-referencing and religious use of castle motifs.

The common structure of the hall also goes alongside other landscape practices that suggest a common set of architectural and social practices. Many socially middling farmers surrounded their houses with moats (Figure 6.2). These moats may have been first dug out in the twelfth and thirteenth centuries, and may have had their origins in other considerations, the need to drain clayland, for example. However, like castle moats, these bodies of water were often carefully maintained and may have come to have quite other meanings by the late Middle Ages. Where they have not been interpreted as purely functional, these moats have been interpreted as markers of 'status'. Again, however, I suggest that their meanings are more complex than this.

All of these architectural elements elicited customary or expected actions, standardised modes of behaviour of the sort we examined in Chapter 3. These standardised modes of behaviour – access or lack of access to certain spaces, movement between the lower and upper end of the hall, the expression of

Figure 6.2 A moated site at Pampisford near Cambridge.

deference – were the linchpin of late medieval social forms, and were articulated and expressed through the use of space in certain ways. They articulated the vertical social relationships between lord and subject, even as those relationships came under strain. I suggest, however, that they were to break down quite fundamentally in the sixteenth century.

Rebuilding social relations

It is now well established that the open hall was lost from peasant housing in the sixteenth century, and that the reasons for this loss were at least partly social ones. Specifically, the loss of the open hall was tied to the changes in certain social values within the sixteenth-century family and household (Mercer 1975; Johnson 1993). What I want to do now is ask what this loss of architectural cross-referencing implied about relations between households up and down the social scale.

The new pattern in which halls had a ceiling rather than being open to the roof, and in which the open hearth was finally abandoned, was not one which started at the top social level and diffused downwards. The very highest levels of the elite were building open halls well into the sixteenth century, for example, at Hampton Court. These halls moreover were of exceptional size and scale. At the same time, socially middling farmers and cloth workers in Kent, Essex and Suffolk were building houses with chimneys and ceilings from at least *c.*1500 onwards (Johnson 1993: 87).

The long-term change in *form* – the abandonment of the hall – went with a long-term change in *pattern of building* – the construction of more permanent, well-appointed peasant farmhouses, of a standard that has enabled many of them to survive to the present day. It is a matter of some controversy what the precise chronology of this process is, and whether it was a long steady process or the narrower Great Rebuilding of 1560–1640 suggested by Hoskins (1953), but what I want to stress here is that by 1640 very different forms of peasant houses were appearing over much of England, a much larger area than that defined for late medieval houses.

These new houses were of a sort that no longer followed the grammatical rules of the open hall. All had chimney-stacks and ceilings, which reduced the size and visual impact of the hall, and increased the amount of living-space upstairs, away from the front doors. Many had lobby entries, so that entry to the house was no longer straight into the hall space. As a result, a socially middling farmer of the early seventeenth century, walking into an elite structure built by Inigo Jones, might well find its architectural organisation quite alien to him.

I am suggesting then that sixteenth- and seventeenth-century peasant rebuilding represented a loss of a common vocabulary of architecture. This loss ran in parallel to, and was just as fundamental as, the loss of architectural cross-referencing represented by artillery fortification and the Reformation discussed in Chapter 4. I am also suggesting that this was as much an active choice by the peasant classes themselves as one imposed on them. Late fifteenth-century open-hall houses and sixteenth-century 'closed' houses represent broadly similar investments of resources; the major difference is in their form. Yeomen and husbandmen *chose* to abandon traditional forms of architecture. The result was a much sharper division between the architectural forms of different social classes, elite and non-elite.

Polite and vernacular

It is this sharp division that is expressed in the division in modern scholarship between 'polite' and 'vernacular' traditions of building. 'Polite' architecture is the central theme of this book: large buildings built by the elite, of national or international importance, employing professional masons who work to a written plan. 'Vernacular' or 'traditional' building, on the other hand, encompasses small or medium-sized buildings built by ordinary people, using semi-professional builders who bring unwritten assumptions of traditional or customary practice to their work.

Clearly these definitions are over-simplified, or represent opposite ends of a spectrum of building practice in which, for example, gentry houses might occupy a position in the middle. Further, ideas of what is or is not polite and vernacular are dialectical: that is, they can only be defined one against the other within a specific historical period.

The sixteenth century marked a decisive shift in the relationship between polite and vernacular buildings. After this date, and until the phenomenon of 'Georgianisation' of the mid-eighteenth century, ordinary buildings might be well constructed, indicative of a certain level of affluence or 'solid sufficiency', and yet of a style and design that clearly marked them off from their social superiors. The illiterate men who built them were expressing a self-confidence in their idea of culture and their view of the world. They built houses, enclosed and improved their fields, and sent their sons to the local grammar school to learn to read and write. As such, vernacular buildings were a statement of class identity before the term 'class identity' was born.

Articulating anxieties

A whole series of overtly articulated ideas rushed in to fill this growing gap between polite and vernacular. What before was taken for granted was now a problem, to be agonised over in poetry, treatises on the manor, and conduct books.

The country house genre of poetry flourished in the decades either side of 1600. It routinely idealised a system of social values characterised by the late medieval castle or great house – the large household, hospitality, meals in the great hall. But it did so in the very act of affirming that this system was threatened. This is most obvious in Ben Jonson's famous 'To Penshurst', where Penshurst is praised for *not* being one of the new species of house of spectacular new architecture and lack of hospitality. In treatises on manorial organisation and farming techniques, traditional practice is for the first time articulated and therefore constituted as a problem – a problem, moreover, that is as much social and ideological as it is economic (Johnson 1996). It should not surprise us to see a social system articulated most coherently at the moment of its dissolution – it is at precisely that moment that its ideas and assumptions cease to be so obvious and taken-for-granted that they need to be expressed overtly. And it is also articulated at a moment of sharp class antagonism. Thomas Lever boomed from the pulpit in 1550 that 'the chief cause why the commons does not love, trust, nor obey the gentlemen and the officers, is because the gentlemen and the officers build many fair houses and keep few good ones' (cited in Thomson 1993: 38).

It is interesting to note that in these discourses, the image of the castle played an increasingly prominent role. Castles became idealised as the 'Englishman's home', in part as a symbol of the free-born Englishman's rights, in part as a symbol of patriarchal order within the household itself. Richard Brathwaite thundered: 'As every man's house is his castle, so is his family a private commonwealth, wherein if due government be not observed nothing but confusion is to be expected' (Amussen 1988: 37). So even as the cultural systems that went with castles were *cracking apart*, so the allusive, symbolic image of the castle was being *set up*. However, the castle image was just that, an image. Crenellation was now an allusion, a metaphor – it no longer held any reality.

This allusive quality can be seen in late sixteenth- and seventeenth-century 'castles' themselves. Buildings like Lulworth, Bolsover and Sherborne, and Leicester's gatehouse at Kenilworth, referred to a medieval past, but it was the past, and as such something to be referred to and played upon, just like the gatehouse at Kenilworth.

Destroying anxieties

By the 1640s, these anxieties had emerged into open conflict, in revolution and civil war. Most destruction during the civil wars was the by-product of military campaigns (Porter 1994). However, towards the end of that conflict, much damage was quite deliberate. The victory of the middling sort of people, and more broadly of new ideas of moral and political order, was expressed in the 'slighting' or destruction of castles.

The slighting of castles is usually presented as one of the hazards of war, as a contingent political event related to military necessity. So many castles had been centres of Royalist resistance to Parliament, and were the focus of tedious and wearing sieges in the latter stages of the Civil War. Parliamentarian victory was delayed by frustrating siege after siege. It is hardly surprising then that after the end of the conflict, many castles were 'slighted' or partly destroyed by order of Parliament. But as we have seen throughout this book, cultural actions are more complex than this.

In the first place, destruction of castles was not a purely contingent event. The destruction of private or civic medieval fortifications occurred in parallel with England in other early modern European states, for example, early seventeenth-century France. Private strongholds were real and symbolic threats to the new Renaissance state; city walls symbolised political independence, and the destruction of such walls represented the subordination of city rights to that of the nation-state. The French royal edict of 1626 reveals a complex set of State and popular impulses behind this destruction:

> Whereas formerly the assemblies of the estates of this realm and those of notable persons chosen to give advice to ourselves, and to the late king, our very honourable lord and father, on important affairs of this realm, and likewise the assembly of the estates of the province of Brittany held by us in the year 1614, have repeatedly requested and very humbly supplicated our said lord and father and ourselves to cause the demolition of many strongholds in divers places of this realm, which, being neither on hostile frontiers nor in important passes and places, only serve to augment our expenses by

the maintenance of useless garrisons, and also serve as retreats for divers persons who on the least provocation disturb the provinces where they are located; . . . for these reasons, we announce, declare, ordain, and will that all the strongholds, either towns or castles, which are in the interior of our realm or provinces of the same, not situated in places of importance either for frontier defence or other considerations of weight, shall be razed and demolished; even ancient walls shall be destroyed so far as it shall be deemed necessary for the well-being and repose of our subjects and the security of this state, so that our said subjects henceforth need not fear that the said places will cause them any inconvenience, and so that we shall be freed from the expense of supporting garrisons in them.

(Robinson 1906: 180–3)

Second, deliberate destruction of castle fabric was not purely random; rather, it was often directed at particular elements of the castle. At Kenilworth, the outer perimeter of the defences was not touched; instead, the lake was drained, and the north face of the *donjon* was slighted. The slighting of the *donjon* was not particularly relevant from a military perspective, but it was the side of the castle most readily visible to ordinary people, and its most potent symbol of lordship (Figure 5.15). At Raglan, the slighting was turned into a community festival. The Yellow Tower of Gwent, the Herberts' most potent symbol, was first undermined, and, when that failed, attacked with picks; one whole face of the tower was destroyed. Again, the face selected for destruction is the most visible face as one approaches the castle. Meanwhile, local people were summoned to dredge the moat (unsuccessfully) for treasure and to break down the fishponds and take the fat carp (Whittle 1990).

Third, the destruction of castles can be viewed in the context of destruction of other symbols of royal and aristocratic authority. The particularly complete and spectacular slighting of the castle of Corfe, leaving what remains today as a surreal landscape of massive chunks of broken wall standing at every angle save the vertical, has been described by Allen Brown as 'vicious' (1989: 101). Much defacing of aristocratic and royal symbols has been seen as casual violence, but can equally well be seen as considered disrespect. When Parliamentary troops used King Arthur's round table hung in the great royal hall at Winchester as target practice, their chosen targets were the Tudor rose and the face of the king (Biddle 2000: Figure 69).

After the destruction of so many symbols of political authority, there was no shortage of symbols to put in its place. The execution of the king meant that a whole series of items of material culture had to be refashioned; these included the Great Seal of the kingdom, its coinage, its coat of arms. Kelsey (1997) has argued that these produced a new set of forms he terms 'vernacular republicanism'. I suggest that ordinary people would have seen the new coins and other items and the new destruction in the land together, and drawn common conclusions.

Conclusion: architecture and resistance

In this chapter, I have argued that we must look at the ideas and attitudes of ordinary people if we want to produce a full account of the meanings of castles. I argued that the lack of documentary evidence for a distinctive 'popular agenda' did not preclude this need; nor did current stress on ideas of social emulation. I did suggest, however, that late medieval architecture expressed a common set of meanings at different social levels. The breakdown of this code was as much the result of ordinary people making their own architectural and social world as it was driven by the elite. The vacuum created by that failure created the space for the emergence of a whole series of written discourses, in whose anxieties (for example, over the physical and social structure of the manor and over gender and master/servant relations within the household) we can see both domination and resistance, political authority and political subversion. The ultimate authority and subversion occurred in the mid-seventeenth century, when a new form of nation-state and a newly assertive middling sort combined to finally destroy the power of the castle, both culturally and physically. Concomitant with this development was the rise of the castle as an image, whether of household order, political freedom or national pride.

Those 'beyond the pale' had complex and varying attitudes to the great castles of their social and political masters. They reacted in different ways at different times. Any account of late medieval and Renaissance society does it a disservice by seeing it anachronistically as either packed full of eighteenth-century-style robotic social emulators or conversely as a seething mass of nineteenth-century-style class hatred. The texts of this period show such complexity and ambiguity that, for example, unpicking the 'vernacular' social commentary of *Piers Plowman*, or for that matter the representation of the popular crowd in the plays of Shakespeare, has become a major scholarly industry (cf. Gross 1990). We must expect illiterate expressions of social attitudes to be at least as complex and ambiguous.

However complex and ambiguous they were, these expressions can be seen in the material forms of vernacular culture. Difficulties of interpretation are of our own making. The choice of a moat, or of a form of a house, are in their own way implicit commentaries on the relationship of polite and vernacular, and through this on social forms of the period.

7

CONCLUSION
Rethinking castles

Looking back through this book, the reader may conclude that more has been left out of its arguments than is really satisfactory. Only a few selected structures have been discussed. Many buildings of great importance have been largely omitted – Baconsthorpe, Bolsover, Herstmonceux, Sheriff Hutton, Wressle, to name a few.

More fundamentally, the arguments presented here lack a comparative European perspective. Castles were built and rebuilt all across Europe; and the set of changes we discussed in Chapter 4 as part of the 'medieval to Renaissance' tradition have to be understood in a broader context. There is a danger implicit in my arguments here. Though I am suggesting we reject the 'ripples from Italy' model, in part because we need to understand what particular architectural forms meant within local contexts and identities, we should not simply turn our back on the larger geographical scale of developments across Europe. The small-scale and local was important, and has been stressed at different points in this book. What is interesting, however, is not how the smaller scale supplants large-scale 'influence' as a way of understanding castles, but how understanding at the smaller scale enriches our understanding of the larger scale.

Indeed, moving beyond 'ripples from Italy' leaves us in a new and challenging position of being able to look comparatively at different regional and national traditions rather than assuming that one is just the product of diffusion from another. We noted in Chapter 4 how architectural traditions in areas such as Ireland have often been seen as somehow peripheral or secondary, in the Irish case the result of English colonial influence (O'Keeffe 1998; 2000). We might instead begin to develop a comparative understanding of how in different European states different elements came together in different combinations. These elements included: an architectural and artistic vocabulary derived from Classical models, reinterpreted in different ways within different regional and national traditions; new technologies associated with the rise of the nation-state, seen for example in the new forms of artillery fortification and in the destruction of 'private' fortresses; and new social forces.

One of these new social forces was a redefined localism – an active state-ment of local identity, seen, for example, in ordinary people actively choosing and maintaining traditions of vernacular building discussed in the last chapter. These forces interacted in different ways in different locations across Europe; the difference in definitions between building types, for example the different meanings of the French term *château* and the way it does not quite approximate in English either to 'castle' or to 'country house', are artefacts of these different trajectories (Girouard 2000).

The net of comparative analysis needs to be cast wider still, across the Atlantic world as a whole and forward into the early modern period. The idea of the castle enclosure, it can be argued, was transmuted into the 'bawn', the central strongpoint in colonial plantations from Ulster and Munster in Ireland to the Caribbean and Virginia (St. George 1990; Delle 1998). The castle, the bawn and the park pale became metaphors for the divide between them and us, the civilised and the savage. As such, they became symbols that were central to nascent colonialism. If we want to trace an archaeology of practices central to nascent colonialism, we must go back to the later medieval castle. Chapter 6 discussed one of the ceremonial episodes in the deerparks of Kenilworth involving a 'Green Man' showing submission to Queen Elizabeth (Cunliffe 1910); the image of the Green Man can be traced backwards into medieval folk belief and forwards into colonial ideas of the natural savage. Elizabeth's acceptance of the Green Man's submission, set within the oak trees of an ancient deerpark a little way from the red walls of the castle, has been read allegorically as an assumption of the mantle of Empire (Doran 1996; Levin 1994; Helgerson 1992).

Rethinking castles

However, these points comprise a research agenda for the future. What have we learnt in this book? The sceptical reader may argue that we have not learnt very much. Much of the obsession with military explanation to the exclusion of all other factors died a death many years ago. Narrow typolo-gies are largely already out of favour. At the same time, many of the theoretical elements in this book have been common currency in medieval and Renaissance studies for some time. I said at the beginning of this book that I wanted to gather together a series of insights that have been familiar, and present them in a new way. This is what I've done – observations of watery landscapes, critiques that show that military views do not work, analyses of circulation patterns, New Historicist work on the Renaissance; all these elements are familiar enough.

As 'familiar' as they are, how far have recent monographs on castles taken them on board? David Stocker made the point in 1992 that the three recent books he was reviewing made little or no acknowledgement of new perspec-tives on castle studies or on archaeology generally. Ten years later the position has hardly changed. Learned journals carry articles on new ideas, but these do not seem to affect the flow of castle studies, even as rocks thrown into a pool create a large splash but do not affect the water's equilibrium. A flow of recent books have no explicit discussion of theory, and appear to be based largely on a typological approach with little or no reference to contemporary social changes.

So despite the flow of pithy papers, the old myths in castle studies live on. The problem has been echoed by Ronald Hutton in his work on folk customs. Hutton was attacked by folklorists for passing over recent work in folklife studies which, they said, anticipated his criticisms of folklore as a discipline: he was, they claimed, saying nothing new. Yet in the same year he noted the publication of '[the same] theory, not delivered as a refutation of the recent attacks upon it, but as though those attacks had never been made' (Hutton 1997: xi).

A more complex response is to point out that part of the problem with archaeology in the period as a whole remains its under-theorised nature. Because medieval and postmedieval archaeologists in particular are rarely behoved to spell out their underlying theoretical and methodological assumptions to any great extent, contradictions and inconsistencies in their underlying attitudes are difficult to identify, dissect and eliminate. The result of this lack of theorisation is a kind of interpretive doublethink. Scholars can assert that they have looked at 'social' factors for a long time, and that such a perspective is therefore 'nothing new', and yet still place primacy on the military in practice, or adopt some of the implicit models of social diffusion, emulation, or of essentialist thinking discussed in Chapter 4. Doublethink is especially apparent if we contrast 'academic' and 'public' understandings of castles. When someone writes 'we all know that castles had social roles', the 'we' referred to does not include Josie and Joe Public. While researching this book, I came into extended contact with the ideas presented to the public. Kenilworth was explained by an English Heritage-sponsored guide as the burnt-out shell of an Iraqi tank; the Welsh heritage agency Cadw claimed that castles in general and Chepstow in particular were evidence of Man's (*sic*) innate aggression. I have even heard an academic colleague tell a large group of undergraduate students that 'castles are just like cruise missiles'.

What goes for military doublethink goes also for other forms of doublethink. While scholars pay careful attention to the niceties of gender politics in some contexts, particularly after the recent election of Pamela Marshall to the Presidency of the Castle Studies Group, they continue to assume that castle studies are largely the preserve of men. In 1997 the *Castle Studies Group Newsletter* noted that the fact that members at a conference in Denmark 'were made to work hard' and spent little time in the bar would be gladly noted by 'wives left behind' (McNeill 1997b: 6). Doublethink is of course insulated from critique, since the response will be 'yes, but this is not serious academic writing' – as if we did not have a responsibility to be consistent in our academic and public writing, or that what we write for the public is somehow less important than what we write academically.

Of course, many castles played important military roles. No-one practising historical archaeology in north-east England could deny the Border castles' 'military role'. The fifteenth- and sixteenth-century remodelling of northern defences at places like Norham and Berwick could hardly suggest anything else. At Norham, there were sieges by the Scots in 1497 and 1513; much of the outer curtain wall was destroyed in 1513 by bombardment by the great Scottish cannon Mons Meg; though repaired and 'well furnyshed and stuffed with artillery, munitions and other necessaries' again by 1542 Norham was in final decay by the end of the century (Hunter Blair and Honeyman 1985: 19).

However, what is 'military reality'? Whatever it is, it can only be seen in very problematic form in the late Middle Ages. There were elements of pageantry in medieval warfare, and many sieges appear largely formal. The Captain of Warkworth surrendered after only seven shots of Henry IV's siege cannon, a decision that suggests that considerations of honour were primary (O'Neill 1960); the siege of Caerlaverock reads like a mass picnic, however savage its final outcome (Prestwich 1996).

Part of the problem here is that just as we must rethink easy and familiar terms like 'display' or 'defence', so we must rethink the nature of war in the Middle Ages. In reviewing the whole sweep of experiences of medieval war, we often simply select out and mark as authentic and 'real' those elements of medieval warfare that appear as authentic to us; and authenticity, for us, is the horror of total mechanised war. Thus Michael Prestwich (1996: 12) selects as 'real' a passage from the medieval chronicles which sounds to us like a World War I narrative. There may be other, very different, passages which will be marked as 'real' and 'authentic' to twenty-first-century ears, according to their experience of warfare.

In any case, what is marked out as 'military' in any given castle is often assumed rather than real. Take, for example, our habit of mind that leads us to assume that at the top of every ruined wall or tower there must have been a crenellated fighting parapet and wall-walk. At Cooling, the thin walls make the existence of a wall-walk questionable; at Bodiam, Coulson has raised the problem of access to it; the evidence for crenellations is quite unclear at Bolton; many more towers may have been capped by roofs rather than parapets, as they were at Farleigh Hungerford. We tend to mentally reconstruct these buildings with fighting parapets and crenellations, whereas a better analogue might be a surviving French *château* with pepperpot roofs.

Such a critique applies equally to the assumptions we make about the use of castles in the Civil War. Many great houses with no military pretensions seem to have undergone sieges. Where castles were used as seriously defensible strongpoints, their character had to be changed drastically. Castle

Donington was surrounded by earthworks which cost £1,000 to make effetcive (Wood 1964: 9: when the plan of this castle is usually presented in syntheses, such as Thompson 1987: 140, the scale is difficult to judge, so the casual reader does not appreciate the tiny nature of the site – it is in fact a small block with angle turrets and a pretentious gatehouse with gargoyles). Places like Ashby de la Zouch were more centres of operations than fortresses as such. Conversely, apparently 'unfortified' structures such as Wingfield, claimed by Thompson (1987: 1–2) to provide a clear contrast to castle design and described by Allen Brown as a 'non-castle', was attacked and defended in 1643 and 1644 and subsequently slighted (Brown 1989: 231–2). Conversely, I argued in the last chapter that when viewed in context, 'slighting' was in part a symbolic act: the concern was in part to make a building untenable and visibly out of action, and by implication announce the political failure and impotence of its owners, not merely to render it militarily indefensible.

If the meanings of castles are complex, in the final analysis they are also unprovable. The balance of evidence might point one way or another, but I have argued that the whole point about castles and great houses is the necessary complexity and ambiguity of their meanings. However, to criticise such an explanation as 'unprovable' is to make a statement that could equally be applied to any explanation of the forms of castles currently on offer. Nor can traditional castle scholars prove or disprove their assertions about what castles 'really were'. However hard either side works to assemble evidence in support of their respective positions, it is doubtful that either side will admit to losing the argument, because by its very nature the evidence itself is open to different interpretations. One person's military causeway is another's processional route; one person's cleared strip around castles is for defence, but is another person's landscaping feature.

One of the unnoticed weaknesses of many explanations of castle design is their lack of falsifiability. Where a castle is built on high ground, this is clearly for defence. Where a castle is not on high ground, it is in order to be able to dam streams to create a wide moat. When Raglan's gunports do not work, it is because they are very early and the science of gunnery is imperfectly understood. When Carisbrooke's do not work, it is merely evidence of 'stagnation' of military thinking (O'Neill 1960: 36). When I showed one castle buff the picture of the rear view of the 'towers' of Cooling, his reply was simply, 'Oh, the towers were open at the back so they could not afford cover to attackers should they force the gate.' Karl Popper (1959) warned us against this type of reasoning when he pointed out that to make progress, scientific statements must be of a form that is falsifiable.

However, this difficulty of proof and disproof should tell us something interesting. It should reinforce the point I have repeatedly made that arguments over castles should not be over-simplified into either/or terms. In this respect archaeology has a great deal to learn from literary criticism. We would not argue about whether, say, Shakespeare's *Macbeth* is 'really' about class or nascent capitalism, 'really' about different constructions of gender, or 'really' just a great work of individual literary genius; clearly it is all of these things, and its interest lies partly in the fact that it is all of them at once. Now a castle or great house, as I argued in the case of Kenilworth, is surely just as complex a creation as a work of literature.

If the reader is still unconvinced of just how diverse and complex such meanings are, he or she might consider for a moment the great diversity of agencies and intentions that go into building and living in a castle. There is the conscious intention of the owner; his or her desire to build a structure of a certain form, which may be constrained or enabled by financial circumstances. There is the ancient form, and the enduring meanings and memories, of any building on the site that the owner inherits. There is then the intention of the builder, who may approximate the owner's imperfectly expressed wishes – 'I want mine to look like such-and-such a castle', 'it should have a large tower in the middle' – to other buildings or indeed to that which he is prepared to build. Both builder and owner work within a framework of ideas and assumptions about what buildings should look like and how they should function; this framework may well be part of what Bourdieu (1977) has called the *habitus*, hidden or implicit, so taken-for-granted that it is never articulated, and it is a framework that allows innovation as well as tradition, otherwise change or diversity would never occur. The building process itself is then variable; spread over many years, it frequently involves changes of mind or *ad hoc* modifications as the original conception is shown to be flawed, requirements change, or the builder/owner simply changes his or her mind. Detailed elements of the building are not necessarily the outcome of conscious decisions of either the builder or the owner; the mannerisms of the gargoyles or the human figures that adorn the battlements were the work of individual members of a team of individual craftsmen, and reflect in part their own identities. Parts of the castle are inscribed with a variety of mason's marks, mundane in form but indicating another kind of authorship.

Once completed, the castle's meanings are still not set in stone, are still open to renegotiation. Its spaces, walls and passages are reused, renegotiated by its household; people take short cuts which after a little time become accepted behaviour, servants move clandestinely around the castle, through passages they were not intended to take. In this process of moving from being created to being lived in, meanings change again. Finally, the builder has little control over the idea and attitudes of those in the village or town beyond the castle.

And all of the above assumes that meanings are somehow produced in the minds of those building and living in the castle. In part they are, but they are produced in more subtle and indirect ways also, through historical associations, unintended consequences of events, the rhythms of time. Castles build up stories around them like layers or blankets, till the whole package of meanings and associations cannot be readily controlled by any one force. At the end of all this, the request for 'proof' of what the castle 'really meant' is misguided. The meaning of the castle has shattered into a thousand fragments, of which we can only retrieve a few.

And if we are to retrieve those few with any kind of rigour, we must be open and self-critical about the theories we are using. To repeat, *any* view of castle development is theoretical, whether or not its author has thought about its intellectual basis. One of the most insidious and problematic notions in historical archaeology is the suggestion that because one has read Foucault or Greenblatt, and takes care to cite their influence on one's work, and more broadly makes one's underlying assumptions as explicit as possible, that one's approach is therefore somehow more 'theoretical' than if one simply did not bother to do any of these things.

It is easy to demonstrate that the traditional scholar draws on a wide variety of theoretical ideas. Many of these as we saw in Chapter 4 are ultimately derived from Hegel and Burckhardt in art history; ideas of technological progress are derived from Enlightenment thought; ideas of warfare are derived from androcentric notions in which certain conceptions of masculinity are taken as obvious and self-evident; and so on. That the traditional scholar does not overtly acknowledge these influences, and further that he or she is in some cases not even consciously aware of them when they write, does not mean they are any less theoretical.

The image appealed to is of the mind of the scholar as a blank slate, ready to be inscribed with direct experiences of the raw data; the 'theorist' is contrasted with this image as having a particular pair of spectacles, spectacles derived from Marxism or feminism or New Historicism or whatever. In the anti-theoretical view these spectacles act as filters, blinding the viewer to contrary evidence. Yet the truth is that we all wear spectacles, and, further, that without them we could not see anything at all. The only choice we have is which pair of spectacles we choose to put on.

This book takes a stand against easy solutions. Castles are not just about defence, not just about class conflict, not just about technological or aesthetic progress, not just about symbolism, and not just about 'a combination of these factors'. If they were, they would be a lot less difficult to write about. Unfortunately we live in an historical age when all such simple stories with an unproblematic baseline have been shown to have very profound problems.

At the end of this book, I have to confess, however, that I am less certain than ever about what castles 'really are'. The problem is that people do not like uncertainty; it makes for unease. People, myself included, find the absence of uncertainty much more emotionally appealing. The assertion of 'no real doubt', both in castle studies and in academic life generally, remains comforting as a philosophical security blanket long after its intellectual basis has been eroded. In this sense, this book is simply an appeal to castle buffs of all shapes, sizes and variety to go out and look at castles afresh. I think that rather than engaging in tiresome quarrels about what castles 'really are' we should instead go and look at some castles together. Maybe as we engage in the actual field experience of wandering around some ruins and comparing notes on what we see, or more accurately what we think we see, maybe we can make an accommodation, construct a picture of castle development that interests us all.

And the ruins may speak to us after all, whatever I said about castles being mute in Chapter 1. When I visit a ruined castle such as Kenilworth, I find it impossible to banish the utterly unacademic suspicion that the ruins are conscious, are looking down on me. This interestingly positioned gunport, that cleverly angled entrance, this emblem or motif – all look down on the visitors milling around them, solitary anorak-clad individuals bearing elaborate photographic equipment, families with picnics gazing anxiously at the greying skies above, screaming babies, scabrous dogs paying their respects in the usual manner, gangs of academics in shabby tweed jackets poring over butt-joints and grassy mounds trying and failing to look more expert and less vulgar than the general crowd.

And the ruins must be looking down with a degree of amusement. The ruins of Kenilworth or Tattershall or Raglan laugh at us. They are amused at our attempts to classify them, to reduce their mysteries to a simplistic rational order. We should listen to them more carefully, hear their laughter, and pay them more respect.

GLOSSARY

Aristocracy   Those families at the very top of the social scale, but below the monarchy.

Ashlar   Stone that is faced and squared.

Bailey   The courtyard of a castle.

Bascule   A bridge formed of a pair of counterpoised drawbridges, as seen at Raglan *donjon*.

Berm   The strip of ground between the bottom of the curtain wall and the moat or ditch.

Buttery   A service room used for storing ale, beer and other liquor.

Caponnier   A covered passage with loopholes for guns, thrown forward from the foot of a rampart to provide raking fire along the walls.

Chequer-work   Squares of flint and ashlar laid in a chequer pattern.

Constable   The officer appointed by the lord or king to oversee the castle.

Crenellation   A battlement of merlons and embrasures.

Demesne   Part of the lord's estate; in the classical feudal model, a 'demesne farm' was worked using the labour services of peasants given as a form of rent, though this practice had largely died out in England by the late fourteenth century.

Diachronic   Through time (as opposed to synchronic).

Diffusion   The spread of ideas between cultural groups.

Donjon   Also 'great tower' or 'keep': used in castle studies of the principal tower of a castle. Some or all of these terms can be taken to suggest that this tower is the principal or the lord's 'residence'; recent studies have tended to move via stress on different forms and functions towards the deconstruction of all such terms as general categories.

Embrasure   Opening.

Enceinte   Enclosure.

Episcopal   Belonging to a bishop.

Essentialism   'The assumption that groups, categories or objects have one or several defining features exclusive to all members of that category' (Ashcroft *et al.* 1998: 77).

Feoffment   The act of investing with an estate of land in return for homage.

Feudal   In this book, used loosely of medieval society, in which ties of lord-ship and ownership of land were central to political power.

Garderobe   A latrine.

Gentry   Members of the elite though below the aristocracy, typically leaders of the local community.

Ha-ha   A form of fence or boundary that does not interrupt the view of an apparently unbounded landscape, for example, by placing a fence at the bottom of a ditch.

Impaling   Of two coats of arms, to place side by side.

Keep   See *donjon*.

Leat   An artificial water channel.

Livery   Forms of dress or of badges, signifying allegiance to a feudal lord.

Machicolations   The projecting parapet of a battlement, enabling defenders to drop missiles or water on those below.

mere   A small lake.

Metonym   A symbol that is linked with what it signifies by a logical link.

Meutrière   A 'murder-hole' in the vaulted ceiling of a gate passageway, to use against attackers passing below.

Motte   An earthen mound.

Munition   In seventeenth-century usage, fortifications.

Newel   Of a circular staircase that winds round a central pillar or 'newel post'.

Oriel window   A projecting window, often found at the upper end of a hall.

Pale   Boundary. Often used as a social metaphor to indicate lack of social acceptability, as in 'beyond the pale'.

Parapet   A wall, usually battlemented in castles, protecting the wall-walk and any roof behind.

Peer   A great lord or baron.

Pele   A tower-like residence, found in the Anglo-Scottish borders.

Peripatetic   Moving periodically from place to place (often used of great medieval households).

Polite   Of architecture that is large in scale and national or international in scope and influence (*contra* vernacular).

Postern   Rear or secondary gate.

Primogeniture   The practice of leaving an estate to the eldest son.

Recusant   A person or family who remained loyal to the Roman Catholic Church after the Reformation.

Reiving   A term applied to organised cattle rustling in the Anglo-Scottish border regions.

Sconce   A small fortification separate from the main mass.

Seignorial   Pertaining to structures of lordship.

Slighting   Deliberate destruction of castle fabric.

Solar   A private chamber, usually at the upper end of a hall.

String course A horizontal line of projecting ashlar.

Synchronic At one specific point or moment in time (as opposed to diachronic).

Vernacular Of regional, local traditions of art, architecture, and culture, for example, ordinary farmhouses.

Whiggish The study of the past with implicit moral reference to the present, in that past people and processes are classified according to whether they helped or hindered 'progress' (i.e. towards the present state of affairs).

Wicket gate A smaller gate set within the larger doors.

BIBLIOGRAPHY

Aberg, F.A. (ed.) 1978. *Medieval Moated Sites*. CBA Research Report 17. London, Council for British Archaeology.

Adams, S. (ed.) 1995. *Household Accounts and Disbursement Books of Robert Dudley, Earl of Leicester, 1558–1561, 1584–1586*. Camden 5th Series vol. 6. Cambridge, Cambridge University Press.

Aers, D. 1992a. 'A whisper in the ears of early modernists: or, reflections on literary critics writing the "history of the subject".' In D. Aers (ed.) *Culture and History 1350–1600*. London, Harvester, pp. 177–202.

Aers, D. (ed.) 1992b. *Culture and History 1350–1600: Essays on English Communities, Identities and Writing*. London, Harvester.

Amussen, S. 1988. *An Ordered Society: Gender and Class in Early Modern England*. Oxford, Oxford University Press.

Anglo, S. (ed.) 1990. *Chivalry in the Renaissance*. Woobridge, Boydell.

Apted, M.R., Gilyard-Beer, R. and Saunders, A.D. (eds) 1977. *Ancient Monuments and their Interpretation: Essays Presented to A.J. Taylor*. London, Phillimore.

Archer, R.E. 1992. '"How ladies . . . who live on their manors ought to manage their households and estates": women as landholders and administrators in the later middle ages.' In P.J.P. Goldberg (ed.) *Woman is a Worthy Wight*. London, Alan Sutton, pp. 149–81.

Ashcroft, B., Griffiths, G. and Tiffin, H. (eds) 1998. *Key Concepts of Post-Colonial Studies*. London, Routledge.

Aston, M. 1970. 'Earthworks at the Bishop's Palace, Alvechurch, Worcestershire.' *Transactions of the Worcestershire Archaeological Society*. Third series, 3, 55–9.

Aston, M. (ed.) 1988. *Medieval Fish, Fisheries and Fishponds in England*. BAR British Series 182. Oxford, British Archaeological Reports.

Aston, M., Austin, D. and Dyer, C.C. (eds) 1989. *The Rural Settlements of Medieval England*. Oxford, Clarendon Press.

Aston, M. and Lewis, C. (eds) 1994. *The Medieval Landscape of Wessex*. Oxbow Monograph 46. Oxford, Oxbow Books.

Aughterson, K. (ed.) 1995. *Renaissance Woman: Constructions of Femininity in England*. London, Routledge.

Austin, D. 1984. 'The castle and the landscape.' *Landscape History* 6, 69–81.

Austin, D. 1990. 'The "proper study" of medieval archaeology.' In D. Austin and L. Alcock (eds) *From the Baltic to the Black Sea*. London, Unwin Hyman, pp. 1–35.

Austin, D. and Alcock, L. (eds) 1990. *From the Baltic to the Black Sea: Studies in Medieval Archaeology*. London, Unwin Hyman.

Austin, D. and Thomas, J. 1990. 'The "proper study" of medieval archaeology: a case study.' In D. Austin and L. Alcock (eds) *From the Baltic to the Black Sea*. London, Unwin Hyman, pp. 43–78.

Barker, P. and Higham, R. 1992. *Hen Domen, Montgomery: A Timber Castle on the English-Welsh Border*. London, Royal Archaeological Insititute.

Barnard, T.C. 1990. 'Gardening, diet and "improvement" in late 17th century Ireland.' *Journal of Garden History* 10, 72–85.

Barnes, J. 1997. 'Dissident eccentricity.' *Heritage Today* 38, 30–2.

Barrell, J. 1990. 'The public prospect and the private view: the politics of taste in eighteenth century Britain.' In S. Pugh (ed.) *Reading Landscape: Country-City-Capital*. Manchester: Manchester University Press, pp. 19–40.

Barry, J. and Brooks, C. (eds) 1994. *The Middling Sort of People: Culture, Society and Politics in England 1550–1800*. Basingstoke, Macmillan.

Barstow, AM. 1974. 'The importance of the Ashmolean Roll of Arms for the study of medieval blazon.' *Antiquaries Journal* 54, 75–84.

Barthes, R. 1977. *Image – Music – Text*. London, HarperCollins.

Barthes, R. 1987. *Michelet*. Oxford, Blackwell. First published 1954 (Paris, Editions du Seuil).

Bath, M. 1994. *Speaking Pictures: English Emblem Books and Renaissance Culture*. London, Longman.

Belsey, A. and Belsey, C. 1990. 'Icons of diversity: portraits of Elizabeth I.' In L. Gent and N. Llewellyn (eds) *Renaissance Bodies*. London, Reaktion, pp. 11–35.

Belsey, C. 1985. *The Subject of Tragedy: Identity and Difference in Renaissance Drama*. London, Methuen.

Bennett, M. 1999. 'Military masculinity in England and Northern France c.1050–1225.' In D.Hadley (ed.) *Masculinity in Medieval Europe*. Harlow, Longman, pp. 71–88.

Beresford, M. and Hurst, J.G. 1979. *Medieval England: An Aerial Survey*. Second edition. Cambridge, Cambridge University Press.

Beretta, I. 1993. *'The World's a Garden': Garden Poetry of the English Renaissance*. Studia Anglista Upsaliensa 84. Uppsala, University of Uppsala.

Bermingham, A. 1987. *Landscape and Ideology: The English Rustic Tradition, 1740–1860*. Berkeley, CA: University of California Press.

Berry, P. 1995. *Of Chastity and Power: Elizabethan Literature and the Unmarried Queen*. London, Routledge.

Biddle, M. (ed.) 2000. *King Arthur's Round Table: An Archaeological Investigation*. Woodbridge, Boydell.

Biddle, M., Clayre, B. and Morris, M. 2000. 'The setting of the Round Table: Winchester Castle and the Great Hall.' In M. Biddle (ed.) *King Arthur's Round Table*. Woodbridge, Boydell, pp. 59–102.

Binford, L.R. 1962. 'Archaeology as anthropology.' *American Antiquity* 11, 198–200.

Binford, L.R. 1972. *An Archaeological Perspective*. New York, Seminar Press.

Blood, N.K. and Taylor, C.C. 1992. 'Cawood: an archiepiscopal landscape.' *Yorkshire Archaeological Journal* 64, 83–102.

Bond, J. 1994. 'Forests, chases, warrens and parks in medieval Wessex.' In M. Aston and C. Lewis (eds) *The Medieval Landscape of Wessex*. Oxford, Oxbow Books, pp. 115–58.

Bonde, S. 1994. *Fortress-Churches of Languedoc: Architecture, Religion and Conflict in the High Middle Ages*. Cambridge, Cambridge University Press.

Bourdieu, P. 1977. *Outline of a Theory of Practice*. Cambridge, Cambridge University Press.

Bowden, M., Mackay, D. and Topping, P. (eds) 1989. *From Cornwall to Caithness*. BAR British Series 209. Oxford, British Archaeological Reports.

Bradley, R. 1993. 'Archaeology: the loss of nerve.' In N. Yoffee and A. Sherratt (eds) *Archaeological Theory: Who Sets the Agenda?* Cambridge, Cambridge University Press, pp. 131–3.

Bradney, J.A. (ed.) 1910. *Llfyr Baglan*. London.

Braun, H. 1936. *The English Castle*. London, Faber.

Breitenberg, M. 1996. *Anxious Masculinity in Early Modern England*. Cambridge, Cambridge University Press.

Brewer, J. and Porter, R. (eds) 1993. *Consumption and the World of Goods*. London, Routledge.

Bristol, M. 1985. *Carnival and Theatre: Plebeian Culture and the Structure of Authority in Renaissance England*. London, Methuen.

Britnell, R.H. and Pollard, A.J. (eds) 1995. *The McFarlane Legacy: Studies in Late Medieval Politics and Society*. Stroud, Alan Sutton.

Brown, R.A. 1970. *English Castles*. London, Batsford.

Brown, R.A. 1973. *The Origins of English Feudalism*. London, Allen and Unwin.

Brown, R.A. 1984. *Proceedings of the Battle Conference on Anglo-Norman Studies*. Ipswich, Boydell Press.

Brown, R.A. 1986. *Rochester Castle, Kent*. Second edition. London, English Heritage.

Brown, R.A. 1989. *Castles From the Air*. Cambridge, Cambridge University Press.

Brück, J. 1999. 'Ritual and rationality: some problems of interpretation in European archaeology.' *European Journal of Archaeology* 2, 3, 313–44.

Brumfiel, E.M. 1992. 'Distinguished lecture in archaeology: breaking and entering the ecosystem – gender, class and faction steal the show.' *American Anthropologist* 94: 551–67.

Brumfiel, E.M. and Earle, T.K. (eds) 1987. *Specialisation. Exchange and Complex Societies*. Cambridge, Cambridge University Press.

Brumfiel, E.M. and Fox, J.W. (eds) 1994. *Factional Competition and Political Development in the New World*. Cambridge, Cambridge University Press.

Burckhardt, J. 1860. *Die Kultur der Renaissance in Italien*. Basle. English translation 1990. Harmondsworth, Penguin.

Burckhardt, J. 1867. *The Architecture of the Italian Renaissance*. English translation 1985. London, Secker and Warburg.

Burke, P. 1969. *The Renaissance Sense of the Past*. London, Edward Arnold.

Bryson, A. 1998. *From Courtesy to Civility: Changing Codes of Conduct in Early Modern England*. Oxford, Clarendon Press.

Camille, M. 1985. 'Seeing and reading: some visual implications of medieval literacy and illiteracy.' *Art History* 8, 26–49.

Camille, M. 1994. 'The image and the self: unwriting late medieval bodies.' In S. Kay and M. Rubin (eds) *Framing Medieval Bodies*. Manchester, Manchester University Press, pp. 62–99.

Campbell, C. 1993. 'Understanding traditional and modern patterns of consumption in 18th century England: a character-action approach.' In J. Brewer and R. Porter (eds) *Consumption and the World of Goods*. London, Routledge, pp. 40–57.

Cannadine, D. and Price, S. (eds) 1987. *Rituals of Royalty: Power and Ceremonial in Traditional Societies*. Cambridge, Cambridge University Press

Carman, J. (ed.) 1997. *Material Harm: Archaeological Studies of War and Violence*. Glasgow, Cruithne Press.

Carruthers, M.J. 1990. *The Book of Memory: A Study of Memory in Medieval Culture*. Cambridge, Cambridge University Press.

Charlton, J. 1977. 'The Lady Ann Clifford (1590–1676).' In M.R. Apted *et al.* (eds) *Ancient Monuments and their Interpretation*. London, Phillimore, pp. 303–12.

Charlton, J. 1985. *Brougham Castle, Cumbria*. London, English Heritage.

Charlton, J. 1986. *Brough Castle, Cumbria*. London, English Heritage.

Chettle, G.H. and Leach, P. 1984. *Kirby Hall, Northamptonshire*. London, English Heritage.

Clark, G.T. 1884. *Medieval Military Architecture in England*. London, Wyman.

Cohen, G.A. 1978. *Karl Marx's Theory of History: A Defence*. Oxford, Clarendon Press.

Cohen, J.J. and Wheeler, B. (eds) 1997. *Becoming Male in the Middle Ages*. London, Garland.

Colvin, H.M. 1983. 'The "court style" in medieval English architecture: a review.' In V.J. Scattergood and J.W. Sherborne (eds) *English Court Culture in the Later Middle Ages*. London, Duckworth, pp. 129–40.

Colvin, M. (ed.) 1963. *History of the King's Works*. Vol. II. London, Her Majesty's Stationery Office.

Contamine, P. 1972. *Guerre, Etat et Société à la Fin du Moyen Age*. Paris, Picard.

Cooper, N. 1997. 'The gentry house in the age of transition.' In D. Gaimster and P. Stamper (eds) *The Age of Transition*. Oxford, Oxbow Books, pp. 115–26.

Cooper, N. 1999. *Houses of the Gentry 1480–1680*. New Haven, CT, Yale University Press.

Cosgrove, D.E. 1984. *Social Formation and Symbolic Landscape*. London, Croom Helm.

Cosgrove, D.E. 1993. *The Palladian Landscape: Geographical Change and its Cultural Representations in 16th Century Italy*. Leicester, Leicester University Press.

Cosgrove, D. and Daniels, S. 1988. *The Iconography of Landscape*. Cambridge, Cambridge University Press.

Cosgrove, D. and Petts, S. (eds) 1990. *Water, Engineering and Landscape: Water Control and Landscape Transformation in the Modern Period*. London, Bellhaven.

Coss, P.R. and Lloyd, S. (eds) 1992. *Thirteenth Century England IV: Proceedings of the Newcastle Upon Tyne Conference*. Woodbridge, Boydell.

Coulson, C. 1979. 'Structural symbolism in medieval castle architecture.' *Journal of the British Archaeological Association* 132, 80–90.

Coulson, C. 1982. 'Hierarchism in conventual crenellation: an essay in the sociology and metaphysics of medieval fortification.' *Medieval Archaeology* 26, 69–100.

Coulson, C. 1992. 'Some analysis of the castle of Bodiam, East Sussex.' In C. Harper-Bill and R. Harvey (eds) *Medieval Knighthood IV: Papers from the Fifth Strawberry Hill Conference*. Woodbridge, Boydell, pp. 51–108.

Coulson, C. 1993. 'Specimens of freedom to crenellate by licence.' *Fortress* 18, 3–15.

Coulson, C. 1994. 'Freedom to crenellate by licence: an historiographical revision.' *Nottingham Medieval Studies* 38, 86–137.

Coulson, C. 1996. 'Cultural realities and reappraisals in English castle-study.' *Journal of Medieval History* 22, 171–208.

Crumley, C.L. 1987. 'A dialectical critique of hierarchy.' In T.C. Patterson and C.W. Galley (eds) *Power Relations and State Formation*. Washington, D.C., American Anthropological Association.

Cunliffe, J.W. (ed.) 1910. *George Gascoigne: The Glasse of Governement, The Princely Pleasures at Kenilworth Castle, The Steele Glas, and Other Poems and Prose Works*. Cambridge, Cambridge University Press.

Currie, C. 1988. 'Time and chance: modelling the attrition of old houses.' *Vernacular Architecture* 19, 1–9.

Daalder, J. (ed.) 1990. *The Changeling* (Thomas Middleton and William Rowley). 2nd edition. London, Black.

Dean, M.A. 1984. 'Early fortified houses: defences and castle imagery 1275–1350 with evidence from the south-east Midlands.' In K. Reyerson and F. Powe (eds) *The Medieval Castle*. Dubugne, University of Iowa Press.

Deetz, J.F. 1977. *In Small Things Forgotten: An Archeology of Early American Life*. New York, Anchor.

Delle, J. 1998. *An Archaeology of Social Space: Analysing Coffee Plantations in Jamaica's Blue Mountains*. New York, Plenum.

Detsicas, A. (ed.) 1981. *Collectanea Historica: Essays in Memory of Stuart Rigold*. Maidstone, Kent Archaeological Society.

Diller, H.-J., Kohl, S., Kornelius, J., Otto, E. and Stratmann, G. (eds) 1992. *Englishness*. Heidelberg, Heidelberg University Press.

Dixon, P. 1979. 'Towers, pelehouses and border society.' *Archaeological Journal* 136, 240–52.

Dixon, P. 1988. *Aydon Castle, Northumberland*. London, English Heritage.

Dixon, P. 1990. 'The donjon of Knaresborough: the castle as theatre.' *Château Gaillard: Etudes de Castellologie Médiévale* 14, 121–39.

Dixon, P. 1992. 'From hall to tower: the change in seignorial houses in the Anglo-Scottish border after c.1250.' In P.R. Coss and S. Lloyd (eds) *Thirteenth Century England*. Woodbridge, Boydell, pp. 85–107.

Dixon, P. 1993. '*Mota, aula et turris*: the manor houses of the Northern border.' In G. Meirion-Jones and M. Jones (eds) *Manorial Domestic Buildings in England and Northern France*. London, Society of Antiquaries, pp. 22–45.

Dixon, P. 1996. 'Design in castle-building: the controlling of access to the Lord.' *Château Gaillard* 18, 47–57.

Dixon, P. and Borne, P. 1978. 'Coparcenary and Aydon Castle.' *Archaeological Journal* 135, 234–8.

Dixon, P. and Lott, B. 1993. 'The courtyard and the tower: contexts and symbols in the development of late medieval great houses.' *Journal of the British Archaeological Association* 146, 93–101.

Dixon, P. and Marshall, P. 1993a. 'The great tower in the twelfth century: the case of Norham castle.' *Archaeological Journal* 150, 410–32.

Dixon, P. and Marshall, P. 1993b. 'The great tower at Hedingham castle: a reassessment.' *Fortress* 18, 16–23.

Dobrer, M.-A. and Robb, J. (eds) 2000. *Agency in Archaeology*. London: Routledge.

Doig, J. 1996. 'Propaganda and truth: Henry V's royal progress in 1421.' *Nottingham Medieval Studies* 40, 167–79.

Dollimore, J. 1992. 'Shakespeare, cultural materialism and the New Historicism.' In R. Wilson and R. Dutton (eds) *New Historicism and Renaissance Drama*. London, Longman, pp. 45–56.

Dollimore, J. and Sinfield, A. (eds) 1985. *Political Shakespeare*. Manchester, Manchester University Press.

Doran, S. 1996. *Monarchy and Matrimony: The Courtships of Elizabeth I*. London, Routledge.

Douglas, M. n.d. 'The parish church as a focus of collective memory.' Unpublished manuscript in possession of author.

Duffy, C. 1979. *Siege Warfare: The Fortress in the Early Modern World 1494–1660*. London, Routledge.

Dyer, C. 1970. 'The consumption of freshwater fish in medieval England.' In M. Aston (ed.) *Medieval Fish, Fisheries and Fishponds in England*. Oxford, British Archaeological Reports, pp. 27–38.

Dyer, C. 1989. *Standards of Living in the Later Middle Ages: Social Change in England c.1200–1520*. Cambridge, Cambridge University Press.

Eagleton, T. 1976. *Criticism and Ideology*. London, Verso.

Eagleton, T. 1991. *Ideology: An Introduction*. London, Verso.

Edelen, G. (ed.) 1968. *The Description of England by William Harrison*. Ithaca, NY, Cornell University Press.

Elias, N. 1978. *The Civilising Process*. Volume One: *The History of Manners*. Oxford, Blackwell.

Ellis, P. (ed.) 2000. *Ludgershall Castle: Excavations by Peter Addyman 1964–1972*. WANHS Monograph 2. Devizes, Wiltshire Archaeological and Natural History Society.

Emery, A. 1975. 'The development of Raglan castle and keeps in late medieval England.' *Archaeological Journal* 132, 151–86.

Emery, A. 1985. 'Ralph, Lord Cromwell's manor at Wingfield (1439–c.1450): its construction, design and influence.' *Archaeological Journal* 142, 276–339.

Emery, A. 1994. 'Saltwood castle.' In N.J.G. Pounds (ed.) *The Canterbury Area*. London, Royal Archaeological Institute, pp. 30–4.

Emery, A. 1996. *Greater Medieval Houses of England and Wales 1350–1500 I: Northern England*. Cambridge, Cambridge University Press.

Emery, A. 2000. *Greater Medieval Houses of England and Wales II: East Anglia, Central England, and Wales*. Cambridge, Cambridge University Press.

Evans, C. 1997. 'Sentimental prehistories: the construction of the Fenland past.' *Journal of European Archaeology* 5, 2, 105–36.

Evans, J. (ed.) 1966. *The Flowering of the Middle Ages*. London, Thames and Hudson.

Everson, P. 1998. '"Delightfully surrounded with woods and ponds": field evidence for medieval gardens in England.' In P. Pattison (ed.) *There By Design*. Oxford, British Archaeological Reports, pp. 32–8.

Everson, P., Brown, G. and Stocker, D. 2000. 'The castle earthworks and landscape context.' In P. Ellis (ed.) *Ludgershall Castle*. Devizes, Wiltshire Archaeological and National History Society, pp. 97–104.

Everson, P., Taylor, C.C. and Dunn, C.J. 1991. *Change and Continuity: rural settlement in north-east Lincolnshire*. London, Her Majesty's Stationery Office.

Evett, D. 1994. *Literature and the Visual Arts in Tudor England*. London, University of Georgia Press.

Fairclough, G. 1992. 'Meaningful constructions: spatial and functional analysis of medieval buildings.' *Antiquity* 66, 348–66.

Farago, C. (ed.) 1995. *Reframing the Renaissance: Visual Culture in Europe and Latin America 1450–1650*. New Haven, CT, Yale University Press.

Faulkner, P.A. 1958. 'Domestic planning from the 12th to the 14th centuries.' *Archaeological Journal* 115, 150–83.

Faulkner, P.A. 1963. 'Castle planning in the 14th century.' *Archaeological Journal* 120, 215–35.

Faulkner, P. 1972. *Bolsover Castle, Derbyshire*. London, Her Majesty's Stationery Office.

Fenton, J. 1999. 'An ardor for armor.' *New York Review of Books* 46, 7, 57–64.

Fernie, E. 1989. 'Archaeology and iconography: recent developments in the study of English medieval architecture.' *Architectural History* 32, 18–29.

Fernie, E. 1995. *Art History and its Methods: A Critical Anthology*. London, Phaidon.

Fernie, E. and Crossley, P. (eds) 1990. *Medieval Architecture and its Intellectual Context*. London, Hambledon.

Fraser, A. 1996. *The Gunpowder Plot: Terror and Faith in 1605*. London, Weidenfeld.

Frazer, W. (ed.) 1999. 'Reconceptualising resistance in the historical archaeology of the British Isles: an editorial.' *International Journal of Historical Archaeology* 3, 1, 1–10.

Friedman, A.T. 1997. 'Wife in the English country house: gender and the meaning of style in early modern England.' In C. Lawrence (ed.) *Women and Art in Early Modern Europe*. University Park, Pennsylvania University Press, pp. 111–25.

Gaimster, D. and Stamper, P. (eds) 1997. *The Age of Transition: The Archaeology of English Culture 1400–1600*. Oxford, Oxbow Books.

Gardiner, M. 2000. 'Vernacular buildings and the development of the later medieval domestic plan in England.' *Medieval Archaeology* 44, 159–80.

Gates, H.L. 1995. *Loose Canons: Notes on the Culture Wars*. Oxford, Oxford University Press.

Geertz, C. 1973. *The Interpretation of Cultures*. New York, Basic Books.

Gent, L. 1981. *Picture and Poetry 1560–1620*. Leamington Spa, James Hall.

Gent, L. and Llewellyn, N. (eds) 1990. *Renaissance Bodies: The Human Figure in English Culture c.1540–1660*. London, Reaktion.

Gilchrist, R. 1993. *Gender and Material Culture: The Archaeology of Religious Women*. London, Routledge.

Gilchrist, R. 1994. 'Medieval bodies in the material world: gender, stigma and the body.' In S. Kay and M. Rubin (eds) *Framing Medieval Bodies*. Manchester, Manchester University Press.

Gilchrist, R. 1999. *Gender and Archaeology: Contesting the Past*. London, Routledge.

Gilchrist, R. 2000. 'Landscapes of the Middle Ages: churches, castles and monasteries.' In J. Hunter and I. Ralston (eds) *The Archaeology of Britain*. London, Routledge, pp. 228–46.

Girouard, M. 1978. *Life in the English Country House*. New Haven, CT, Yale University Press.

Girouard, M. 1981. *The Return to Camelot: Chivalry and the English Gentleman*. New Haven, CT, Yale University Press.

Girouard, M. 2000. *Life in the French Country House*. London, Cassell.

Given-Wilson, C. 1986. *The Royal Household and the King's Affinity: Service, Politics and Finance in England*. New Haven, CT, Yale University Press.

Goffman, E. 1959. *The Presentation of Self in Everyday Life*. New York, Anchor Press.

Goffman, E. 1971. *Relations in Public: Microstudies of the Public Order*. Harmondsworth, Penguin.

Goldberg, J. (ed.) 1994. *Queering the Renaissance*. London, Duke University Press.

Goldberg, P.J.P. (ed.) 1992. *Woman is a Worthy Wight: Women in English Society c.1200–1500.* London, Alan Sutton.

Goodall, J. 2000. 'Lulworth Castle, Dorset.' *Country Life* cxciv, 2, 34–9.

Graves, C.P. 1989. 'Social space in the English medieval parish church.' *Economy and Society* 18, 3, 297–322.

Graves, C.P. 2000. *The Form and Fabric of Belief: An Archaeology of the Lay Experience of Religion in Medieval Norfolk and Devon.* BAR British Series 311. Oxford, British Archaeological Reports.

Greenblatt, S. 1980. *Renaissance Self-Fashioning: From More to Shakespeare.* London, University of Chicago Press.

Greenblatt, S. 1985. 'Invisible bullets: Renaissance authority and its subversion, Henry IV and Henry V.' In J. Dollimore and A. Sinfield (eds) *Political Shakespeare.* Manchester, Manchester University Press, pp. 18–47.

Greenblatt, S. 1988. *Shakespearian Negotiations: The Circulation of Social Energy in Renaissance England.* Berkeley, CA: University of California Press.

Greenblatt, S. 1994. 'The eating of the soul.' *Representations* 48, 97–116.

Grenville, J. 1997. *Medieval Housing.* Leicester, Leicester University Press.

Gross, A. 1990. 'Langland's rats: a moralist's vision of parliament.' *Parliamentary History* 9, 286–301.

Guillaume, J. (ed) 1999. *Architecture, Jardin, Paysage: L'Environnement du Château et de la Villa aux 15 et 16 Siècles.* Paris, Picard.

Hackett, H. 1994. *Virgin Mother, Maiden Queen: Elizabeth I and the Cult of the Virgin Mary.* London: Macmillan.

Hadley, D. (ed.) 1999. *Masculinity in Medieval Europe.* Harlow: Longman.

Harvey, I.M.W. 1995. 'Was there popular politics in 15th century England?' In R.H Britnell and A.J. Pollard (eds) *The McFarlane Legacy.* Stroud, Alan Sutton, pp. 155–74.

Harvey, J. 1944. *Henry Yevele: The Life of an English Architect.* London, Batsford.

Harvey, J. 1984. *English Medieval Architects: A Biographical Dictionary down to 1500.* Revised edition. London, Sutton.

Hayter, W. 1970. *William of Wykeham.* London.

Heal, F. 1990. *Hospitality in Early Modern England.* Oxford, Clarendon Press.

Helgerson, R. 1992. *Forms of Nationhood: The Elizabethan Writing of England.* Chicago, University of Chicago Press.

Heslop, T.A. 1991. 'Orford Castle: nostalgia and sophisticated living.' *Architectural History* 34, 36–58.

Heslop, T.A. 1994. *Norwich Castle Keep.* Norwich, Centre of East Anglian Studies.

Higham, R. and Barker, P. 1992. *Timber Castles.* London, Batsford.

Hill, C. 1964. *Society and Puritanism in Pre-Revolutionary England.* London, Secker and Warburg.

Hill, C. 1972. *The World Turned Upside Down: Radical Ideas During the English Revolution.* London, Templeton.

Hill, P.R. n.d. *The Story of Caister Castle and Car Collection.* Caister, no publisher stated.

Hillier, R. and Hanson, J. 1984. *The Social Logic of Space.* Cambridge, Cambridge University Press.

Hilton, R. 1973. *Bond Men Made Free: Medieval Peasant Movements and the English Rising of 1381.* London, Methuen.

Hinton, D. 1999. '"Closing" and the later Middle Ages.' *Medieval Archaeology* 43, 172–82.

Hislop, M. 1991. 'The date of the Warkworth donjon.' *Archaeologica Aeliana* 5th Series, 19, 79–92.

Hislop, M. 1997. 'Bolton Castle and the practice of architecture in the Middle Ages.' *Journal of the British Archaeological Association* 149, 10–22.

Hohler, C. 1966. 'Kings and castles: court life in peace and war.' In J. Evans (ed.), The Flowering of the Middle Ages. London, Thames and Hudson pp. 133–78.

Hoskins, W.G. 1953. 'The rebuilding of rural England, 1570–1640.' *Past and Present* 4, 44–59.

Howard, J.E. 1991. 'Women as spectators, spectacles, and paying customers.' In D.S. Kastan and P. Stallybrass (eds) *Staging the Renaissance*. London, Routledge, pp. 68–74.

Howard, M. 1987. *The Early Tudor Country House: Architecture and Politics 1490–1550*. London, George Philip.

Howard, M. 1990. 'Self-fashioning and the classical moment in mid sixteenth century architecture.' In L. Gent and N. Llewellyn (eds) *Renaissance Bodies*. London, Reaktion, pp. 180–217.

Huizinga, J. 1924. *The Waning of the Middle Ages*. 1965 edition. Harmondsworth, Penguin.

Hunter, J. and Ralston, I. (eds) 2000. *The Archaeology of Britain*. London, Routledge.

Hunter Blair, C.H. and Honeyman, H.L. 1966. *Norham Castle, Northumberland*. London, English Heritage.

Hutton, R. 1994. *The Rise and Fall of Merry England: The Ritual Year 1400–1700*. Oxford, Oxford University Press.

Hutton, R. 1997. *The Stations of the Sun*. Oxford, Oxford University Press.

Impey, E. and Parnell, G. 2000. *The Tower of London: The Official Illustrated History*. London, Merell.

Isaac, R. 1982. *The Transformation of Virginia, 1760–1820*. Chapel Hill, NC, University of North Carolina Press.

James, S. 1986. *Society, Politics and Culture: Studies in Early Modern England*. Cambridge, Cambridge University Press.

Jardine, L. 1983. *Still Harping on Daughters*. Brighton, Harvester.

Jardine, L. 1991. 'Boy actors, female roles, and Elizabethan eroticism.' In D.S. Kastan and P. Stallybrass (eds) *Staging the Renaissance*. London, Routledge, pp. 57–67.

Jardine, L. 1996a. *Reading Shakespeare Historically*. London, Routledge.

Jardine, L. 1996b. *Worldly Goods: A New History of the Renaissance*. London, Macmillan.

Johnson, M.H. 1993. *Housing Culture: Traditional Architecture in an English Landscape*. London, University College London Press.

Johnson, M.H. 1996. *An Archaeology of Capitalism*. Oxford, Blackwell.

Johnson, M.H. 1997. 'Rethinking houses, rethinking transitions: of vernacular architecture, ordinary people and everyday culture.' In D. Gaimster and P. Stamper (eds) *The Age of Transition*. Oxford, Oxbow Books, pp. 145–56.

Johnson, M.H. 1999. 'A fragment of architecture at Kenilworth Castle, and its implications.' *Durham Archaeological Journal* 14–15, 173–6.

Jones, P.N. and Renn, D.F. 1982. 'The military effectiveness of arrow loops: some experiments at White Castle.' *Château Gaillard* 9–10, 445–56.

Jones, T.L. 1953. *Ashby de la Zouch Castle, Leicestershire*. London, Her Majesty's Stationery Office.

Kabir, A. and Williams, D. (eds) forthcoming. *Post-Colonial Medieval Studies*. London, Routledge.

Kaeuper, R.W. 1999. *Chivalry and Violence in Medieval Europe*. Oxford, Oxford University Press.

Kastan, D.S. and Stallybrass, P. (eds) 1991. *Staging the Renaissance: Reinterpretations of Elizabethan and Jacobean Drama*. London, Routledge.

Kay, S. and Rubin, M. (eds) 1994. *Framing Medieval Bodies*. Manchester, Manchester University Press.

Kean, M.H. 1984. *Chivalry*. New Haven, CT, Yale University Press.

Kelsey, S. 1997. *Inventing a Republic: The Political Culture of the English Commonwealth 1649–1653*. Manchester, Manchester University Press.

Kendall, H.P. 1948. *History of the Old Castle of Mulgrave in Yorkshire*. Hull, Brown.

Kenyon, J.R. 1981. 'Early artillery fortifications in England and Wales: a preliminary survey and appraisal.' *Archaeological Journal* 138, 205–40.

Kenyon, J.R. 1982. 'The Civil War earthworks around Raglan Castle, Gwent: an aerial view.' *Archaeologia Cambrensis* 131, 151–86.

Kenyon, J.R. 1987. 'The gunloops at Raglan Castle, Gwent.' In J.R. Kenyon and R. Avent (eds) *Castles in Wales and the Marches*. Cardiff, University of Wales Press, pp. 161–72.

Kenyon, J.R. 1988. *Raglan Castle*. Cardiff, Cadw.

Kenyon, J.R. and Avent, R. (eds) 1987. *Castles in Wales and the Marches: Essays in Honour of D.J. Cathcart King*. Cardiff, University of Wales Press.

Klukas, A.W. 1984a. 'Liturgy and architecture: Deerhurst Priory as an expression of the *Regularis Concordia*.' *Viator* 15, 81–106.

Klukas, A.W. 1984b. 'The architectural implication of the *Decreta Lanfranci*.' In R.A. Brown (ed.) *Proceedings of the Battle Conference on Anglo-Norman Studies*. Ipswich, Boydell Press, pp. 136–71.

Knowles, D. 1974. *Bare Ruined Choirs: The Dissolution of the English Monasteries*. Cambridge, Cambridge University Press.

Lange, B.P. 1992. 'The English garden and the patriotic discourse.' In H.-J. Diller *et al.* (eds) *Englishness*. Heidelberg, Heidelberg University Press, pp. 49–70.

Lawrence, C. (ed.) 1997. *Women and Art in Early Modern Europe: Patrons, Collectors and Connoisseurs*. University Park, Pennsylvania University Press.

Leach, E. 1976. *Culture and Communication*. Cambridge, Cambridge University Press.

Leone, M. 1984. 'Interpreting ideology in historical archaeology: using the rules of perspective in the William Paca garden in Annapolis, Maryland.' In D. Miller and C. Tilley (eds) *Ideology, Power and Prehistory*. Cambridge, Cambridge University Press, pp. 25–36.

Leone, M. and Potter, P. (eds) 1988. *The Recovery of Meaning: Historical Archaeology in the Eastern United States*. Washington, D.C., Smithsonian Institution.

Leone, M. and Potter, P. (eds) 1999. *Historical Archaeologies of Capitalism*. New York, Plenum.

Le Patourel, H.E.J. and Roberts, B.K. (eds) 1978. 'The significance of moated sites.' In F.A. Aberg (ed.) *Medieval Moated Sites*. London, Council for British Archaeology, pp. 46–55.

Leslie, M. 1992. 'Sidney, Spenser and the Renaissance garden.' *English Literary Renaissance* 22, 3–36.

Leslie, M. 1993. 'An English landscape garden before the "English landscape garden"?' *Journal of Garden History* 13, 2–18.

Leslie, M. and Raylor, T. (eds) 1992. *Culture and Cultivation in Early Modern England: Writing and the Land*. Leicester, Leicester University Press.

Levin, C. 1994. *'The Heart and Stomach of a King': Elizabeth 1st and the Politics of Sex and Power*. Philadelphia, PA, University of Pennsylvania Press.

Lewis, M.J. 1994. 'Utopia and the well-ordered fortress: JM von Schwalbach's town plans of 1635.' *Architectural History* 37, 24–36.

Lindley, P. 1995. *Gothic to Renaissance: Essays in Sculpture in England*. Stamford, Paul Watkins.

Lindley, P. 1996. 'The Black Death and English art: a debate and some assumptions.' In W.M. Ormrod and P.G. Lindley (eds) *The Black Death in England*. Stamford, Paul Watkins, pp. 125–46.

Llewellyn, N. 1993. *Chivalry in the Renaissance*. Woodbridge, Boydell.

Loomis, C. 1996. 'Elizabeth Southwell's manuscript account of the death of Queen Elizabeth (with text).' *English Literary Renaissance* 26, 482–509.

McBride, I. 1997. *The Siege of Derry in Ulster Protestant Mythology*. Dublin, Four Courts Press.

McFarlane, K.V. 1973. *The Nobility of Later Medieval England*. Oxford, Clarendon Press.

MacIvor, I. 1972. *The Fortifications of Berwick-upon-Tweed*. London, Her Majesty's Stationery Office

MacIvor, I. 1977. 'Craignethan Castle, Lanarkshire: an experiment in artillery fortification.' In M.R. Apted *et al.* (eds) *Ancient Monuments and their Interpretation*. London, Phillmore, pp. 237–61.

McNeill, T. 1990. 'Trim Castle, Co Meath: the first three generations.' *Archaeological Journal* 147, 308–36.

McNeill, T. 1997a. *Castles in Ireland: Feudal Power in a Gaelic World*. London, Routledge.

McNeill, T. 1997b. '18th Château Gaillard Conference: Denmark, August 1996.' *Castle Studies Group Newsletter* 10, 6.

Maitland, F.W. 1897. *Domesday Book and Beyond: Three Essays in the Early History of England*. Cambridge, Cambridge University Press.

Maley, W. 1997. *Salvaging Spenser: Colonialism, Culture and Identity*. London, Macmillan.

Marks, R. 1978. 'The glazing of Fotheringhay church and college.' *Journal of the British Archaeological Association* CXXXI, 79–109.

Marks, R. 1984. *The Stained Glass of the Collegiate Church of the Holy Trinity, Tattershall*. London, Garland.

Mathieu, J.R. 1999. 'New methods on old castles: generating new ways of seeing.' *Medieval Archaeology* 43, 115–42.

Meirion-Jones, G. and Jones, M. 1993. *Manorial Domestic Buildings in England and Northern France*. London, Society of Antiquaries.

Mercer, E. 1962. *English Art 1553–1625*. Oxford, Clarendon Press.

Mercer, E. 1975. *English Vernacular Houses*. London, Her Majesty's Stationery Office.

Mertes, K. 1988. *The English Noble Household 1250–1600*. Oxford, Blackwell.

Miller, D. and Tilley, C. (eds) 1984. *Ideology, Power and Prehistory*. Cambridge, Cambridge University Press.

Miller, M.C. 1995. 'From episcopal to communal palaces: palaces and power in northern Italy 1000–1250.' *Journal of the Society of Architectural Historians* 54, 2, 175–85.

Millett, M. 1990. *The Romanisation of Britain*. Cambridge, Cambridge University Press.

Milner, L. 1990. 'The dating of Warkworth donjon.' In E. Fernie and P. Crossley (eds) *Medieval Architecture and its Intellectual Context*. London, Hambledon, pp. 219–37.

Morley, B.M. 1976. 'Hylton castle.' *Archaeological Journal* 133, 118–34.

Morley, B.M. 1981. 'Aspects of 14th century castle design.' In A. Detsicas (ed.) *Collectanea Historica*. Maidstone, Kent Archaeological Society, pp. 104–13.

Morley, B.M., Brown, P. and Crump, T. 1995. 'The Elizabethan gardens and Leicester's stables at Kenilworth Castle: excavations between 1970 and 1984.' *Birmingham and Warwickshire Archaeological Society Transactions* 99, 72–116.

Mullaney, S. 1991. 'Civic rites, city sites: the place of the stage.' In D.S. Kastan and P. Stallybrass (eds) *Staging the Renaissance*. London, Routledge, pp. 17–26.

NAU (Northamptonshire Archaeological Unit) n.d. 'Geophysical Survey at Fotheringhay Castle, Fotheringhay, Northamptonshire, 1991.' Unpublished report, Northamptonshire County Council.

Nelson, J.L. 1999. 'Monks, secular men and masculinity, c.900.' In D. Hadley (ed.) *Masculinity in Medieval Europe*. Harlow, Longman, pp. 121–42.

Nenk, B.S. Margeson, S. and Hurley, M. 1993. 'Medieval Britain and Ireland in 1992.' *Medieval Archaeology* 37, 240–313.

Newman, J. 1969. *The Buildings of England: West Kent and the Weald*. Harmondsworth, Penguin.

Newman, K. 1991. *Fashioning Femininity and English Renaissance Drama*. Chicago, University of Chicago Press.

Oakley, T. 1896. Guide to Kenilworth Castle. No place or publisher given. Copy in NMR Records.

O'Keeffe, T. 1998. 'The fortifications of western Ireland, AD 1100–1300, and their interpretation.' *Journal of the Galway Archaeological and Historical Society* 50, 184–200.

O'Keeffe, T. 2000. 'Castle-building and the construction of identity: contesting narratives about medieval Ireland.' *Irish Geography* 33:2, 69–88.

O'Keeffe, T. forthcoming. 'Castellology as postcolonial discourse.' In A. Kabir and D. Williams (eds) *Post-Colonial Medieval Studies*. London, Routledge.

O'Neill, B.H. St. J., 1960. *Castles and Cannon: A Study of Early Artillery Fortifications in England*. Oxford, Clarendon Press.

Oosthuizen, S. and Taylor, C.C. 2000. '"John O'Gaunt's House", Bassingbourn, Cambridgeshire: a 15th century landscape.' *Landscape History* 22, 61–71.

Ormrod, W.M. (ed.) 1986. *England in the 14th Century: Proceedings of the 1985 Harlaxton Symposium*. Woodbridge, Boydell.

Ormrod, W.M. and Lindley, P.G. (eds) 1996. *The Black Death in England*. Stamford, Paul Watkins.

Patterson, T.C. and Galley, C.W. (eds) 1987. *Power Relations and State Formation*. Washington, DC, American Anthropological Association.

Pattison, P. (ed.) 1998. *There By Design: Field Archaeology in Parks and Gardens*. BAR 268. Oxford, British Archaeological Reports.

Payling, S.J. 1992. 'Social mobility, demographic change, and landed society in late medieval England.' *Economic History Review* 95, 1, 51–73.

Payling, S.J. 1995. 'The politics of family: late medieval marriage contracts.' In R.H. Britnell and A.J. Pollard (eds) *The McFarlane Legacy*. Stroud, Alan Sutton, pp. 21–48.

Pearson, S. 1994. *The Medieval Houses of Kent: An Historical Analysis*. London, Her Majesty's Stationery Office.

Peers, C. 1957. *Kirby Muxloe Castle, Leicestershire*. London, Her Majesty's Stationery Office.

Percy, T. 1827. *The Regulations and Establishment of the Household of Henry Algernon Percy, the Fifth Earl of Northumberland, at his Castles of Wresill and Lekinfield in Yorkshire*. London, Pickering.

Pevsner, N. 1956. *The Englishness of English Art*. Harmondsworth, Penguin.

Pevsner, N. 1957. *The Buildings of England: Northumberland*. Harmondsworth, Penguin.

Pevsner, N. 1976. *A History of Building Types*. London, Thames and Hudson.

Phillips, J. 1973. *The Reformation of Images: Destruction of Art in England, 1535–1660*. Berkeley, CA, University of California Press.

Platt, C. 1982. *The Castle in Medieval England and Wales*. London, Batsford.

Poklewski-Zoziell, T. 1996. 'Le vocabulaire castéllogique dans les sources médiévales polonaises et la réalité archéologique.' *Château Gaillard* 18, 181–5.

Pollard, A.J. 1990. *North-Eastern England During the Wars of the Roses: Lay Society, War, and Politics 1450–1500*. Oxford, Clarendon Press.

Popper, K. 1959. *The Logic of Scientific Discovery*. London, Hutchinson.

Porter, S. 1994. *Destruction in the English Civil Wars*. London, Sutton.

Poulsen, C. 1984. *The English Rebels*. London, The Journeyman Press.

Pounds, N.G.J. 1990. *The Medieval Castle in England and Wales: A Social and Political History*. Cambridge, Cambridge University Press.

Pounds, N.J.G. (ed.) 1994. *The Canterbury Area: Proceedings of the 140th Summer Meeting of the Royal Archaeological Institute*. London, Royal Archaeological Institute.

Prestwich, M. 1980. *The Three Edwards: War and State in England, 1272–1377*. London, Weidenfeld & Nicholson.

Prestwich, M. 1996. *Armies and Warfare in the Middle Ages: The English Experience*. New Haven, CT, Yale University Press.

Putter, A. 1997. 'Transvestite knights in medieval life and literature.' In J.J. Cohen and B. Wheeler (eds) *Becoming Male in the Middle Ages*. London, Garland, pp. 279–302.

Rawcliffe, C. 1978. *The Staffords, Earls of Stafford and Dukes of Buckingham*. Cambridge, Cambridge University Press.

RCHME 1959. *An Inventory of the Historical Monuments of the City of Cambridge*. London, Her Majesty's Stationery Office.

RCHME 1975. *An Inventory of the Historical Monuments in the County of Northampton*. London, Her Majesty's Stationery Office.

Renfrew, A.C. 1973. *Before Civilisation*. Harmondsworth, Penguin.

Reyerson. K. and Powe, F. (eds) 1984. *The Medieval Castle: Romance and Reality*. Dubuque, University of Iowa Press.

Riddy, F. 1995. 'Nature, culture and gender in *Sir Gawain and the Green Knight*.' In F. Wolfzettel (ed.) *Arthurian Romance and Gender*. Amsterdam, Rudopi, pp. 215–25.

Rigold, S.E. 1966. *Baconsthorpe Castle, Norfolk*. London, Her Majesty's Stationery Office.

Roberts, B.K. 1987. *The Making of the English Village*. London, Longman.

Roberts, E. 1986. 'The Bishop of Winchester's fishponds in Hampshire, 1150–1400: their development, function and management.' *Proceedings of the Hampshire Field Club and Archaeological Society* 42, 123–38.

Roberts, E. 1993. 'The Bishop of Winchester's fishponds and deerparks.' *Proceedings of the Hampshire Field Club and Archaeological Society* 49, 229–31.

Robin, C. 2001. 'Kin and gender in Classic Maya society: a case study from Yaxchilán, Mexico.' In I. Stone (ed.) *New Directions in Anthropological Kinship*. New York, Rowman and Littlefield, pp. 204–28.

Robinson, J.H. (ed.) 1906. *Readings in European History*. Boston, Ginn.

Rosenthal, J.T. 1996. *Old Age in Late Medieval England*. Philadelphia, PA, University of Pensylvania Press.

Ross, C. 1997. *The Custom of the Castle: From Malory to Macbeth*. Berkeley, CA: University Press of California.

Ruggles, D.F. 1994. 'Vision and power at the Qala Bani Hammad in Islamic North Africa.' *Journal of Garden History* 14, 1, 28–41.

Salch, Ch.-L. 1979. *Dictionnaire des Châteaux et les fortifications du Moyen Age en France*. Strasbourg, Publitotal.

Samples, S. 1995. 'The rape of Ginover in Heinrich von dem Turlin's *Diu Crone*.' In F. Wolfzettel (ed.) *Arthurian Romance and Gender*. Amsterdam, Rodopi, pp. 196–205.

Sands, H. 1903. 'Bodiam Castle.' *Sussex Archaeological Collections* 46, 114–33.

Saul, N. 1990. 'The commons and the abolition of badges.' *Parliamentary History* 9, 302–15.

Saul, N. 1995. 'Richard II and the vocabulary of kingship.' *English Historical Review* 110, 854–77.

Saunders, A.D. 1967. *Upnor Castle, Kent*. London, Her Majesty's Stationery Office.

Saunders, A.D. 1978. 'Five castle excavations: reports on the Institute's research project into the origins of the castle in England.' *Archaeological Journal* 134, 1–11.

Saunders, A.D. and Pugh, R.B. 1968. *Old Wardour Castle, Wiltshire*. London, Her Majesty's Stationery Office.

Sawday, J. 1995. *The Body Emblazoned: Dissection and the Human Body in Renaissance Culture*. London, Routledge.

Scattergood, V.J. and Sherborne, J.W. (eds) 1983. *English Court Culture in the Later Middle Ages*. London, Duckworth.

Sherborne, J. 1994. *War, Politics and Culture in 14th Century England*. London, The Hambledon Press.

Simpson, W.D. 1938. 'Warkworth: a castle of Livery and Maintenance.' *Archaeologica Aeliana* 15, 115–36.

Simpson, W.D. 1941. 'The Warkworth donjon and its architect.' *Archaeologia Aeliana* 19, 93–104.

Simpson, W.D. 1946. 'Bastard feudalism and the later castles.' *Antiquaries Journal* 26, 145–71.

Simpson, W.D. 1960. *The Building Accounts of Tattershall Castle 1434–72*. Lincoln, Lincoln Record Society 55.

Sinfield, A. 1992a. 'Macbeth: history, ideology and intellectuals.' In R. Wilson and R. Dutton (eds) *New Historicism and Renaissance Drama*. London, Longman, pp. 167–80.

Sinfield, A. 1992b. *Faultlines: Cultural Materialism and the Politics of Dissident Reading*. Oxford, Oxford University Press.

Skretowicz, V. 1990. 'Chivalry in Sidney's Arcadia.' In S. Anglo (ed.) *Chivalry in the Renaissance*. Woodbridge, Boydell, pp. 161–74.

Smith, L.D.W. 1980. 'A survey of building timber and other trees in the hedgerows of a Warwickshire estate, c.1500.' *Birmingham and Warwickshire Archaeological Society Transactions* 90, 65–74.

Society for Medieval Archaeology 1987. 'Archaeology and the Middle Ages: Recommendations by the Society for Medieval Archaeology to the Historic Buildings and Monuments Commission for England.' *Medieval Archaeology* 31, 1–12.

Sponsler, C. 1997. 'Outlaw masculinities: drag, blackface, and late medieval labouring-class festivities.' In J.J. Cohen and B. Wheeler (eds) *Becoming Male in the Middle Ages*. London, Garland, pp. 321–48.

Stafford, P. 1995. 'More than a man, or less than a woman? Women rulers in early modern Europe.' *Gender and History* 7, 3, 486–90.

Starkey, D. 1982. 'Ightham Mote: politics and architecture in early Tudor England.' *Archaeologia* 107, 153–63.

Starn, R. and Partridge, L. 1992. *Arts of Power: Three Halls of State in Italy, 1300–1600*. Berkeley, CA, University of California Press.

Steane, J. 1993. *The Archaeology of the Medieval English Monarchy*. London, Batsford.

Stein, R.M. 1998. 'Making history English: cultural identity and historical explanation in William of Malmesbury and Lazamon's Brut.' In S. Tomasch and S. Gilles (eds) *Text and Territory*. Philadelphia, University of Pennsylvania Press, pp. 97–115.

Stell, G. 1985. 'The Scottish medieval castle: form, function and evolution.' In K.J. Stringer (ed.) *Essays on the Nobility of Scotland*. Edinburgh, Edinburgh University Press, pp. 195–209.

Stewart, A. 1995. 'The early modern closet discovered.' *Representations* 50, 76–100.

St. George, R.B. 1990. 'Bawns and beliefs: architecture, commerce and conversion in early New England.' *Winterthur Portfolio* 25, 4, 89–125.

Stocker, D. 1992. 'The shadow of the general's armchair.' *Archaeological Journal* 149, 415–20.

Stocker, D. and Stocker, M. 1996. 'Sacred profanity: the theology of rabbit breeding and the symbolic landscape of the warren.' *World Archaeology* 28, 2, 265–72.

Stone, L. (ed.) 2001. *New Directions in Anthropological Kinship*. New York, Rowman and Littlefield.

Stone, L. and Stone, J.C. 1984. *An Open Elite? England 1540–1880*. Oxford, Clarendon Press.

Stringer, K.J. (ed.) 1985. *Essays on the Nobility of Scotland*. Edinburgh, Edinburgh University Press.

Strong, R. 1958. *Eltham Palace, London*. London, Her Majesty's Stationery Office.

Strong, R. 1984. *Art and Power: Renaissance Festivals, 1450–1650*. Woodbridge, Boydell.

Strong, R. and van Dorsten, J.A. 1964. *Leicester's Triumph*. Leiden, Leiden University Press.

Sullivan, M.A. 1994. *Brueghel's Peasants: Art and Audience in the Northern Renaissance*. Cambridge, Cambridge University Press.

Swanson, R.N. 1999. 'Clergy, masculinity and transgression in late medieval England.' In D. Hadley (ed.) *Masculinity in Medieval Europe*. Harlow, Longman, pp. 178–96.

Sweetman, D. 1999. *The Medieval Castles of Ireland*. Cork, Collins Press.

Tabbaa, A. 1988. 'Towards an interpretation of the use of water in Islamic courtyards and countryard gardens.' *Garden History* 7.

Tait, H. 1997. 'The great divide?' In D. Gaimster and P. Stamper (eds) *The Age of Transition*. Oxford, Oxbow Books, pp. 1–8.

Tarlow, S. and West, S. (eds) 1999. *The Familiar Past?* London, Routledge.

Taylor, A.J. 1974. *The King's Works in Wales 1277–1330*. London, Her Majesty's Stationery Office.

Taylor, A.J. 1979. *Raglan Castle, Gwent*. 14th impression. Cardiff, HMSO.

Taylor, C.C. 1989. 'Somersham Palace, Cambridgeshire: a medieval landscape for pleasure?' In M. Bowden *et al.* (eds) *From Cornwall to Caithness*. Oxford, BAR, pp. 211–14.

Taylor, C. 1998. *Parks and Gardens of Britain: A Landscape History from the Air*. Edinburgh, Edinburgh University Press.

Tealdi, J. n.d. *La France Médiévale: Romantisme et Renouveau.* Publitotal, place and date not stated.

Thackray, D. 1991. *Bodiam Castle.* London, The National Trust.

Thirsk, J. 1992. 'Making a fresh start: 16th-century agriculture and the classical inspiration.' In M. Leslie and T. Raylor (eds) *Culture and Cultivation in Early Modern England.* Leicester, Leicester University Press, pp. 15–34.

Thomas, K. 1983. *Man and the Natural World: Changing Attitudes in England 1500–1800.* London, Allen Lane.

Thompson, A.H. 1912. *Military Architecture in England During the Middle Ages.* Oxford, Oxford University Press.

Thompson, M.W. 1964. 'Reclamation of waste ground for the pleasance at Kenilworth Castle.' *Medieval Archaeology* 8, 222–3.

Thompson, M.W. 1965. 'Two levels of the mere at Kenilworth Castle, Warwickshire.' *Medieval Archaeology* 8, 222–3.

Thompson, M.W. 1966. 'The origins of Bolingbroke castle.' *Medieval Archaeology* 10, 152–8.

Thompson, M.W. 1977. 'Three stages in the construction of the hall at Kenilworth Castle.' In M.R. Apted *et al.* (eds) *Ancient Monuments and their Interpretation.* London, Phillimore, pp. 211–18.

Thompson, M.W. 1987. *The Decline of the Castle.* Cambridge, Cambridge University Press.

Thompson, M.W. 1994. 'The military interpretation of castles.' *Archaeological Journal* 151, 439–45.

Thompson, M.W. 1995. *The Medieval Hall: The Basis of Secular Domestic Life, 600–1600 AD.* Aldershot, Scolar Press.

Thompson, M.W. 1998. *Medieval Bishops' Houses in England and Wales.* Aldershot, Ashgate.

Thomson, D. 1993. *Renaissance Architecture: Critics, Patrons, Luxury.* Manchester, Manchester University Press.

Thornton, D. 1997. *The Scholar in His Study: Ownership and Experience in Renaissance Italy.* London, Yale University Press.

Thurley, S. 1993. *The Royal Palaces of Tudor England.* London, Yale University Press.

Tinniswood, A. 1989. *A History of Country House Visiting: Five Centuries of Tourism and Taste.* Oxford, Blackwell.

Tomasch, S. and Gilles, S. (eds) 1998. *Text and Territory: Geographical Imagination in the European Middle Ages.* Philadelphia, PA. University of Pennsylvania Press.

Tristram, E.W. 1955. *English Wall Painting of the 14th Century.* London, Routledge.

Turner, D.J. 1986. 'Bodiam, Sussex: true castle or old soldier's dream house?' In W.M. Ormrod (ed.) *England in the 14th Century.* Woodbridge, Boydell, pp. 267–77.

Vale, J. 1982. *Edward III and Chivalry: Chivalric Society and its Context 1270–1350.* Woodbridge, Boydell.

Virgoe, R. 1973. 'Walter Tailboys and Lord Cromwell: crime and politics in Lancastrian England.' *Bulletin of the John Rylands Library* 55.

Wagner, A. 1939. *Heralds and Heraldry in the Middle Ages.* Oxford, Oxford University Press.

Wall, W. 1995. *The Imprint of Gender: Authorship and Publication in the English Renaissance.* Ithaca, NY, Cornell University Press.

Warnke, M. 1994. *Political Landscape: The Art History of Nature.* London, Reaktion.

Way, T. 1997. 'The victim or the crime: park focussed conflict in Cambridgeshire and Huntingdonshire 1200–1556.' In J. Carman (ed.) *Material Harm*. Glasgow, Cruithne Press, pp. 143–66.

Weaver, P. 1993. *Middleham Castle, Yorkshire*. London, English Heritage.

White, H. 1973. *Metahistory*. Baltimore, Johns Hopkins University Press.

White, H. 1978. *Tropics of Discourse*. Baltimore, Johns Hopkins University Press.

White, H. 1987. *The Content of the Form*. Baltimore, Johns Hopkins University Press.

Whiteley, M. 1999. 'Relationship between garden, park and princely residence in medieval France.' In J. Guillaume (ed.) *Architecture, Jardin, Paysage*. Paris, Picard, pp. 91–102.

Whittick, C. 1993. 'Dallingridge's bay and Bodiam Castle millpond – elements of a medieval landscape.' *Sussex Archaeological Collections* 131, 119–23.

Whittle, E.H. 1990. 'The 16th and 17th century gardens at Raglan Castle.' *Monmouthshire Antiquary* 6, 69–75.

Wicker, N. 1999. 'Archaeology and art history: common ground for the new millennium.' *Medieval Archaeology* 43, 161–71.

Williams, D. 1974–5. 'Fortified manor houses.' *Transactions of the Leicestershire Archaeological and Historical Society* 1, 1–16.

Williams, I. and Williams, J.L. 1965. *Medieval Welsh Lyrics*. Trans. J.P. Clancy. London, Macmillan.

Williams, J.H. 1992. 'Excavations at Brougham Castle, 1987.' *Transactions of the Cumberland and Westmorland Archaeological Society* 92, 105–22.

Williams, R. 1973. *The Country and the City*. London, Chatto.

Williams, R. 1980. *Problems in Materialism and Culture*. London, Verso.

Williams, T. 1990. '"Magnetic Figures": polemical prints of the English Revolution.' In L. Gent and N. Llewellyn (eds) *Renaissance Bodies*. London, Reaktion, pp. 86–110.

Williamson, T. 2000. 'Understanding enclosure.' *Landscapes* 1, 1, 56–79.

Williamson, T.M. 1993. 'The landscape park: economics, art and ideology.' *Journal of Garden History* 13, 49–55.

Wilson, R. and Dutton, R. (eds) 1992. *New Historicism and Renaissance Drama*. London, Longman.

Wolfzettel, F. (ed.) 1995. *Arthurian Romance and Gender*. Amsterdam, Rodopi.

Wood, M. 1964. *Donnington Castle, Berkshire*. London, Her Majesty's Stationery Office.

Woolgar, C.M. 1999. *The Great Household in Late Medieval England*. New Haven, CT, Yale University Press.

Worsley, G. 1993. 'Inigo Jones: lonely genius or practical examplar?' *Journal of the British Archaeological Association* 146, 102–12.

Wrightson, K. 1982. *English Society 1580–1680*. London, Hutchinson.

Yentsch, A.E. and Beaudry, M.C. (eds) 1992. *The Art and Mystery of Historical Archaeology: Essays in Honour of James Deetz*. Boca Raton, FL, CRC Press.

Yoffee, N. and Sherratt, A. (eds) 1993. *Archaeological Theory: Who Sets the Agenda?* Cambridge, Cambridge University Press.

Youngs, S.M., Clark, J., Gaimster, D.R.M. and Barry, T. 1988. 'Medieval Britain and Ireland in 1987.' *Medieval Archaeology* 32, 225–314.

Zimmerman, S. (ed.) 1992. *Erotic Politics: Desire on the Renaissance Stage*. London, Routledge.

INDEX

Printed in the USA/Agawam, MA
April 4, 2012

565123.062